# ST. THÉRÈSE OF LISIEUX

## HER LAST CONVERSATIONS

# ST. THÉRÈSE OF LISIEUX

## HER LAST CONVERSATIONS

*Translated by*
JOHN CLARKE, O.C.D.

**ICS Publications**
INSTITUTE OF CARMELITE STUDIES
*Washington, D.C.*
1977

*ST. THÉRÈSE OF LISIEUX, Her Last Conversations* is a translation of *J'ENTRE DANS LA VIE,* Derniers Entretiens (Editions du Cerf—Desclée de Brouwer 1973)
Photos are from *Visage de Thérèse de Lisieux* (© Office Central de Lisieux—51 rue du Carmel)

ISBN 0-9600876-3-X
Library of Congress Catalog Card Number 76-27207
Copyright © by Washington Province of Discalced Carmelites, Inc., 1977.
ICS Publications, 2131 Lincoln Road, N.E., Washington, D.C. 20002

# TABLE OF CONTENTS

## Introduction

> I love to read the lives of the saints very much; the account of their heroic deeds inflames my courage and spurs me on to imitate them. I must admit, however, that I've envied at times the happy lot of their relatives who had the good fortune to live in their company and enjoy their holy conversations.[1]

These words, written by St. Thérèse of Lisieux to her aunt, Mme. Isidore Guérin, July 20, 1895, express a desire that was fully realized by those who had the "good fortune" of knowing Thérèse. A glance at the content of this letter shows that she was congratulating her relatives on their own conduct—saintly in her estimation—with regard to the entrance of their daughter Marie into the Lisieux Carmel the following month. Within a short period after she'd written these words, Thérèse herself had died and her reputation for sanctity was becoming world-wide. Her own relatives, therefore, especially her sisters who attended to her during her last illness, had been living in the "company" of one of God's saints—one prepared for our times. Fortunately for us, they didn't simply listen to "her holy conversations," but they wrote them down, totally unconscious that eventually a great multitude of yet unborn friends of St. Thérèse would hunger for her words.

After the passing of so many years since her death, September 30, 1897, and her canonization, May 17, 1925, there is still a great interest in this humble nun from the Lisieux Carmel. The words of Pius XI still ring with the same conviction as when they were first spoken. On February 11, 1923, upon the occasion of the approval of the miracles attributed to the intercession of the Venerable Thérèse of the Child Jesus, he stated:

> The voice of God and the voice of His people have joined in extolling the Venerable Thérèse of the Child Jesus. The voice of God first made itself heard, and the faithful, recognizing the divine call, added their voices to the hymn of praise. We repeat, the voice of God was the first to speak, as is clear from the magnificent preparation of that soul whose splendor dazzles us today. It is God Himself we exalt when we praise the heroic virtue of this heavenly work of His hands. Scarcely, however, had the divine voice gone forth than there arose the voice of

---

[1]  Thérèse de l'Enfant-Jésus et de la Sainte-Face, Ste., *Correspondance Générale*, 2 vols. (Paris: Cerf-Desclée de Brouwer, 1973), 1:811.

the people of God, urgent, insistent, and a great multitude of pilgrims flocked to the tomb of Sister Thérèse. . . . God it is who by His astounding miracles has revealed what a treasure house of grace He had hidden away in the heart of Thérèse.

Pius XI went on to describe God's almighty power as it is clearly manifested in His material creation, in great as well as in little things, how the same divine hand formed huge monsters and minute organisms invisible to the eye. He continued:

It is not otherwise in the spiritual world. Confining ourselves to the saints whose centenary the Church has lately kept, we find that God created such giants of zeal and holiness as Ignatius Loyola and Francis Xavier. Behind these, on the far horizon, we catch a glimpse of Peter and Paul, of Athanasius, Chrysostom, and Ambrose. But behold! the same heavenly Artist has secretly fashioned, with a love well-nigh infinite, this maiden so modest, so humble—this child.

These are not simply words of empty praise. They contain the teaching of a truth which is really believed by those who know St. Thérèse. To them she is still "a most exquisite miniature of spiritual perfection," and her heart is really "a treasure house of grace." Recent publications on St. Thérèse have only served to impress this truth more deeply in the minds of her friends. One newly translated work: *St. Thérèse of Lisieux by those who knew her,*[2] contains a description of how she practiced the Christian virtues to a heroic degree. When reading it, we are reminded again and again of those other words of Pope Pius XI, in this same allocution, when he refers to her as "a miracle of virtues and a prodigy of miracles."

*Last Conversations of St. Thérèse* is the translation of a recent publication entitled: *J'entre dans la Vie, Derniers Entretiens.*[3] This present book, we might say, could serve as a sequel to St. Thérèse's autobiography, *Story of a Soul.*[4] It contains her final interviews with her three sisters during the last months of her life, especially those three critical months in the Carmel infirmary from July to September,

---

[2] *St. Thérèse of Lisieux by those who knew her, Testimonies from the process of beatification,* edited and translated by Christopher O'Mahony, O.C.D. (Dublin: Veritas Publications, 1975).

[3] Thérèse de l'Enfant-Jésus et de la Sainte-Face., Ste., *J'Entre dans la Vie, Derniers Entretiens.* (Paris: Cerf-Desclée de Brouwer, 1973).

[4] Thérèse of Lisieux, St., *Story of a Soul,* trans. John Clarke, O.C.D. (Washington, D.C.: ICS Publications, Institute of Carmelite Studies, 1975).

1897. Furthermore, it contains these "conversations" in their entirety. We have the opportunity, then, of living in her "company" and of enjoying her "holy conversations." When we are reading her words, we can almost sense her presence at our side, speaking directly to us, sharing with us her human experience, her joys, her sufferings, her views on a variety of topics, her love for God, and especially her trust in Him in spite of her terrible ordeal.

We must, however, keep in mind that this translation is that of the popular edition of a much more extensive work entitled: *Derniers Entretiens*.[5] This is a very complete and scholarly production which made its appearance in 1971 in the form of two volumes: the first (922 pages) contains the "last conversations," plus excellent introductions, various charts, extensive footnotes; the second (504 pages) is a supplement, containing a synopsis of Mother Agnes' four versions of Thérèse's "conversations." (These versions will be explained later.)

This work was eight years in the making and is the result of a critical and painstaking examination of all the original documents of the saint's conversations. It was produced by a team made up of the Carmelite nuns of Lisieux, Fathers Bernard Delalande, O.C.D., Guy Gaucher, O.C.D., Albert Patfoort, O.P., Sister Geneviève, O.P., of Clairefontaine monastery, and Sister Anne of the Carmel of Boulogne-sur-Seine. While their work is invaluable for anyone desirous of studying St. Thérèse more deeply, we are assured by the editors of the present popular edition that it contains the essential elements of this larger work. In other words, we are sure we are reading the following:

a) the entire text of the words collected by the three main witnesses: Mother Agnes of Jesus (Pauline), Sister Geneviève (Céline), and Sister Marie of the Sacred Heart (Marie);

b) the testimony of other witnesses when this does not repeat that of the three main ones;

c) additional words of St. Thérèse as they were quoted in letters written during her critical illness.

We should take note of the fact that we are reading the whole text of the "words" collected by the three main witnesses, Thérèse's three sisters. It is really the first time these have been published in their

---

[5] Thérèse de l'Enfant-Jésus et de la Sainte-Face, Ste., *Derniers Entretiens avec ses soeurs et temoignages divers,* 2 vols. (Paris: Cerf-Desclée de Brouwer, 1971).

present form. This is quite understandable when we consider the personal feelings of Mother Agnes. After all, she was the one responsible for the major portion of this collection, a fact quite evident when we examine her "Yellow Notebook."[6] The very existence of Thérèse's many statements is the outcome of her own attitude towards Pauline, her "little Mother," in whom she'd confided from the age of four and a half. Because of the nature of their conversations, often bordering on strict confidences, Mother Agnes always felt they should not be published indiscriminately. Her attitude persisted over the many years she was to outlive Thérèse (she died July 28, 1951), and this attitude was shared by both Céline and Marie. It was only after the death, then, of all Thérèse's sisters (Céline was the last to die on February 25, 1959) that the reasons for withholding total publication of the "conversations" were no longer considered valid.

In spite of their sensitivity in the matter, however, Mother Agnes and Sister Geneviève did provide many of St. Thérèse's "conversations" for the reading public. Many of us, for example, are already quite well acquainted with a small book in its English translation called: *Novissima Verba* (Latin for Last Words).[7] This was printed for the first time in France on January 15, 1927, under the title: *Novissima Verba—Derniers Entretiens de Ste. Thérèse de l'Enfant-Jésus—Mai-Septembre 1897*. This book came out less than two years after Thérèse's canonization on May 17, 1925, and it was Mother Agnes' way of answering a demand being made by so many of the newly-canonized saint's friends. She did this reluctantly for the reasons already mentioned, and consequently *Novissima Verba* was a rather restrained publication, containing as we now know only slightly over half the "conversations" Mother Agnes had in her possession. Nevertheless, this work was instantly popular, and was eventually translated into eleven languages. It went out of print in its French edition in 1960. An interesting note to the first edition reads:

> These words of St. Thérèse of the Child Jesus were gathered from the lips of the saint herself by Reverend Mother Agnes of Jesus. Written

[6]   The term "Yellow Notebook" will be explained later when we are dealing wtih the different versions of Mother Agnes' notes. See appendix, p. 311.

[7]   *Novissima Verba, Last Conversations and Confidences of St. Thérèse of the Child Jesus, May-September, 1897,* trans. Carmelite Nuns of New York. (New York: P. J. Kenedy & Sons, 1952).

down from day to day, they were submitted to the ecclesiastical tribunal during the process of beatification and canonization. Certain well-known words of the saint, not heard by Mother Agnes of Jesus, do not appear in these conversations.[8]

In addition to *Novissima Verba,* there was a second source from which St. Thérèse's "conversations" could be drawn. This was as old as the first printing of the saint's autobiography, *Histoire d'une Ame,* 1898. In the English translations, we were always able to read her words in the section usually entitled: *Counsels and Reminiscences.*[9] A rather lengthy section, almost 40 pages, it contained many of the dying nun's last words, but it also had many of her kindly words of advice and encouragement to her five novices (she was placed in charge of the novices in 1893, without being given the office of Novice Mistress). This source left much to be desired as it was rather incomplete and the identity of Thérèse's interlocutors was never disclosed, a fact which renders conversation less interesting and sometimes meaningless.

There was still a third source from which we could glean her "conversations," and this was a particularly rich one. It was a little book (249 pages in translation) written by Thérèse's sister Céline (Sister Geneviève). As we are perhaps aware, Céline was one of the saint's novices, having entered Carmel on September 14, 1894, after her father's death. Thérèse had preceded her there by six years, and during this time she had acquired much religious knowledge, much virtue, and deep insights into certain scriptural passages. Although it must not have been easy for the older and more worldly-wise Céline (she was already twenty-five) to listen to her younger sister, she nevertheless realized the value of much of what she was being taught. Many of these things she wrote down even while Thérèse was still alive.

With the very early death of Thérèse, a death that was so swiftly followed by her beatification and canonization only twenty-eight years later, these teachings of her former Novice Mistress became invaluable reference notes for Sister Geneviève. She read them over and even made a copy of them to send to her sister Léonie in the Visitation

---

[8]    *Derniers Entretiens,* 1:92, note 128.
[9]    *St. Thérèse of the Child Jesus, The Little Flower of Jesus,* a revised translation of her autobiography by Rev. T. N. Taylor. (New York: P. J. Kenedy & Sons, 1927), pp. 293 ff.

convent at Caen. Eventually she succeeded in gathering all these notes, added to them some of her testimony at the beatification process, and then published the whole in 1952, under the title of: *Sainte Thérèse de l'Enfant-Jésus, Counseils et Souvenirs.* This appeared in English translation as: *A Memoir of My Sister, St. Thérèse.* [10] Its final chapter contains substantially the last conversations between Thérèse and Céline from the month of May up until the former's death, September 30, 1897. The preceding chapters contain an excellent study of St. Thérèse's spiritual teachings to her novices.

This brings us, then, to the present publication of *Last Conversations* of St. Therese. As we glance through the pages of this book, we may wonder why so many of St. Thérèse's words were so meticulously written down and preserved. This was done long before she came to be considered "as the greatest saint of modern times." When Mother Agnes of Jesus was painstakingly writing down these conversations on little scraps of paper, she could not possibly have suspected that less that twenty-five years later, August 14, 1921, Pope Benedict XV would state in his allocution concerning Thérèse's heroic practice of Christian virtue:

> It is our special desire that the secret of her sanctity may be disclosed to all our children. . . . The more the knowledge of this new heroine is spread abroad, the greater will be the number of her imitators giving glory to God by the practice of the virtues of spiritual childhood.

What is particularly interesting about this pope's words is his desire that knowledge of Thérèse be spread abroad throughout the world. God's ways are strange indeed, for at a very early age He had inspired Thérèse Martin with the desire to remain "hidden," "forgotten," and even "unknown." This desire did not spring from any unhealthy fear in her of facing up to life's problems but from a firm conviction that God was calling her to Himself in a life of complete immolation through prayer and sacrifice, with an emphasis on her remaining "hidden." She explains this very clearly in her autobiography. As a little child of nine, she had accidentally learned that her favorite sister Pauline was about to enter Carmel (she entered on October 2, 1882), and recalling her grief years later, Thérèse writes:

---

[10] Sister Geneviève of the Holy Face (Céline Martin), *A Memoir of My Sister, St. Thérèse,* authorized translation by the Carmelite Nuns of New York of *Conseils et Souvenirs.* (New York: P. J. Kenedy & Sons, 1959).

I shall always remember, dear Mother, with what tenderness you consoled me. Then you explained the life of Carmel to me and it seemed so beautiful! When thinking over all you had said, I felt Carmel was the *desert* where God wanted me to go also to hide myself. I felt this with so much force that there wasn't the least doubt in my heart; it was not the dream of a child led astray but the certitude of a divine call; I wanted to go to Carmel not for *Pauline's sake* but for *Jesus alone.* I was thinking *very much* about things which words could not express but which left a great peace in my soul.[11]

A few years later, still very young and doing a good deal of reading, she began to dream about herself in the light of France's past heroines. About this period she wrote:

When reading the accounts of the patriotic deeds of French heroines, especially the *Venerable* JOAN OF ARC, I had the same burning zeal with which they were animated, the same heavenly inspiration. Then I received a grace which I have always looked upon as one of the greatest in my life because at that age I wasn't receiving the *lights* I'm now receiving when I am flooded with them. I considered that I was born for *glory* and when I searched out the means of attaining it, God inspired in me the sentiments I have just described. He made me understand my glory would not be evident to the eyes of mortals, that it would consist in becoming a great saint! This desire could certainly appear daring if one were to consider how weak and imperfect I was, and how, after seven years in the religious life, I am still weak and imperfect. I always feel, however, the same bold confidence of becoming a great saint because I don't count on my merits since I have none, but I trust in Him who is Virtue and Holiness. God alone, content with my weak efforts, will raise me to Himself and make me a saint, clothing me in His infinite merits. I didn't think then that one had to suffer very much to reach sanctity, but God was not long in showing me this was so and in sending me the trials I have already mentioned.[12]

Usually our childhood dreams pass away, and undoubtedly the reason for this is that this is what they are: dreams. The inspirations Thérèse was having in those very early years were not empty dreams or foolish delusions. These inspirations to remain "hidden," "unknown," took on greater depth when she entered Carmel, the "desert" to which she felt God was calling her. This is what she writes about this period of her development:

[11] See *Story of a Soul,* p. 58.
[12] See *Story of a Soul,* p. 72.

The little flower transplanted to Mount Carmel was to expand under the shadow of the cross. The tears and blood of Jesus were to be her dew, and her Sun was His adorable Face veiled with tears. Until my coming to Carmel, I had never fathomed the depths of the treasures hidden in the Holy Face. It was through you, dear Mother, that I learned to know these treasures. Just as formerly you had preceded us to Carmel, so also you were the first to enter deeply into the mysteries of love hidden in the Face of our Spouse. You called me and I understood. I understood what *real glory* was. He whose Kingdom is not of this world (John 13:36) showed me that true wisdom consists in "desiring to be unknown and counted as nothing," (Imitation of Christ, I, 2:3) in "placing one's joy in the contempt of self." (Ibid., III, 49:7) Ah! I desired that, like the Face of Jesus, "my face be truly hidden, that no one on earth would know me." (Isaias 53:3) I thirsted after suffering and I longed to be forgotten.[13]

We don't know exactly when Mother Agnes introduced her sister Thérèse to this devotion, but we do know the latter added this title to her name as early as January 10, 1889, when she received the Habit. We might recall that it was in those months shortly after her entrance on April 9, 1888, that her father suffered his breakdown. Knowing how deeply she loved him, we can well imagine her agony during those months and years of his illness as he became progressively worse. She was to compare his condition to the humiliations Jesus suffered in His Passion.[14]

However, there is an interesting development that takes place around this time. In a letter addressed to her sister Céline, July 18, 1890,[15] she enclosed certain passages of scripture on the sufferings of Christ. Among these were the texts from Isaias, chapter 53: 1-5 and 63: 1-5. These lines served to deepen her devotion to the Holy Face and to console her in her father's mental affliction. Father Guy Gaucher, O.C.D. makes the following observation on Thérèse's discovery of the Isaian texts:

It would be interesting to follow the development of this discovery from the year 1890 to 1897. Let us point out that Thérèse's intuitive genius comes to the fore once again. Instinctively, she goes to the essential texts of the Old Testament, the importance of which modern

[13] See *Story of a Soul,* p. 152.
[14] Ibid., pp. 45-47, 156-157.
[15] *Correspondance Générale,* 1:539.

exegesis has pointed out. Jesus had frequently quoted from the Songs of the Suffering Servant, which were essential prophecies concerning His mission, and these were forgotten, consciously or not, by His disciples who rebelled at the idea of a persecuted Messias, rejected by His people, and crucified. Thérèse, who had no knowledge whatsoever of this scholarly research, who did not even have a bible at her disposition, had nevertheless declared:

"These words of Isaias: 'Who has believed our report? . . . There is no beauty in him, nor comeliness . . . ' have been the whole foundation of my devotion to the Holy Face, or, to express it better, the foundation of my whole piety. I also have desired to be without beauty, to tread the winepress alone, unknown to every creature."[16]

St. Thérèse made this significant statement to Mother Agnes on August 5, 1897, when she was lying sick in the infirmary. Father Guy brings out its importance in his comments on her words:

We cannot place enough emphasis on this confidence which at this date takes on the appearance of a "last will and testament." We have here an inexhaustible source of study: She whom we customarily call St. Thérèse of the Child Jesus—and who, in this way, is made to symbolize only childhood—was able to say, at the moment of her death, that the foundation of her whole piety was nourished on the texts of Isaias, chapter 53, concerning the "Suffering Servant." When we mutilate her name, we mutilate her message, to say nothing of her entire life. If we rely on the testimony of Mother Agnes given at the beatification process, we have good reason to call her Sister Thérèse of the Holy Face. Mother Agnes stated:

"Devotion to the Holy Face was the Servant of God's special attraction. As tender as was her devotion to the Child Jesus, it cannot be compared to her devotion to the Holy Face."[17]

A mutilation of her name leads necessarily to a mutilation of her message, her whole life. In order not to make this mistake, let us keep in mind that St. Thérèse's devotion to the Holy Face can be traced back to her entrance into Carmel, as was already pointed out. However, her devotion to the Passion of Christ, and her desire to use the merits of Christ to bring salvation to others, owed its origin to a

[16] Guy Gaucher, O.C.D., *La Passion de Thérèse de Lisieux,* (Paris: Cerf-Desclée de Brouwer, 1972), p. 205.
[17] Ibid., pp. 205-206.

grace she received in July, 1887, before her entrance into Carmel. She describes it in *Story of a Soul:*

> One Sunday, looking at a picture of Our Lord of the Cross, I was struck by the blood flowing from one of the divine hands. I felt a pang of great sorrow when thinking this blood was falling to the ground without anyone's hastening to gather it up. I was resolved to remain in spirit at the foot of the Cross and to receive the divine dew. I understood I was then to pour it out upon souls. The cry of Jesus on the Cross sounded continually in my heart: "I thirst!" (John 19:28). These words ignited within me an unknown and very living fire. I wanted to give my Beloved to drink and I felt myself consumed with a *thirst for souls.*[18]

We know her story of Henri Pranzini, a criminal whose name was very much on people's lips around the time Thérèse received this grace. He had committed several murders, was brought to trial, and condemned to death. He was to die on August 31, 1887. According to the newspaper reports, he refused to repent. Thérèse began to pray for his conversion, even begging God to give her a sign that her prayers for him were answered in order to increase her zeal in praying for others. She writes:

> My prayer was answered to the letter! In spite of Papa's prohibition that we read no papers, I didn't think I was disobeying when reading the passages pertaining to Pranzini. The day after his execution, I found the newpaper "La Croix." I opened it quickly and what did I see? Ah! my tears betrayed my emotion and I was obliged to hide. Prānzini had not gone to confession. He had mounted the scaffold and was preparing to place his head in the formidable opening, when suddenly, seized by an inspiration, he turned, took hold of the *crucifix* the priest was holding out to him and kissed the *sacred wounds three times!* Then his soul went to receive the *merciful* sentence of Him who declares that in heaven there will be more joy over one sinner who does penance than over ninety-nine just who have no need of repentance! (Luke 15:7)[19]

Thus began a real apostolate of prayer and sacrifice for the conversion of sinners. Thérèse often spoke of Henri Pranzini in later years, calling him her first child. Up to the end of her life she continued to pray and suffer for others. In fact, so great was her suffering

---

[18] See *Story of a Soul*, p. 99.
[19] See *Story of a Soul*, p. 100.

that towards the end she cried out:

> No, I could never have believed it possible to have suffered so much! never! never! I can explain it only by the ardent desires I had to save souls.

These words—practically the last she ever spoke—came from her a few hours before she expired at 7:20 p.m., September 30, 1897. When Sister Geneviève (Céline) was commenting on them, she gave an excellent summary of the whole meaning of her saintly sister's life:

> The saint's voluntary participation in the Passion of Christ (a participation foreseen, to be sure, in her Act of Oblation according to the degree willed by Our Lord) is the reason for her extraordinary sufferings, especially during those last years of her life. The two burning ideals of Thérèse's vocation, therefore—ideals which, while not opposed, are situated on two different planes—might be expressed in this way:
>
> a) from July, 1887, when she was fourteen years old, she voiced the desire to suffer and to help save souls by the Cross;
>
> b) on June 9, 1895, the feast of the Most Holy Trinity, when, at the summit of her spiritual ascent, she offered herself as a victim to the merciful love of God, to make amends to this love which is ignored on all sides.[20]

We have reached a point where we should consider the circumstances under which St. Thérèse's "last conversations" were taken down. Nevertheless, I would like to deal with the matter of what others thought about this young Carmelite. Who exactly was Sister Thérèse of the Child Jesus and the Holy Face on the threshold of her last illness in those early days of April, 1897?

She was only twenty-four years of age. In spite of her youth, however, she had already lived the rather austere Carmelite Rule for nine years, having entered the Lisieux Carmel on April 9, 1888. She had won the love and respect of the majority of the nuns. Two rather vivid descriptions of Thérèse made by Mother Marie de Gonzague, Prioress for the greater part of Thérèse's life in Carmel, give us a fair idea of what others thought about her. In a letter to the Tours Carmel, September 9, 1890, the day after Thérèse's Profession, she wrote:

> This angelic child is only seventeen and a half; yet she has the judgment of a woman of thirty, the religious perfection of an old and ac-

---

[20] See *A memoir of My Sister, St. Thérèse*, pp. 83-84.

complished novice, and very good self-mastery; she is a perfect religious.[21]

Just three years later, in 1893, when Thérèse was twenty, the same Mother Marie wrote to the Visitation convent at Le Mans:

> Tall and robust, with a childlike face, and with a tone of voice and expression that hide a wisdom, a perfection, and a perspicacity of a woman of fifty. . . . She is a little innocent thing to whom one would give Holy Communion without previous confession, but whose head is filled with tricks to be played on anyone she pleases. A mystic, a *comedienne,* she is everything! She can make you shed tears of devotion, and she can as easily make you split your sides with laughter during recreation.[22]

Both evaluations are rather complimentary, each describing a Thérèse who comes across to others as a rather mature person. When only seventeen, she has the judgment of one of thirty; when twenty, the wisdom, perfection, perspicacity of a woman of fifty. Is it any wonder, then, that when Mother Agnes became Prioress on February 20, 1893, she begged her young sister to help train and edify the novices?

There is still a more interesting observation made by Mother Marie de Gonzague. Testifying at the process of beatification, Sister Marie of the Trinity, a former novice of the saint, stated that several times Mother Marie told her:

> If it were necessary to choose a prioress in the community, I would not hesitate to choose Sister Thérèse of the Child Jesus, in spite of her young age. She is perfect in everything, her only fault being that she has her three sisters with her.[23]

If we ask, then, who Sister Thérèse was when she became seriously ill in April, 1897, we must answer: She was a highly respected member of her community, much trusted, already in charge of the novices, a possible candidate for the office of Prioress. The presence of her sisters—there were three—was not really a fault. After all, the same Mother Marie was responsible for allowing so many to be admitted to the same convent.

In spite of all this, we still have to say that Sister Thérèse was not really "known" in her community, even by her three sisters, sur-

---

[21]  See *Derniers Entretiens,* 1:25, note 12.
[22]  Ibid., 1:137, note 149.
[23]  See *St. Thérèse of Lisieux by those who knew her.* p. 253.

prising as this may seem. We get a confirmation of this when reading
the testimonies given at the beatification process. For example, the
same Sister Marie of the Trinity, who deeply admired her young
Novice Mistress, testified:

> During her life in Carmel, the Servant of God passed by unnoticed in
> the community. Only four or five of the nuns, including myself, got
> close enough to her to realize the perfection hidden under the humility
> and simplicity of her exterior. For most of the nuns, she was a very
> regular religious, always above reproach.[24]

Similar testimony was given by another former novice, Sister Mary
Magdalene:

> Generally speaking, the Servant of God was unknown and even misun-
> derstood in the convent. Apart from some novices who were close to
> her, no one noticed the heroism of her life.[25]

Her own sister Céline (Sister Geneviève) testified at the same process:

> During her first six years in Carmel, I had to remain in the world to be
> at my father's side. I have reason to believe by what I learned after my
> entrance into the Carmel that during this period her simplicity and
> humility made her pass unnoticed by the Sisters, who looked upon her
> as very careful about her Rule. During her last three years which I spent
> in Carmel with her, I noticed that certain Sisters, more discerning than
> the others, respected her exceptional sanctity. Sister St. Pierre, a poor
> invalid, wanted us to perpetuate the memory of the love the Servant of
> God had practiced towards her; she maintained even that "Sister
> Thérèse of the Child Jesus would be spoken of later on." Another old
> Sister, since deceased, Sister Marie Emmanuel, told me: "This child
> has such a maturity and so much virtue that I would like her to be
> Prioress if she were not only twenty-two." Finally, two other old
> Sisters used to ask her advice in secret. But, in general, even during her
> last years, she continued to lead a hidden life, the sublimity of which
> was known more to God than to the Sisters around her.[26]

The kindness of St. Thérèse towards Sister St. Pierre was un-
consciously described by herself in the *Story of a Soul* on page 247.

Mother Agnes of Jesus, who knew Thérèse better than anyone else,
including Thérèse's other two sisters, was apparently unaware of
anything exceptional on her sister's part. True, she believed her to be

---

[24] See *St. Thérèse of Lisieux by those who knew her*, p. 253.
[25] Ibid., p. 264.
[26] See *St. Thérèse of Lisieux by those who knew her*, p. 154.

an excellent and examplary religious, but her admiration stopped there. How else can we interpret her utter astonishment when she read Sister Thérèse's manuscript? This manuscript was to form the major portion of the future *Histoire d'une Ame (Story of a Soul),* so soon to become famous. We know the impact it had on its readers in 1898. However, those first eight chapters, those "childhood memories," written explicitly for Mother Agnes, were lying untouched and unread for fully three months after Thérèse had handed them to her on January 20, 1896. Keeping in mind that she is speaking of the elections that took place in the Carmel in late March, 1896, let us read her reaction:

> I did not take the time to read it until after the elections in the spring of that same year. Oh! then, how I regretted not having thanked her sooner, for she so much deserved this! my little Thérèse! But she, once her act of obedience was accomplished, was no longer concerned about it. This holy indifference touched me so much that I found the reading of her life all the more beautiful. I said to myself: And this blessed child, who wrote these heavenly pages, is still in our midst! I can speak to her, see her, touch her. Oh! how she is unknown here! And how I am going to appreciate her more now![27]

We may assume, then, that Mother Agnes was reading through these "childhood memories" around the end of March and the beginning of April, 1896. When she says, "Oh! how she is unknown here," she is repeating what has been said already by the witnesses at the process, and she is including herself in this general lack of knowledge of one who would soon attract world-wide attention. She is determined to take advantage of her sister's presence: "And how I am going to appreciate her more now!" However, she and the community were not to enjoy Thérèse's presence for very long. Simultaneously with Mother Agnes' rude awakening, Thérèse herself was discovering that her death was not far off, that she was already receiving warnings of its swift approach.

Sister Geneviève (Céline), in her testimony at the beatification process, said there were a few nuns who realized Sister Thérèse's depth of spirituality, her sanctity even; however, she concluded: "But, in general, even during the last years, she continued to lead a hidden life, the sublimity of which was known more to God than to the Sisters

---

[27] See *Derniers Entretiens,* 1:35.

around her.'' Let us try to recall the highlights of this sublimely hidden life in Carmel, known only to God. (The page references are to the *Story of a Soul*.)

a) From her entrance into Carmel, April 9, 1888, Thérèse met with suffering. ''Suffering opened its arms to me, and I threw myself into them with love'' (p. 149). Her father's illness began almost immediately (p. 157); aridity in prayer; she makes St. John of the Cross her only reading in those early years (p. 174); she makes her Profession on September 8, 1890, fully determined to become a ''great saint'' (p. 166).

b) The following year, during the October retreat, 1891, Father Alexis ''. . . launched me full sail upon the waves of *confidence* and *love* which so strongly attracted me, but upon which I dared not advance'' (p. 174). This was the beginning of her living out her future teaching on ''spiritual childhood,'' the virtues of which are love for God and confidence in His mercy.

c) Thérèse was only twenty when Mother Agnes of Jesus—just elected Prioress on February 20, 1893—placed her in charge of the novices. She is now in a position to teach her ''little doctrine'' to her sister Céline, who has joined her in Carmel, September 14, 1894, after their father's death which occurred on July 29.

d) The year 1895 is a very important year for Sister Thérèse. She has now lived her doctrine of ''spiritual childhood'' and has gained much experience from it. Upon the request of her sister Marie, Mother Agnes tells her to write down her ''childhood memories,'' and she begins her first manuscript with the words:

> The day you asked me to do this, it seemed it would distract my heart by too much concentration on myself, but since then Jesus has made me feel that in obeying simply, I would be pleasing Him; besides, I'm going to be doing only one thing: I shall begin to sing what I must sing eternally: *''The Mercies of the Lord''* (p. 13).

Perhaps when dwelling upon these innumerable graces of God's mercy she was inspired to make her Act of Oblation to Merciful Love. This she did on June 9, 1895, after receiving permission to do so from Mother Agnes of Jesus. She concludes her long Act of Oblation with this prayer:

> In order to live in one single act of perfect Love, I OFFER MYSELF AS A VICTIM OF HOLOCAUST TO YOUR MERCIFUL LOVE, asking You to consume me incessantly, allowing the waves of *infinite*

*tenderness* shut up within You to overflow into my soul, and that thus I may become a *martyr* of Your *Love,* O my God!

May this martyrdom, after having prepared me to appear before You, finally cause me to die and may my soul take its flight without delay into the eternal embrace of *Your Merciful Love.*

I want, *O my Beloved,* at each beat of my heart to renew this offering to You an infinite number of times, until the shadows having disappeared I may be able to tell You of my *Love in an Eternal Face to Face!*

Some months before, on February 26, 1895, she had composed her poem: *Vivre d'Amour,* and one verse expressed the following:

> To die of Love, this is truly sweet martyrdom,
> And it is what I wish to suffer.
> O Cherubim! bring me your lyre,
> For I feel my exile is about to end.
> Divine Jesus, bring my dream to fruition:
> To die of Love . . . this is my sole desire.*

e) Spiritually mature, purified, she welcomes with joy her first hemoptysis of April 3, 1896 (p. 210). A few days later, she entered into the "thick darkness" of the trial of her faith, and begins to "sit at the table of sinners" (pp. 211-214).

f) The swift development of her love is beautifully expressed in her famous letter to her sister, Sister Marie of the Sacred Heart, dated September 8, 1896. Thérèse has finally come to realize her true vocation:

> Then, in the excess of my delirious joy, I cried out: O Jesus, my Love . . . my vocation, at last I have found it . . . MY VOCATION IS LOVE!
> Yes, I have found my place in the Church, and it is You, O my God, who have given me this place; in the heart of the Church, my Mother, I shall be love. Thus I shall be everything, and thus my dream will be realized (pp. 188-200).

From now on Thérèse seems to live in expectation. Who could possibly suspect the fire of love which gradually consumes her? As she goes about her prayers and her daily tasks no one realizes that soon she will no longer be among them. It is only her illness which suddenly

---

*Mourir d'Amour, c'est un bien doux martyre,*
*Et c'est celui que je voudrais souffrir.*
*O Chérubins! accordez votre lyre,*
*Car je le sens, mon exil va finir.*
*Divin Jésus, réalise mon rêve:*
*Mourir d'Amour . . . Mourir d'Amour, voilà mon espérance.*

becomes very grave in the first week of April, 1897, that finally draws attention to her, and the community begins to realize its loss.[28]

Ever since her entrance into Carmel, Sister Thérèse's health had never been very good. However, over the years the nuns had grown accustomed to her coughing spells, sore throat, fatigue, etc., and none of them, with the exception of her own sisters, ever dreamed that one so young and so apparently robust could be seriously ill. We may be justified in saying that Thérèse was rather misleading in this whole matter of her health, without being in any way at fault. She was, for instance, the last in her community to complain about anything, especially about the food and the cold, two factors which must certainly have contributed to her poor physical condition. In fact, we shall find her, in these "last conversations," actually singling out these two things, even advising Mother Agnes, should she become Prioress again, to provide good food for the nuns and enough blankets against the cold winter months. Again, in this matter of her health, when Thérèse experienced her first "coughing up of blood," April 4, 1896, she made so little of the incident, saying she did not feel weak, etc., that Mother Marie de Gonzague permitted her to carry on with the usual austerities of Carmel and with her assigned tasks.[29] The Prioress did not even judge it necessary to inform Thérèse's older sisters about the incident. Finally, in a letter to her aunt, Mme. Guérin, who had inquired about her health, Thérèse wrote the following on July 16, 1896, three months after coughing up blood:

> You ask me, dear Aunt, to give you some news about my health just as I would to a "mother," and this I will do. But if I were to tell you I was doing marvelously well, you wouldn't believe me. So I will leave the word up to the celebrated Dr. de Cornière, to whom I had the *distinguished honor* of being presented yesterday in the speakroom. This illustrious personage, after having honord me with a look, declared I was very well![30]

With an attitude such as this, and Thérèse undoubtedly didn't know her real condition, we can readily understand why the nuns, particularly Mother Agnes, were very much puzzled and stunned at her

---

[28] For a description of St. Thérèse's illness and its progress, the reader is referred to the short introductions in the "Yellow Notebook" before each month; also to the "Letters" written during this period, pp. 271-292; and to the chronological chart on pp. 293-296.

[29] See *Story of a Soul*, pp. 210-211.

[30] See *Correspondance Générale*, 2:868.

rapid decline in health. As early as April 25, 1897, her sister Céline (Sister Geneviève) was writing to a friend at Rome, Brother Simeon, informing him that Thérèse (he'd met her on her trip there) was not expected to live very long. Under these circumstances, Mother Agnes began to pay short visits to her sick sister during the months of April and May, and these visits were soon to become daily occurrences from the first week of June until Thérèse's death on September 30, 1897. It was during these visits that Mother Agnes began to record the "last conversations."

Why did she write down so many of these private interviews with her dying sister, the future St. Thérèse of Lisieux? We are certain she didn't see into the future, hence she was completely unaware of the world-wide attention Thérèse would receive shortly after her death. This attention would be drawn to her because of two things: the publication of her autobiography, *Histoire d'une Ame (Story of a Soul),* in 1898, and the working of so many miracles attributued to her intercession. Mother Agnes could never vaguely have guessed at these extraordinary events. Why, then, did she consider Thérèse's "conversations" important enough to write down?

One answer lies, I think, in the proper understanding of her deeply emotional response to the reading of St. Thérèse's "childhood memories" written, we must remember, explicitly for her. We have already considered how, at first, because of her busy schedule as Prioress, she paid no attention to the manuscript, and how later on when she did read it attentively, she was overwhelmed by its spiritual content. She was to explain her reaction candidly at the beatification process:

> . . . And this blessed child, who has written these heavenly pages, is still in our midst! I can speak to her, see her, touch her. Oh! how she is unknown here! And how I am going to appreciate her more now!

This reaction of Mother Agnes, strange as it may seem, is identical with that of the many who were to read St. Thérèse's "childhood memories" in the *Story of a Soul* (the first eight chapters). She, too, like so many others, was very much affected by the account of God's dealings with Thérèse, even though she herself was very much part of the many graces received by Thérèse. When she was reading, for example, the following passage:

> It is with great happiness, then, that I come to sing the mercies of the Lord with you, dear Mother. It is for *you alone* I am writing the story

of the *little flower* gathered by Jesus. I will talk freely and without any worries as to the digressions I will make. A mother's heart understands her child even when it can but stammer, and so I'm sure of being understood by you, who formed my heart, offering it up to Jesus!

Mother Agnes was able to recall how she taught Thérèse to lift up her heart to God when rising in the morning; she could remember, too, the many other things she'd taught her, for example, how to appreciate the sacrament of Penance, the Holy Eucharist, etc. And still when this same mature Thérèse was reflecting upon those early years and was striving to sing "the mercies of the Lord" granted to her in those childhood days, Mother Agnes was astounded at how God worked in this child's heart.

She realized, we might say, for the first time that Thérèse was very close to God, that she was literally "possessed" by Him, hence she was to be treasured. It was all there in those pages which described so simply but so clearly the workings of God's "Merciful Love" in this child who had surrendered herself totally to Him. How great must have been her sorrow, then, when she learned that her younger sister would not be long with her. It is easy for us to understand, therefore, how she would take advantage of these few remaining months to profit by the presence of one so "close" to God, attending to her needs at her sickbed, listening to her views on many spiritual subjects, questioning her about her own religious experiences, and writing down the many things Thérèse was to say to her. Mother Agnes undertook this work seriously on June 2, 1897, for it was then that she was fully authorized to be at her sister's bedside daily. However, we shall discover when reading through her "Yellow Notebook" that she made entries for April, eight of them, and quite a number for May. Why did she begin so far back? *Derniers Entretiens* gives an excellent answer:

> Several reasons can be advanced. We should not consider it something extraordinary that a Carmelite should keep track of the spiritual conversations of another religious. And it cannot be doubted that, even before June 3, Mother Agnes wanted to preserve certain of Thérèse's teachings for her personal consolation.[31] Had not Sister Geneviève,

---

[31] Sister Marie of the Sacred Heart (Marie) wrote to Sister Françoise-Thérèse (Thérèse's sister Léonie) on July 24, 1910, that Mother Agnes of Jesus had written down Thérèse's words for her "personal consolation." See *Derniers Entretiens,* 1:76, note 68.

with Thérèse's consent, collected her "reminiscences of a novice?" But from June 4, Mother Agnes felt that she was carrying out an official mission. Without having any presentiment of the "storm of glory"[32] that was to descend upon Lisieux, she was aware of her sister's exceptional maturity.

We must mention, too, certain family reasons. The Guérins, deprived of any direct contact with Thérèse, wanted to know all her conversations, her actions, and even more so, Léonie Martin, who wrote to her sister Céline: ". . . How she must edify you with her virtues! If you could only put everything she says in writing, how consoling it would be for me to have all that, for I haven't as you do, dear little sisters, the good fortune to be near my dear sister. . . ."

Two days before this,[33] Mother Agnes had transmitted to the Guérins several of Thérèse's conversations heard and written down in the infirmary. Sister Marie of the Eucharist did the same thing. All had the same feeling that nothing must be lost.[34]

The Guérins, along with Léonie Martin, during the last three months of Thérèse's life, were away on vacation, a fact which necessitated the writing of so many letters on the part of their daughter Marie, Sister Marie of the Eucharist.

Early in the evening of May 30, 1897, Thérèse very discreetly told Mother Agnes of the incident of her "coughing up of blood," April 3, 1896. Needless to say, her older sister was very much disturbed by this news and expressed her feelings, telling Thérèse how pained she was at not being informed immediately. The latter tried to console her, but it was not until after the exchange of a number of notes between them that an understanding was reached. Thérèse's first note read:

> Don't be troubled, dear little Mother, because *your* little girl *seemed* to have hidden something from you, for you know well enough, although she hid a little corner of the *envelope,* she has never hidden from you one single line of the *letter.* Who then knows better than you this little letter that you love so much? To others, I can show the envelope on all its sides, since they can see only this much; but to you! . . . Oh, little Mother, you know now, it was on Good Friday that Jesus began to tear

---

[32] Pius XI, addressing the Lisieux and Bayeux pilgrims, May 18, 1925, said: ". . . Industrially, too, it is a place of importance, but what is that beside the storm, the deluge of glory that has descended today upon Lisieux!—a glory that will not pass away but will endure forever. . . ."

[33] See p. 280.

[34] See *Derniers Entretiens,* 1:40.

a little the envelope of YOUR little letter; are you not happy that He is getting ready to read this letter you have been writing for twenty-four years? Ah! if you only knew how it will be able to speak of your love all through eternity![35]

Finally convinced that her sister does not have long to live, Mother Agnes has one thought in mind: Thérèse has not completed her autobiography, because she's written almost nothing about her nine years as a Carmelite nun. She soon takes steps to remedy the matter by approaching Mother Marie de Gonzague and asking her to have Thérèse finish her little "life." The Prioress agrees immediately, and at the same time gives Mother Agnes permission to spend time with Thérèse when the infirmarians are attending the Divine Office in the evenings.

Thérèse began writing her last manuscript, June 4, 1897, and she was to continue this rather difficult assignment until her strength gave out and she was brought down to the infirmary. We find her, therefore, all through the month of June, spending a little time each day filling the pages of a little copybook with her fine handwriting. She does this either in her room or out under the chestnut trees, sitting in the wheelchair her father used when he was sick. What she wrote at this time can be read in the two concluding chapters of the *Story of a Soul,* addressed to Mother Marie de Gonzague. It is impossible, I think, to have any real understanding of St. Therese without a careful reading of these closing pages of her "life." In fact, they should be read in conjunction with the "last conversations," for they are contemporaneous with them. Among some of the interesting subjects she deals with are:

a) her "little way"; in her search for the road to sanctity she discovered in the texts of Scripture what she calls her "little way" with its "lift" or "elevator" raising one to God, namely, the "arms of Jesus" (pp. 207-208).

b) her first "coughing up of blood" which occurred in the early hours of Good Friday, April 3, 1896; she calls this "the distant murmur" announcing the Bridegroom's arrival (pp. 210-211).

c) her "trial of faith"; this is perhaps one of the most difficult things in her life to understand because she speaks very little about it,

[35] See p. 53.

and yet it was with her constantly for a period of eignteen months. It came immediately after the first warnings of her approaching death, on Easter Sunday or within Easter week. When writing about it on June 9, 1897, she said: "This trial was to last not a few days or a few weeks; it was not to be extinguished until the hour set by God Himself, and this hour has not yet come." It finally ended a few moments before her death (pp. 211-214; 271).

Mother Agnes tells us that Thérèse did not find it easy to write those final pages of her "life." There was the suffering from her sickness to cope with, but besides this there were innumerable interruptions from the infirmarians, the novices, and nuns who came to chat when they saw her sitting under the chestnut trees. Thérèse tried to take all these distractions in stride, but she explained to Mother Agnes that her work was a "jumble" and that it would have to be touched up. She said:

> I am writing about charity, but I have not been able to do it as well as I should have liked to; in fact, I couldn't have done worse if I'd tried. Still, I have said what I think. But you must touch it all up, for I assure you it is like a jumble.[36]

In spite of her dissatisfaction, however, we find these pages on this virtue flawless, containing a teaching on charity that was never perhaps better expressed before:

> This year, dear Mother, God has given me the grace to understand what charity is; I understood it before, it is true, but in an imperfect way. I had never fathomed the meaning of these words of Jesus: *"The second commandment is* LIKE *the first: You shall love your neighbor as yourself."* (Matt. 22:39) I applied myself especially to *loving* God, and it is in loving Him that I understood my love was not to be expressed only in words, for: *"It is not those who say: 'Lord, Lord!' who will enter the kingdom of heaven, but those who do the will of my Father in heaven."* (Matt. 7:21) Jesus has revealed this several times or I should say on almost every page of His Gospel. But at the Last Supper, when He knew the hearts of His disciples were burning with a more ardent love for Him who had just given Himself to them in the unspeakable mystery of the Eucharist, this sweet Savior wished to give them *a new commandment.* He said to them with inexpressible tenderness: *"A new commandment I give to you that you love one another:* THAT AS I HAVE LOVED YOU, YOU ALSO LOVE ONE ANOTHER. *By this*

---

[36] See *St. Thérèse of Lisieux by those who knew her,* p. 34.

*will all men know that you are my disciples, if you have love for one another.'' (John 13:34-35)*[37]

Again, the reader is referred to these pages on "charity" written by the dying saint in those final months of her life. She goes on to explain how she tried to apply these teachings to herself in her dealings with the nuns in her community. We can learn from these pages how even a saint finds it difficult to carry out this all-important commandment of fraternal charity.

There are two statements made by St. Thérèse in the early part of June, 1897, which merit our attention. Both have to do with her deep appreciation of God's "Merciful Love" as it is manifested in her life. The first was made orally on June 7. She was walking in the garden with Mother Agnes when her attention was drawn to a little white hen sitting under a tree, sheltering her little chicks underneath her wings. Thérèse was moved to tears at the sight, and she was unable to speak when Mother Agnes questioned her on the reason for her crying. Later she explained:

> I cried when I thought how God used this image in order to teach us His tenderness towards us. All through my life, this is what He has done for me! Earlier in the day when I was leaving you, I was crying when going upstairs; I was unable to control myself any longer, and I hastened to our cell. My heart was overflowing with love and gratitude.[38]

How deep was the humility manifested by Thérèse when she told Mother Agnes later in the evening:

> Had you not brought me up well, you would have seen sad things. I would never have cried when seeing the little white hen.

The second statement was written. It was made on June 9, and it appears in her *Story of a Soul*. When describing her "trial of faith" (the longest explanation she has made of this) to Mother Marie de Gonzague, she wrote:

> Never have I felt before this, dear Mother, how sweet and merciful the Lord really is, for He did not send me this trial until the moment I was capable of bearing it. A little earlier I believe it would have plunged me into a state of discouragement. Now it is taking away everything that could be a natural satisfaction in my desire for heaven. Dear Mother, it seems to me that nothing could prevent me from flying away, for I no

---

[37] See *Story of a Soul,* p. 219.
[38] See p. 60; see Matt. 23:37.

longer have any desires except that of loving to the point of dying of love. June 9.[39]

When reading this statement in the copybook in which Thérèse wrote it, we see that she inserted the date "June 9" at the bottom of the page, slightly to the side of the words ". . . dying of love." We may recall that it was on June 9, 1895, only two years before, that Thérèse had made her now famous *Act of Oblation to Merciful Love.* It was this special anniversary that was in her mind when she wrote this. However, it appears after she was explaining her "trial of faith," and so we may conclude that she had made this explanation on this date.

With this in mind, we should find rather intriguing the following entry made by Mother Agnes in her "Yellow Notebook" for this same date of June 9:

"How happy I am today!"
*I asked: "Has your trial of faith passed away?"*
"No, but it seems to be suspended; the ugly serpents are no longer hissing in my ears."[40]

We have the following excellent explanation of this conversation in *Derniers Entretiens.*[41] When explaining the possible reason why Thérèse said: "How happy I am today," and ". . . the ugly serpents are no longer hissing in my ears," it says that perhaps she was permitted a momentary respite in order to be able to objectify her interior martyrdom when she was writing about it; or she may have experienced some slight relief when she had finally expressed herself at such length to Mother Marie de Gonzague, bringing it out into the open. (See pages 211-214, *Story of a Soul.)*

It is very difficult, however, to understand St. Thérèse's "trial of faith." She seems to give us a slight glimpse of its purpose when she writes: ". . . Now it [the trial] is taking away everything that could be a natural satisfaction in my desire for heaven." Perhaps we remember how her ideas on the future happiness of heaven were formed, at least in part, by Father Arminjon's "Conferences."[42] We may also recall

---

[39] See *Story of a Soul,* p. 214.
[40] See pp. 61-62.
[41] See *Derniers Entretiens,* 1:431.
[42] See *Story of a Soul,* p. 102.

that in the explanation she gave of her "trial of faith," she began by saying:

> At this time I was enjoying such a living faith, such a clear *faith,* that the thought of heaven made up all my happiness, and I was unable to believe there were really impious people who had no faith. I believed they were actually speaking against their inner convictions when they denied the existence of heaven, that beautiful heaven where God Himself wanted to be their Eternal Reward.[43]

Thérèse goes on to explain how Jesus made her understand that there were people without any faith, that through the abuse of His grace they had lost this real treasure. He permitted her soul, she tells us, to be invaded with the "thickest darkness" and that the thought of heaven be nothing but "the cause of struggle and torment." She also says that this trial was still with her when she was actually writing these words, i.e., June 9, 1897.

And yet we can read the following statements made by her on May 15, 1897, and entered into Mother Agnes' "Yellow Notebook":

> I have formed such a lofty idea of heaven that, at times, I wonder what God will do at my death to surprise me. My hope is so great, it is such a subject of joy to me, not by feeling but by faith, that to satisfy me fully something will be necessary which is beyond all human conception. Rather than be disappointed, I prefer to keep an eternal hope.
>
> So, I'm already thinking that, if I am not surprised enough, I will pretend to be surprised just to please God. There isn't any danger that I'll allow Him to see my disappointment; I will be able to go about it in such a way that He won't notice anything. Besides, I'll always contrive ways of being happy. To succeed in this, I have my little rubrics that you know about and that are infallible. Then, just to see God happy will be fully sufficient for my own happiness.[44]

There are those who will be horrified at the poor theology expressed in these simple words; nevertheless, Thérèse was by no means a poor theologian. She enjoyed the "wisdom" of the little children of God and could have expressed herself more exactly. However, my own reason for making this particular quotation is to point out how difficult it is to understand her "trial of faith." She could make such a statement as the above even when her mind was flooded with the

---

[43] See *story of a Soul,* p. 211.
[44] See p. 43.

"thickest darkness" and when she was enjoying no consolations what-soever. We shall find similar statements throughout her "last con-versations."

Her "trial" was very real. She was able to say in the same month of May: "If I didn't have this spiritual trial that is impossible to un-derstand, I really believe I'd die of joy at the thought of leaving this earth." In the month of July, when Mother Agnes asked: "How is it that you want to die with your trial of faith that doesn't come to an end?" Thérèse answered: "Ah! but I really believe in the Thief! (Matt. 24:34) It's upon heaven that everything bears. How strange and incomprehensible it is!"

She has stated twice that the "trial" is incomprehensible to her, and so I think we should not try to understand it ourselves. Before leaving the subject, however, I would like to make the following quotations from three witnesses who testified at Thérèse's beatification process. The first, Sister Marie of the Sacred Heart (Thérèse's oldest sister Marie) stated:

> During an intimate conversation (Easter, 1897), Thérèse asked me whether I sometimes had temptations against faith. I was surprised at her question, for I was unaware of her trials against faith. I knew about these only later, and especially through the reading of *Histoire d'une Ame* (Story of a Soul). I then asked her if she had any temptations like this herself, but she answered in a vague way, changing the subject.

Sister Geneviève of the Holy Face (her sister Céline) also testified at the same process:

> She didn't speak about it to anyone for fear of communicating her inexpressible torment to others. She was a little more explicit with Mother Agnes of Jesus, although this was ony through some in-complete sentences.

Finally, Sister Marie of the Trinity, her former novice, had this to say at the process:

> One day when she was speaking to me about the temptations she was suffering, I said to her, very much surprised: "But those beautiful poems that you are composing give the lie to what you're telling me!" She answered: "I sing of what I want to believe, but it is without any feeling. I would not even want to tell you the degree of blackness the night is in my soul for fear of making you share in my temptations."[45]

---

[45] See *Derniers Entretiens,* 1:134-135.

Thérèse enjoyed peace in the midst of this "trial." She admits this on different occasions in her "last conversations" when speaking to Mother Agnes about it. On the occasion, for instance, of the seventh anniversary of her Profession, September 8, 1897, she said when looking at her gifts:

> "It's all God's own tenderness towards me: exteriorly, I'm loaded down with gifts; interiorly, I'm always in my trial (of faith) . . . but also in peace."[46]

She was to receive no consolation from the chaplain, Father Youf. Thérèse said of him:

> "Father Youf told me with reference to my temptations against the faith: 'Don't dwell on these; it's very dangerous.' This is hardly consoling to hear, but happily I'm not affected by it. . . ."[47]

One of the greatest trials she was to endure was being deprived of Holy Communion during her illness. She was able to receive up to a point, but she always feared some accident because of her coughing up of blood, her breathing difficulties, and her extreme weakness. There came a time, August 19, when she received for the last time, not even having the comfort of receiving before her death. This was perhaps her greatest trial because of her great love for the Eucharist. The reader is referred to Mother Agnes' note on this in her "Yellow Notebook," August 20.

With regard to St. Thérèse's physical sufferings, I think that here, too, we meet with something that is not easily grasped. When speaking to Mother Agnes in the month of August, she said: " . . . Oh! if one only knew." And in September: "O Mother, it's very easy to write beautiful things about suffering, but writing is nothing . . . nothing. One must suffer in order to know!" However, when we read through the pages of the "Yellow Notebook," we can easily realize the authenticity of Thérèse's cry: "Never would I have believed it was possible to suffer so much! Never! never! I cannot explain this except by the ardent desires I have had to save souls." These words were spoken on September 30, just a few hours before her death. (We must keep in mind that all through her sufferings she was not given any injections of morphine.)

---

[46] See p. 186.
[47] See p. 58.

I don't want to go into these sufferings at any great length. The reader is referred to the following three sources in which the progress of St. Thérèse's illness can be carefully followed: the short introductions at the beginning of each month in the "Yellow Notebook"; the "chronological chart" on page 293; and the "Letters concerning the sickness of Sister Thérèse of the Child Jesus" on page 271.

I would like to bring this Introduction to a conclusion by recalling the words of Monsignor Dubosq, the promoter of the faith in St. Thérèse canonization process. After Mother Agnes published the *Novissima Verba* in 1926, Monsignor Dubosq wrote the following congratulatory words to her:

> . . . With what loving care did you not, as you took your station at her bedside, note down, day by day, and hour by hour, during her last months of agony, all she said and did! You did not omit the shortest syllable or overlook the least gesture which might reveal the dispositions of her heart. . . . Perhaps you hesitated to divulge without further consideration the pages of a diary which you instinctively felt contained sacred confidences of a very intimate nature. . . . But now you realize that the numerous souls whom your little sister must conquer and guide in "her way" are eager to know her better. . . . Yet, this little book you have given us is a treasure, in truth, the very testament of our dear saint. We find here her character more truly manifested than in any other record. Thank you for not having kept the treasure for yourself alone.[48]

How much more can this be said of this present book, containing as it does the complete record of St. Thérèse's "last words and actions." May it be a source of real comfort to all its readers as they, too, struggle to understand God's will in their own sufferings and the complications of life.

I would like to express my gratitude to those who, in one way or another, helped me to bring this book into being. First of all, I am extremely grateful to the Carmelite nuns of Morristown, New Jersey, for so kindly allowing me to reside on their premises over a period of many months, thus providing the atmosphere of peace and quiet so necessary for this type of work. I want to express my thanks to Mother Marie-Thérèse, who read over my manuscript after translation and whose own knowledge of French was so helpful in detecting errors,

[48] See *Novissima Verba*, pp. v. vi.

omissions, etc. I thank also Sister Agnes for her expert work in typing the manuscript. I greatly appreciate the hard work done by the Carmelite nuns of Cleveland, Ohio, in getting together an index for this publication. Finally, I owe much thanks to Father Kieran Kavanaugh, O.C.D., who was so helpful in so many ways by providing me with his expert advice.

John Clarke, O.C.D.
July 16, 1976

# THE "YELLOW NOTEBOOK"

## OF MOTHER AGNES

*Very intimate*

# WORDS SET DOWN
# DURING THE LAST MONTHS

## of our saintly Little Thérèse

Sister Agnes of Jesus
c.d.i.

# APRIL

*The eight statements dated for April, 1897, give us only a few of Thérèse's experiences acquired in the formation of the novices. These statements belong to the "Counsels and Reminiscences" published in the original Histoire d'une Ame.*

*A few family letters make reference to repeated vesicatories [an extremely painful remedy in the form of hot plasters applied to the skin to induce blistering] given to Thérèse; these proved useless in arresting her coughing spells.\** *There is mention made, too, of some hemoptyses [coughing up of blood] that took place towards the end of this month in the mornings. Her general state of health was very poor.*

---

(\*) *It is interesting to note that as far back as November, 1876, when Thérèse was only three, her mother, Zélie Martin, mentioned in a letter that Thérèse was already having trouble with her breathing. When she walked fast, there was a kind of whistling sound that could be heard in her chest. Mme. Martin states that one remedy suggested by the doctor proved useless, and that she feared she would have to apply a vesicatory, but the mere thought of it made her shudder. [Translator's note].*

April 6, 1897

1. "When we're misunderstood and judged unfavorably, what good does it do to defend or explain ourselves? Let the matter drop and say nothing. It's so much better to say nothing and allow others to judge us as they please! We don't see in the Gospel where Mary explained herself when her sister accused her of remaining at Jesus' feet, doing nothing![1] She didn't say: 'Oh, Martha, if you only knew the joy I am experiencing, if you only heard the words I hear! And besides, it's Jesus who told me to remain here.' No, she preferred to remain silent. O blessed silence that gives so much peace to souls!"

\* \* \*

2. " 'Let the sword of the Spirit which is the word of God remain in our mouth and heart.'[2] If we come in conflict with a disagreeable person, let us never grow discouraged or abandon her. Let us always have 'the sword of the Spirit' in our mouths in order to correct her faults. Don't allow the matter to pass over just for the sake of peace, but fight on even when there is no hope of gaining victory. What does it matter whether we're successful or not? What God asks of us is not to give up the struggle because of our weariness, not to become discouraged saying: 'That's that! There's nothing to be gained here and she's to be left to herself!' Oh, this is only laziness, and we have to do our duty to the bitter end."

\* \* \*

3. "Ah! how we should never pass judgments on this earth. Here is something that happened to me during recreation a few months ago.[3] It's an insignificant thing, but it taught me very much.

"The bell was rung twice, and since Procuratrix[4] was absent, a third

---

[1]   Luke 10:39-40.

[2]   Ephesians 6:17; quoted in Carmelite Rule. See *Rule of St. Albert,* eds. H. Clarke, O. Carm. and B. Edwards, O.C.D. (Aylesford: Carmelite Priory, 1973), p. 89.

[3]   December, 1896. See Thérèse of Lisieux, St., *Story of a Soul,* trans. John Clarke, O.C.D. (Washington, D.C.: ICS Publications, Institute of Carmelite Studies, 1975), p. 221.

[4]   Mother Agnes of Jesus was procuratrix.

party[5] was required to accompany Sister Thérèse of St. Augustine. It's usually tedious to serve as third party, but this time I was tempted because the large gate had to be opened to bring in some trees for the crib.

"Sister Marie of St. Joseph was at my side and I guessed she shared my childish desire. 'Who is coming as my companion?' asked Sister Thérèse of St. Augustine. I immediately began untying our apron, but I did this slowly so that Sister Marie of St. Joseph would be ready ahead of me and take the place, which is what happened. Then Sister Thérèse of St. Augustine said with a smile, looking at me: 'Well, it's Sister M. of St. J. who will have this pearl for her crown. You were going too slowly.' I answered simply with a smile and began my work again, saying to myself: Oh, my God, how different are Your judgments from those of men! It's in this way we are so often mistaken in this life, taking for an imperfection in our sisters what is meritorious in Your sight!"

* * *

April 7

*Allowing her to see my fears, I asked her what sort of death I would die. She answered with a very tender smile:*

"God will sip you up like a little drop of dew."[6]

* * *

April 18

1. *She had just confided to me some painful humiliations some Sisters had given her:*

"It is in this way that God gives me the means of remaining very little; however, this is exactly what is needed. I'm always happy, for I always manage in the midst of the tempest to preserve interior peace. If one tells me about her fights with the Sisters, I am careful not to work myself up against this or that Sister. I must, for example, while listening to her, be able to look out the window and enjoy interiorly

---

[5]   The nun accompanying the procuratrix in transaction of business.
[6]   Mother Agnes died July 28, 1951, after being in a coma for several days.

the sight of the sky, the trees, etc. Understand? Just now, during my struggle with regard to Sister X, I was watching with pleasure two beautiful magpies playing in the field, and I was as much at peace as if I were at prayer. I really fought with Sister, and I am very tired, but I don't fear the struggle. It is God's will that I fight right up until death. Oh! little Mother, pray for me!''

\* \* \*

2.   ''When I pray for you, I don't say a 'Pater' or an 'Ave' for you, I say simply, lifting up my heart to God: 'O my God, grant my little Mother all kinds of good things; and if You can, love her even more.' ''

\* \* \*

3.   ''I was still very little when Aunt gave me a story to read that surprised me very much. I saw where they were praising a boarding school teacher because she was able to extricate herself cleverly from certain situations without offending anyone. I took note above all of this statement: 'She said to this one: You're not wrong; to that one: You are right.' And I thought to myself: This is not good! This teacher should have had no fear and should have told her little girls that they were wrong when this was the truth.

''And even now I haven't changed my opinion. I've had a lot of trouble over it, I admit, for it's always so easy to place the blame on the absent, and this immediately calms the one who is complaining. Yes, but . . . it is just the contrary with me. If I'm not loved, that's just too bad! I tell the whole truth, and if anyone doesn't wish to know the truth, let her not come looking for me.''

\* \* \*

4.   ''We should never allow kindness to degenerate into weakness. When we have scolded someone with just reason, we must leave the matter there, without allowing ourselves to be touched to the point of tormenting ourselves for having caused pain or at seeing one suffer and cry. To run after the afflicted one to console her does more harm than good. Leaving her to herself forces her to have recourse to God

in order to see her faults and humble herself. Otherwise, accustomed to receiving consolation after a merited reprimand, she will always act, in the same circumstances, like a spoiled child, stamping her feet and crying until her mother comes to dry her tears.''

# MAY

The correspondence for this month of May is silent on the matter of Thérèse's health. The few details given in the "Yellow Notebook" show that her coughing persisted, exhausting her especially at night. To the painful remedy of the vesicatories were added sessions of what were called "pointes de feu" [a cauterizing remedy for tuberculosis, consisting in the repeated puncturing of the skin with red-hot needles]. Her resistance weakened and, in the middle of the month, she had to give up attending the community acts, for example, the recitation of the Divine Office in choir, recreation, etc.

However, all hope of a cure was not given up. During this period of uncertainty, the Saint's abandonment to the will of God reached its highest degree. This is the dominant note of this month.

Thérèse wrote eight letters and four poems during the month of May, among which was her Marian testament: Pourquoi je t'aime, ô Marie.

May 1

1. "It's not 'death' that will come in search of me, it's God. Death isn't some phantom, some horrible spectre, as it is represented in pictures. It is said in the catechism that 'death is the separation of the soul from the body' and that is all it is."

* * *

2. "My heart was filled entirely with a heavenly peace today. I prayed so much to the Blessed Virgin last night, thinking that her beautiful month was about to begin!

"You weren't at recreation this evening. Reverend Mother told us that one of the missionaries[1] who embarked with Father Roulland[2] was dead before he reached his mission. This young missionary received Communion on the ship with hosts from our Carmel that were given Father Roulland . . . . And now he is dead! . . . He didn't have to carry out any apostolate whatsoever, nor go to any trouble, for example, learning Chinese. God gave him the palm of desire; see how He needs no one."

*I was unaware, then, that Mother Marie de Gonzague had assigned Father Roulland as a second spiritual brother to her. The words I've just reported above were written to her by Father Roulland, but since she was forbidden to confide it to me by Reverend Mother, she spoke to me only about what she had heard in recreation.*

*Reverend Mother had asked her to paint a picture for him on a piece of parchment. Since I was in charge of painting, she could have profited by the circumstance by asking my advice, thus letting me in on the whole secret. Instead, she hid from me as well as she could, even coming in secret to borrow the burnisher, as I learned later, for polishing the gold and which I kept on the table. She returned it when I was absent.*

*It was only three months before her death when Mother Prioress told her to speak to me freely about this matter as well as all others.*

---

[1] Fr. Frederick Mazel: missionary, fellow-student of Fr. Roulland; was assassinated in China on April 1, 1897.

[2] Fr. Adolphe Roulland, of the Foreign Mission of Paris, given as spiritual brother to Thérèse by Mother Marie de Gonzague, 1896.

May 7
1.  *Seven o'clock in the morning.*
   "It's a free day[3] today, and so I sang *'Ma joie'*[4] while I was getting dressed."

* * *

2.  "Our family won't remain a long time on this earth; when I am in heaven, I'll call all of you very quickly. Oh, how happy we shall be! We are all predestined."

* * *

3.  "I cough and cough! I'm just like a locomotive when it arrives at the station; I'm arriving also at a station: heaven, and I'm announcing it!"

* * *

May 9
1.  "We can say, without any boasting, that we have received very special graces and lights; we stand in the truth and see things in their proper light."

* * *

2.  *With regard to certain feelings beyond our control at times, such as, when we have performed a service for someone and receive no thanks:*
   "I assure you, I too experience the feeling you are speaking about. However, I don't allow myself to be trapped by it, for I expect no reward at all on earth. I do everything for God, and in this way I can lose nothing, and I'm always very well repaid for the trouble I go to for my neighbor."

---

[3]   A day of "extraordinary recreation" during which the nuns could communicate with each other more freely, sing, etc.
[4]   A poem composed by Thérèse for Mother Agnes of Jesus, January 21, 1897.

3. "It is impossible, I know, but if God were not to see my good actions, I would not be the least bit disturbed by it. I love Him so much that I'd like to please Him without His being aware of it. When He knows it and sees it, He is obliged to reward me, and I don't want Him to have to go to this trouble."

\* \* \*

May 15.
1. "I am very happy to go to heaven very soon, but when I think of these words of God: 'My reward is with me, to render to each one according to his works,'⁵ I tell myself that He will be very much embarrassed in my case. I haven't any works! He will not be able to reward me 'according to my works.' Well, then. He will reward me 'according to His own works.' "

\* \* \*

2. "I have formed such a lofty idea of heaven that, at times, I wonder what God will do at my death to surprise me. My hope is so great, it is such a subject of joy to me, not by feeling but by faith, that to satisfy me fully something will be necessary which is beyond all human conception. Rather than be disappointed, I prefer to keep an eternal hope.

"So, I'm already thinking that, if I am not surprised enough, I will pretend to be surprised just to please God. There isn't any danger that I'll allow Him to see my disappointment; I will be able to go about it in such a way that He won't notice anything. Besides, I'll always contrive ways of being happy. To succeed in this, I have my little rubrics that you know about and that are infallible. Then, just to see God happy will be fully sufficient for my own happiness."

\* \* \*

3. *I was speaking to her about certain practices of devotion and perfection counseled by the saints, which were a source of discouragement to me:*

⁵  Apocalypse 22:12.

"As for me, with the exception of the Gospels, I no longer find anything in books. The Gospels are enough. I listen with delight to these words of Jesus which tell me all I must do: 'Learn of me for I am meek and humble of heart';[6] then I'm at peace, according to His sweet promise: 'and you will find rest for your souls.' "

*She quoted the last sentence, her eyes raised with a heavenly expression in them; she added the word: 'little' to Our Lord's words, thus giving them even more charm:*

"And you will find rest for your *little* souls."

\* \* \*

4.  *She had been given a new habit (the one which is preserved). And she put it on for the first time at Christmas, 1896. This habit, the second since her clothing, did not fit her very well. I asked her if this caused her any annoyance:*

"Not the least bit! Not any more than if this were a habit belonging to a Chinese, over there, two thousand leagues from us."

\* \* \*

5.  "To the right and to the left, I throw to my little birds the good grain that God places in my hands.[7] And then I let things take their course! I busy myself with it no more. Sometimes, it's just as though I had thrown nothing; at other times, it does some good. But God tells me: 'Give, give always, without being concerned about the results.' "

\* \* \*

6.  "I would really love to go to Hanoi,[8] to suffer very much for God. I'd like to go there in order to be all alone, having no earthly consolations. As for the thought of making myself useful there, it doesn't even enter into my mind; I know very well I would do nothing at all."

---

[6]   Matthew 11:29.
[7]   A reference to the novices under her care.
[8]   To the Carmel founded by the Saigon Carmel in 1895.

7. "After all, it's the same to me whether I live or die. I really don't see what I'll have after death that I don't already possess in this life. I shall see God, true; but as far as being in His presence, I am totally there here on earth."

\* \* \*

May 18.
1. "All my duties were taken away from me; I was thinking that my death would cause no disturbance in the community because of this."
   *I asked her: "Does it cause you any pain to pass as a useless member in the minds of the nuns?"*
   "As far as that is concerned, it is the least of my worries; it makes no difference to me at all."

\* \* \*

2. *When I saw she was so sick, I did everything possible to have Mother Prioress dispense her from reciting the Office of the Dead.*[9]
   *She said:*
   "I beg you, don't prevent me from saying my 'little' Offices of the Dead; it's the only thing I can do for the Sisters who are in purgatory, and it doesn't tire me out in the least. Sometimes at the end of silence,[10] I have a moment; this is a relaxation for me."

\* \* \*

3. "I must always have some work to prepare, for, in this way, I'm not preoccupied and don't waste my time."

\* \* \*

4. "I begged God to permit me to follow the community acts right up to my death, but He did not will it! I really could have attended

---

[9] The Divine Office prescribed by the Constitutions to be recited upon the death of a nun.

[10] Free time between Compline and Matins, i.e., between eight and nine in the evening.

them all, and I would not have died a moment sooner. I'm certain of this. Sometimes, it seems to me, that if I had said nothing, no one would have discovered that I was sick.''

\* \* \*

May 19.
   *I asked her: "Why are you so happy today?"*
   "Because this morning I had two 'little' pains. Oh! very sharp ones! . . . Nothing gives me 'little' joys like 'little' pains. . . .''

\* \* \*

May 20.
1.   "Someone told me I shall fear death. This could very well be true. There isn't anyone here more mistrustful of her feelings than I am. I never rely on my own ideas; I know how weak I am. However, I want to rejoice in the feeling that God gives me at the present moment. There will always be time to suffer the opposite.''

\* \* \*

2.   *I was showing her a photo of herself:*
"Yes, but . . . this is the envelope; when will we see the letter? Oh! how I want to see the letter! . . . ''

\* \* \*

From May 21 to 26.
1.   "Théophane Vénard[11] pleases me much more than St. Louis de Gonzague [St. Aloysius Gonzaga], because the life of the latter is extraordinary, and that of Théophane is very ordinary. Besides, he is the one who is talking, whereas for the Saint someone is telling the story and making him speak; so we know practically nothing about his 'little' soul!
   "Théophane Vénard loved his family very much, and I, too, love my 'little' family very much. I don't understand the saints who don't

11 See p. 309.

love their family. . . . My little family of today, oh! I love it very much! I love my little Mother very, very much.''

\* \* \*

2. "I'm going to die very soon, but when! Oh! when? . . . It doesn't come! I'm like a little child who has been always promised a cake. He is shown it at a distance, and when he approaches to take it, a hand withdraws it. . . . But, at the bottom of my heart, I am resigned to living, dying, being cured, and even going to Cochin-China,[12] if God wills it.''

\* \* \*

3. "After my death, I don't want to be surrounded with wreaths of flowers as Mother Geneviève was.[13] To those who want to give these, you will say that I would rather they spend this money in the ransom of little black babies. This will please me.''

\* \* \*

4. "There was a time when I had trouble taking expensive remedies, but, at present, it makes no difference to me; it's just the contrary. This is ever since the time I read in St. Gertrude's life that she enjoyed these for herself, saying that this would be to the advantage of those who do good to us. She relied on Our Lord's words: 'Whatever you do to the least of my brethren, you do to me.' ''[14]

\* \* \*

5. "I'm convinced of the uselessness of remedies to cure me; but I have made an agreement with God so that He will bring profit from them for poor, sick missionaries who have neither the time nor the means to take care of themselves. I've asked Him to cure them instead of me through the medicines and the rest that I'm obliged to take.''

---

[12] To the Saigon Carmel founded by the Lisieux Carmel in 1861.

[13] See p. 300.

[14] Matthew 25:40.

6. "I've been told so much that I have courage, and this is so far from the truth, that I have said to myself: Well, then, you mustn't make a liar out of everybody! And so I set myself, with the help of grace, to the acquisition of courage. I've acted just like a warrior who, hearing himself always being praised for his bravery, and knowing that he's nothing but a coward, ends up by being ashamed of the compliments and wants to be deserving of them."

\* \* \*

7. "When I'm up in heaven, how many graces I will beg for you! Oh! I'll torment God so much that, if He wanted to refuse me at first, my importunity will force Him to grant my desires. This story is in the Gospel."[15]

\* \* \*

8. "If the saints show me less affection than my sisters have shown me, this will appear very hard for me . . . and I'll go and cry in a little corner."

\* \* \*

9. "The Holy Innocents will not be little children in heaven; they will have only the indefinable charms of childhood. They are represented as 'children' because we need pictures to understand spiritual things. . . . Yes, I hope to join them! If they want, I'll be their little page, holding up their trains."

\* \* \*

10. "If I didn't have this spiritual trial[16] that is impossible to understand, I really believe I'd die of joy at the thought of leaving this earth."

---

[15] Luke 11:5-8.

[16] Thérèse's "trial of faith," lasting from Easter, 1896 until her death, September 30, 1897. See *Story of a Soul,* pp. 211-214.

May 21 to 26.[a]

11. "I was a little sad this morning, wondering whether God was really pleased with me. I was thinking of what each Sister would say about me, if she were questioned. One would say: 'She is a good little soul.' Another: 'She is very gentle, very pious, but . . . ' And still others would have different ideas; several would find me very imperfect, which is true. . . . As for my little Mother, she loves me so much that this blinds her, and so I can't believe her. Oh! what God thinks, who will tell me? I was in these reflections when your little note reached me. You were telling me that everything in me pleased you, that I was especially loved by God, that He had not made me, as He did others, climb the rough ladder of perfection, but that he had placed me in an elevator so that I might be brought to Him more speedily. Already, I was much touched, but always the thought that your love made you see what wasn't there hindered me from rejoicing fully. Then I took my little Gospels, asking God to console me, to answer me Himself, and my glance fell upon this passage which I'd never noticed before: 'For he whom God sent speaks the words of God, for not by measure does God give the Spirit.'[17] Oh! then I shed tears of joy, and this morning, when awakening, I was still filled with joy. It is you, little Mother, whom God has sent for me; it is you who brought me up, who had me enter Carmel. All the great graces of my life I have received through you. You speak the same words as God, and now I believe that God is very much content with me since you have said so.''

* * *

May 26. *Eve of the Ascension.*

"This morning, during the procession,[18] I was in the hermitage of St. Joseph, and I was looking out the window at the community in the garden. It was beautiful, this procession of religious in white mantles; it made me think of the procession of virgins in heaven. At the turn in the chestnut walk, I saw you all half-hidden by the tall grass and the buttercups in the meadow. It was more and more delightful. But then

---

(a)   *"I no longer recall the exact date."* [Mother Agnes of Jesus' note]

[17]   John 3:34.

[18]   Procession for the Rogation Days.

among these religious, I saw one, the nicest of all, who was looking in my direction, who was bending over, giving me a smile of recognition. It was my little Mother! I recalled the dream immediately: the smile and the caresses of Mother Anne of Jesus[19] and the same impression of sweetness invaded me. I said to myself: This is the way in which the saints know me, love me, and smile upon me from above, inviting me to join them!

"Then the tears came. It has been many years since I cried as much as I did then. Ah! but these were tears of consolation!"

\* \* \*

May 27. *Ascension.*
1.  "I really want a 'circular,'[20] because I've always been of the opinion that I must pay for the Office of the Dead that each Carmelite nun will recite for me. I don't understand too well why there are those who don't want any circular; it's so sweet to know one another, and to know a little about those with whom we shall live for all eternity."

\* \* \*

2.  "I haven't any misgivings whatsoever about the final struggles or sufferings of this sickness, no matter how great they may be. God has always come to my aid; He has helped me and led me by the hand from my childhood. I count upon Him. I'm sure He will continue to help me until the end. I may really become exhausted and worn out, but I shall never have too much to suffer; I'm sure of this."

\* \* \*

3.  "I don't know when I will die, but I believe it will be soon; I have many reasons for expecting it."

\* \* \*

4.  "I don't want to die more than to live; that is, if I had the choice,

---

[19] See *Story of a Soul,* p. 190.
[20] A biographical account sent to the Carmels after the death of a nun.

I would prefer to die. But since it's God who makes the choice for me, I prefer what He wills. It's what He does that I love.''

* * *

5. "Let no one believe that if I were to be cured it would throw me off my course or destroy my little plans. Not in the least! Age means nothing in the eyes of God, and I'd manage to remain a little child, even were I to live for a long time.''

* * *

6. "I always see the good side of things. There are some who set about giving themselves the most trouble. For me, it's just the opposite. If I have nothing but pure suffering, if the heavens are so black that I see no break in the clouds, well, I make this my joy! I revel in it![21] I did this during Papa's trials[22] which made me more glorious than a queen.''

* * *

7. "Did you notice during the reading in the refectory, the letter addressed to the mother of St. Louis de Gonzague, in which it was said of the Saint that had he lived to the age of Noah he would not have learned more or become more holy?''

*She said this because of some remarks that were made about the necessity of a long life in the service of God.*

* * *

8. *With reference to her approaching death:*
"I'm like a person who, having a lottery ticket, runs the chance of winning, more so than one who hasn't a ticket; but still the person is not sure of obtaining a prize. So I have a ticket, my illness, and I can keep up my hopes!''

---

[21] *"Faire jabot"* has the meaning of (i) to pout; (ii) to swell with importance, to put on airs, to strut.

[22] M. Martin's mental illness.

9. "I recall a little neighbor at Les Buissonnets, aged three, hearing herself called by other children, said to her mother: 'Mamma, they want me! let me go, I beg you. . . . They want me!'

"Well, it appears to me that today the little angels are calling me, and I, like the little girl, say to you: 'Let me go, then, they want me! . . .'"

"I don't hear them, I feel them."

\* \* \*

10. "At the time when my departure for Tonkin was planned, around the month of November,[23] you recall how we began a novena to Théophane Vénard in order to have a sign of God's will? At this time, I returned to all the community exercises, even Matins. Well! during the novena precisely, I began to cough again, and since then I've gone from bad to worse. He's the one who's calling me. Oh! I would love to have his portrait; he's a soul that pleases me. St. Louis de Gonzague was serious, even during recreation, but Théophane Vénard was always cheerful."

*At this time we were reading the life of St. Louis de Gonzague in the refectory. [This is the same person as St. Aloysius Gonzaga.]*

\* \* \*

May 29.

*"Pointes de feu" [a cauterizing remedy for tuberculosis, consisting of repeated puncturing of the skin with red-hot needles] applied for the second time. In the evening I was sad, and seeking consolation, I opened the Gospels in her presence. My eyes fell upon these words which I read to her: "He is risen; he is not here; see the place where they laid him."[24]*

"Yes, that's really true! I am no longer, in fact, as I was in my childhood, open to every sorrow; I am as one risen; I am no longer in the place where they think I am. . . . Oh! don't be troubled about me, for I have come to a point where I cannot suffer any longer, because all suffering is sweet to me."

---

[23] 1896.
[24] Mark 16:6.

May 30.

1.   *On this day she received permission to confide to me her coughing up of blood on Good Friday, 1896. When I showed her how pained I was at not being told immediately, she consoled me as well as she could, writing me this note in the evening:*

"Don't be troubled, dear little Mother, because *your* little girl *seemed* to have hidden something from you; for you know well enough, although she hid a little corner of the *envelope,* she has never hidden from you one single line of the *letter.* Who then knows better than you this little letter that you so much love? To others, I can show the envelope on all its sides, since they can see only this much; but to you! . . . Oh! little Mother, you know now, it was on Good Friday that Jesus began to tear a little the envelope of YOUR little letter; are you not happy that He is getting ready to read this letter you have been writing for twenty-four years? Ah! if you only knew how it will be able to speak of your love all through eternity!''

* * *

2.   *"You will perhaps suffer very much before you die," I said:*
"Oh! don't worry about it; I have a great desire to suffer.''

* * *

3.   "I don't know what I'll do in heaven without you!''

# JUNE

*The first days of June were marked with rapid decline in the patient's health. Anxiety was great on June 5, the eve of Pentecost, and the Prioress, along with her dismayed community, began a novena in honor of Our Lady of Victories.*

*The doctor prescribed a milk diet to make up for her food deficiency. Up until June 15, Thérèse frequently spoke about her approaching death, and then her condition improved. June appeared as the month of painful waiting.*

*Mother Agnes of Jesus obtained from Mother Marie de Gonzague permission for Thérèse to complete her autobiography, and the patient dedicated her remaining strength to the writing of Manuscript C from June 4 onward. Those around her did not suspect that she was writing her spiritual testament which, one year later, was to capture the hearts of so many.*

*On Pentecost Monday, June 7, Sister Geneviève (Céline) photographed her sister in three different poses. She did this in anticipation of the feast of Mother Marie de Gonzague, and, as Thérèse wrote in a letter, "in view of my approaching death." These three photos have become important historical documents. The Saint wrote sixteen letters during this month.*

June 4.

1. *She was bidding us her adieux\* in Sister Geneviève's cell, the one which leads out onto the terrace on the side of the Chapter room. She was lying on Sister Geneviève's paillasse. That particular day, she was no longer suffering and her face was transfigured. We weren't able to stop looking at her and listening to her sweet words.*

"I've asked the Blessed Virgin that I be not so tired and withdrawn as I have been all these days; I really felt that I was causing you pain. This evening, she answered me.

"Oh! little sisters, how happy I am! I see that I'm going to die very soon, I am sure of this now.

"Don't be astonished if I don't appear to you after my death, and if you see nothing extraordinary as a sign of my happiness. You will remember that it's 'my little way' not to desire to see anything. You know well what I've said so often to God, to the angels, and to the saints:

> My desire is not\*\*
> To see them here on earth.[1]

*"The angels will come looking for you," said Sister Geneviève. "Oh! perhaps we shall really see them!"*

"I don't believe you'll see them, but that doesn't prevent their being there. . . .

"I would , however, like to have a beautiful death to please you. I asked this from the Blessed Virgin. I didn't ask God for this because I want Him to do as He pleases. Asking the Blessed Virgin for something is not the same thing as asking God. She really knows what is to be done about my little desires, whether or not she must speak about them to God. So it's up to her to see that God is not forced to answer me, to allow Him to do everything He pleases.

"This evening I obtained the favor of being able to console you a little and of being very nice, but you mustn't expect to see me like this at the moment of death. I don't know! Right now the Blessed Virgin

(\*)   *It was during the novena to Our Lady of Victories to obtain her cure.*

( \*\* )   *Que mon désir n'est pas*
        *De les voir ici-bas.*

[1]   Poem by Thérèse entitled: *Jésus, Mon Bien-Aimé, rappelle-toi!* Composed October 21, 1895.

was able to do this herself, without saying anything to God, but this proves nothing for later on!

"I don't know whether I'll go to purgatory or not, but I'm not in the least bit disturbed about it; however, if I do go there, I'll not regret having done nothing to avoid it. I shall not be sorry for having worked solely for the salvation of souls. How happy I was to learn that our holy Mother, St. Teresa, thought the same way![2]

"Little Mother, if you are Prioress again one day,[3] don't worry about it; you will see that you will not experience the same trials as you did before. You will be in control of things. You will allow others to think and say what they want, but you will carry out your duties in peace, etc., etc.

"Do nothing to become Prioress, and do nothing not to be in this position. Moreover, I promise you I'll not allow you to become Prioress if this is prejudicial to your soul."

*When I kissed her:*

"I've said everything! in particular to my little Mother for later on. . . .

"Don't be troubled, little sisters, if I suffer very much and if you see in me, as I've already said, no sign of happiness at the moment of my death. Our Lord really died as a Victim of Love, and you see what His agony was! . . . All this says nothing."

* * *

2. *A little later, being alone with her, and seeing her suffer very much, I said: "Well, you wanted to suffer, and God hasn't forgotten it."*

"I wanted to suffer and I've been heard. I have suffered very much for several days now. One morning, during my act of thanksgiving after Communion, I felt the agonies of death . . . and with it no consolation!"

---

[2]  Teresa of Avila, St., *Way of Perfection*. See *the Complete Works of St. Teresa*, trans. and ed. by E. Allison Peers, from the critical edition of P. Silverio de Santa Teresa, O.C.D., 3 vols. (London: Sheed & Ward Ltd., 1946), 2:12.

[3]  Mother Agnes of Jesus was prioress from 1902 until her death (1951), with the exception of eighteen months, in 1908-1909.

3. "I accept everything out of love for God, even all sorts of extravagant thoughts that come into my mind."

\* \* \*

June 5.
1. *During Matins:*
"Little Mother, I've seen that you love me with an unselfish love. Well! if I know that you are my little Mother, you will one day know that I'm your little girl. Oh! how I love you!"

\* \* \*

2. "I have read over again the play on Joan of Arc that I composed.[4] You will see there my sentiments on death; they are all expressed; this will please you. But don't believe I'm like Joan of Arc when she was afraid for a moment. . . . She was tearing her hair out![5] . . . I myself am not tearing out my 'little' hair. . . ."

\* \* \*

3. "Little Mother, it's you who prepared me for my First Communion; prepare me now for my death. . . ."

\* \* \*

4. "If you find me dead one morning, don't be troubled: it is because Papa, God, will have come to get me. Without a doubt, it's a great grace to receive the sacraments; but when God doesn't allow it, it's good just the same; everything is a grace."

\* \* \*

June 6.
1. "I thank you for having asked that I be given a particle of the sacred Host. I still have very much trouble swallowing it. But how

---

[4] *"Jeanne d'Arc accomplissant sa mission,"* written by Thérèse, January 1, 1895.
[5] Thérèse could have read this detail in *Jeanne d'arc,* H. Wallon.

happy I was to have God in my heart! I cried as on the day of my First Communion.''[6]

* * *

2. "Father Youf[7] told me with reference to my temptations against the faith: 'Don't dwell on these, it's very dangerous.' This is hardly consoling to hear, but happily I'm not affected by it. Don't worry, I'm not going to break my 'little' head by torturing myself.

"Father Youf also said: 'Are you resigned to die?' I answered: 'Ah! Father, I find I need resignation only to live. For dying, it's only joy I experience.' "

* * *

3. "I wonder how I will do when dying. I would like, nevertheless, to come off 'with honor!' But I believe this doesn't depend on oneself."
*(She was thinking of us.)*

* * *

4. "In my childhood, the great events of my life appeared to me as insurmountable mountains. When I saw little girls make their First Communion, I said to myself: How will I do at my First Communion? . . . Later: How will I do at entering Carmel? . . . And afterwards: at taking the Habit? at making Profession? At present, it's: How will I do at dying?"

* * *

5. *"I'm going to take your photograph to please Mother Prioress."*[8]
*She smiled mischievously:*
"Say rather that it's for yourself! . . . 'Little north wind, cease your blowing! It's not for me, it's for my comrade, who has no coat. . . .' "

---

6   See *Story of a Soul,* p. 77.
7   See p. 309.
8   Mother Marie de Gonzague.

*She thus recalled a little Auvergnat story that Papa used to tell us. She made a perfect application, for the comrade who appeared so charitable was pleading for himself.*

\* \* \*

6. *We didn't want to tell her, for fear of causing her any disgust, that the syrup she was taking was snail-syrup, but she noticed this and laughed at our fears.*

"What does it matter if I take snail-syrup as long as I can't see their horns! Now I'm eating snails just like the little ducks! Yesterday, I was acting like the ostriches, I was eating eggs raw!"

\* \* \*

7. "I love you very much, very much!"

\* \* \*

8. *I said to her: "The angels will bear you up lest you dash your foot against a stone."[9] She answered:*

"Ah! that's good for right now; for later on, after my death, I will not be encumbered!"

\* \* \*

9. *After Dr. de Cornière's[10] visit, when he found her better, I said: "Are you sad?"*

"Oh! no. . . . I drew this from the Gospel: 'Soon you will see the Son of Man seated on the clouds of heaven.'[11]

"I answered: 'When, Lord?' And on the opposite page, I read: 'This very day.'[12]

"From all this, I learn to be disturbed about nothing, not to wish to live or to die . . ."

---

[9]   Psalm 90:12.
[10]   See p. xxx.
[11]   Luke 22:69.
[12]   Ibid., 22:43.

*And after a few moments, she said:*

"However, I do want to go! I've told the Blessed Virgin so, and she can do what she pleases with my little wish."

* * *

June 7.

*Sunday.*[13] *She was taking a little rest on a bench in the cemetery, sitting by my side; after a while, she placed her head tenderly on my heart, singing softly:*

I forget you, dear Mother,*
No, no, never![14]

*Descending the steps leading into the garden, she saw a little white hen under a tree, protecting her little chicks under her wings; some were peeping out from under. Thérèse stopped, looking at them thoughtfully; after a while, I made a sign that we should go inside. I noticed her eyes were filled with tears, and I said: "You're crying!" She put her hand over her eyes and cried even more.*

"I can't explain it just now; I'm too deeply touched."

*That evening, in her cell, she told me the following, and there was a heavenly expression on her face:*

"I cried when I thought how God used this image in order to teach us His tenderness towards us.[15] All through my life, this is what He has done for me! He has hidden me totally under His wings! Earlier in the day, when I was leaving you, I was crying when going upstairs; I was unable to control myself any longer, and I hastened to our cell. My heart was overflowing with love and gratitude."

* * *

2.   "It's ten years ago today since Papa gave me that little white flower, when I spoke to him for the first time about my vocation."[16]

*Then she showed me the little flower.*

(*)   *Moi t'oublier, Mère chérie,*
*Non, non, jamais!*

[13]  June 6, Pentecost Sunday.
[14]  A passage from a contemporary hymn: *Nous t'oublier, Mère chérie?*
[15]  Matthew 23:37.
[16]  May 27, 1887, Pentecost Sunday. See *Story of a Soul*, p. 107.

3. "Had you not brought me up well, you would have seen sad things.[17] I would never have cried today when seeing the little white hen."

\* \* \*

June 8.
1. "Very soon you will all come with me; it won't be long, you'll see!"
*To Sister Marie of the Trinity, one of her novices, who was asking her to remember her in heaven:*
"Thus far you've only seen the shell; soon you'll see the little chick."

\* \* \*

2. *I was telling her I had no support here on earth:*
"But you do; you have a support, me!"

\* \* \*

3. *We were speaking to her about long-term illnesses that often tired the infirmarians out and were the cause of great suffering to the patients who were aware of this:*
"I wish to remain like this until the end of a very long life; I would even wish to be taken by influenza if it were pleasing to God."

\* \* \*

June 9.
1. "It's said in the Gospel that God will come like a Thief.[18] He will come to steal me away very gently. Oh, how I'd love to aid the Thief!"

\* \* \*

2. "How happy I am today!"

[17] Thérèse used the words "tistes choses" instead of "tristes choses."
[18] Matthew 24:43-44.

*I asked: "Has your trial of faith passed away?"*[19]

"No, but it seems to be suspended; the ugly serpents are no longer hissing in my ears."

\* \* \*

3.  "With what peace I allow it said around me that I'm getting better! Last week, I was up and around and some found me very sick; this week, I'm no longer able to stay up; I'm exhausted; and they judge me to be on the mend! What does it all mean!"

*I asked: "You hope to die soon in spite of everything?"*

"Yes, I hope to go soon; I'm certainly not getting better. My side aches very much, But I shall always say, if God cures me, I'll not be the least bit disappointed."

*To Sister Marie of the Sacred Heart, who said: "What sorrow we'll experience when you leave us!"*

"Oh, no, you will see; it will be like a shower of roses."

\* \* \*

4.  "I'm not afraid of the Thief. I see Him in the distance, and I take good care not to call out: 'Help, Thief!' On the contrary, I call to Him, saying: 'Over here, over here!' "

\* \* \*

5.  "I'm like a little child at a railway station, waiting for her Papa and Mamma to put her on the train; alas, they don't come, and the train pulls out! However, there are others, and I'll not miss all of them!"

\* \* \*

June 10.

*She was getting well and this surprised her; she was forced to get hold of herself in order not to become sad:*

"The Blessed virgin really carried out my messages well; I'll give her

---

[19] See note 16 for May.

some once more!

"I tell her very often: 'Tell Him never to put Himself out on my account.'[20]

"He has heard this, and this is exactly what He's doing. I no longer understand anything about my sickness. Here I am getting better! However, I abandon myself to Him and I'm happy just the same. What would become of me if I did not nourish the hope of soon dying? What disappointments! But I don't have a single one, because I am totally content with what God does; I desire only His will."

\* \* \*

June 11.
1. *She had cast some flowers at a statue of St. Joseph which was in the garden at the end of the chestnut walk, saying in a childish tone of voice:*
"Take them!"
*I asked: "Why are you throwing flowers at St. Joseph? To obtain a special favor?"*
"Ah, no! It's just to please him; I don't want to give in order to receive."

\* \* \*

2. "I'm not breaking my head over the writing of my 'little' life;[21] it's as though I were fishing with a line: I write whatever comes to the end of my pen."

\* \* \*

June 12.
1. "They don't believe I'm as sick as I am. So it makes it all the harder to be deprived of Holy Communion, the Divine Office. However, it's all the better if no one is worried about me. I was suffering very much, and I asked the Blessed Virgin to arrange things in order that others would be in no way inconvenienced. She answered my prayer.

---

[20] Poem written by Thérèse and entitled: *Pourquoi je t'aime, ô Marie,* in May, 1897.
[21] Manuscript "C" in *Story of a Soul.*

"As far as I am concerned, what does it matter what others think or say? I don't see why I should be disturbed about it."

\* \* \*

2. "Tomorrow, I shall not receive Holy Communion! And so many little girls will be receiving God!"[22]
*It was First Communion Day at the parish of St. Jaques, Lisieux.*

\* \* \*

June 13.
*In the garden.*
"I'm reminded of a piece of cloth stretched over a frame to be embroidered; then nobody shows up to embroider it! I wait and wait! It's useless! . . . However, this isn't really surprising since little children don't know what they want!

"I'm saying this because I'm thinking of little Jesus; He is the one who has stretched me over a frame of sufferings in order to have the pleasure of embroidering me; then He loosens me so that he can go up to heaven and show them His beautiful work.

"Whenever I am speaking of the Thief, I'm not thinking of little Jesus; I'm thinking of the 'great' God."

\* \* \*

June 14.
*This was the last day of the novena in honor of Our Lady of Victories, and she was greatly improved in health, much to her disappointment. She said with a smile:*
"I'm a cured little girl!"
*"Are you sad about it?" I asked:*
"Oh, no, we can put up with very much from one moment to the next!"

---

[22] See p. 262. This was a testimony given by Sister Marie of the Sacred Heart at the diocesan process of beatification of Sister Thérèse of the Child Jesus.

June 15.

1. "On June 9, I saw very clearly the beacon that was announcing to me heaven's port; but now I no longer see anything. It's as if my eyes were blindfolded. That day I saw the Thief; at present I no longer see anything at all. What anyone says to me about death no longer penetrates; it slides over me as it would over smooth glass. It's finished! The hope of death is all used up. Undoubtedly, God does not will that I think of it as I did before I became sick. At that time, this thought was necessary for me and very profitable; I really felt it. But today it's just the contrary. God wills that I abandon myself like a very little child who is not disturbed by what others will do to him."

* * *

2. *I asked: "Are you tired out because of your present state that seems to be prolonged? You must be suffering very much!"*
"Yes, but this pleases me."
*"Why?"*
"Because it pleases God."
*She used this word and several others that didn't fit in with the simple way she usually expressed herself. It was evident that she wanted to cloak her thoughts in order to distract us. She also adopted certain very simple expressions that she used in our presence; these took on much charm when coming from her.*

* * *

3. "I don't know when I shall die; I no longer have any confidence in this sickness. Even though I were to receive Extreme Unction, I still believe I could recover. I will not be sure of success until I shall have taken the final step and shall see myself in God's arms.

* * *

4. *In the evening:*
"How I'd like to say something nice to you!"
*I said: "Tell me simply whether you'll forget me when you're in heaven."*

"Ah, if I were to forget you, it seems to me that all the saints would chase me out of heaven just as they would an ugly owl. Little Mother, when I'm up there, 'I shall come to take you with me, so that where I am, there also you will be.' "[23]

\* \* \*

5. "I'm very happy; I don't offend God at all during my illness. Recently, I was writing on charity *(in the copybook of her Life)*[24] and, very often, the nuns came to distract me; then I was very careful not to become impatient, to put into practice what I was writing about."

\* \* \*

June 19.
*Our cousin, Mother Marguerite (Superior General of the Religious Auxiliary Nurses of Paris) had sent me a beautiful basket filled with artificial lilies for Mother Marie de Gonzague's feast day. I brought her this basket, saying with great joy: "It's the Superior General of the Auxiliary Nurses, who sent me this!"*
*She answered suddenly with verve and affection:*
"Well, then, you are the Superior General of my heart."

\* \* \*

June 20.
*I was showing her little pictures I had painted of the Blessed Virgin and the Child Jesus for the feast of Mother Prioress. She placed her hands on the miniatures spread out before her, and, spreading her fingers, she touched each of the heads of the Child Jesus, saying:*
"I'm holding them all under my dominion."

\* \* \*

June 22.
*She was seated in the garden in the wheelchair.*[25] *When I came out to her in the afternoon, she said:*

[23] John 14:3.
[24] See *Story of a Soul*, p. 219.
[25] A wheelchair used by M. Martin, Thérèse's father, during his illness; was donated to the Carmel later.

"How well I understand Our Lord's words to St. Teresa, our holy Mother: 'Do you know, my daughter, who are the ones who really love me? It's those who recognize that everything that can't be referred to me is a lie.'[26]

"Oh, little Mother, I really feel that this is true! Yes, everything outside of God is vanity."

\* \* \*

June 23.
*I was telling her: "Alas, I'll have nothing to offer to God when I die; my hands will be empty, and this saddens me very much."*

"Well, you're not like 'baby' (she called herself this at times) who finds herself in the same circumstances, nevertheless. Even if I had accomplished all the works of St. Paul, I would still believe myself to be a 'useless servant.'[27] But it is precisely this that makes up my joy, for having nothing, I shall receive everything from God."

\* \* \*

June 25.
1. *The Feast of the Sacred Heart. She had been placed in the library because of the sun that was shining in her room. During the sermon, she was glancing through a book on the Propagation of the Faith. Afterwards, she showed me a passage where there was mention made of a beautiful woman dressed in white and appearing to a baptized child. She said:*

"Later on, I'll go to little baptized children just like this."

\* \* \*

2. "I played truant during the sermon because I felt it was a feast day. I would not permit myself this every day. I consider my copybook *(her Life)* as my *little* assignment."

---

[26] Teresa of Avila, St., *Life.* See *The Complete Works of St. Teresa,* 1:290.
[27] Luke 17:10.

June 26.

"Yesterday, great pain in my side! Then . . . finished this morning! Ah! When shall I be with God! How I would like to go to heaven!"

\* \* \*

June 27.

"When I am in heaven, I'll say so many beautiful things about my little Mother to all the saints that they will really want to take her. I'll always be with my little Mother; I'll ask the saints to come with me into the terrible cellars to protect her, and, if they don't want to come, I will come all alone."

*This has reference to a little incident that had happened to me that day in the sacristy cellar.*

\* \* \*

June 29.

1.   "This is what has happened: When I was about to die, the little angels made all sorts of beautiful preparations to receive me; but they got tired and fell asleep. Alas! little children sleep a long time! We don't know when they will get up."

*She often told us little stories like this to distract us from her sufferings of soul and body.*

\* \* \*

2.   "How unhappy I shall be in heaven if I cannot do little favors on earth for those whom I love."

\* \* \*

3.   *In the evening she was feeling her trial of faith a little more and certain reflections had caused her pain. She said to me:*

"My soul is exiled, heaven is closed for me, and on earth's side it's all trial too.

"I understand very well that they don't believe I'm sick, but it's God who permits this."

4. "I shall be happy in heaven if you compose some pretty verses for me; it seems to me that this must give pleasure to the saints."

\* \* \*

June 30.
1. *I was speaking to her about certain saints who had led extraordinary lives, such as St. Simon Stylites.*[28] *She said:*
"I myself prefer the saints who feared nothing, for example, St. Cecilia, who allowed herself to be married and didn't fear."

\* \* \*

2. *Uncle had asked her to come to the parlor with us to visit him, and, as usual, she had said practically nothing.*
"How shy I was in the parlor with Uncle! When I came out, I scolded a novice very much, and I didn't recognize myself. What contrasts there are in my character! My timidity comes from an extreme shyness which I experience when anyone pays any attention to me."[29]

---

[28] An Eastern saint who lived on top of a column for years.
[29] See *Story of a Soul,* p. 34.

# JULY

*Two sources furnish us with a rich documentation for the month of July: the two hundred and thirty-eight statements that form one-third of the "Yellow Notebook," and the thirty-four letters that speak of Thérèse, the greater part addressed to the Guérin family on vacation at La Musse. The latter permit us to follow the progress of the tuberculosis step by step.*

*After an apparent respite at the end of June, great and repeated hemoptyses began on July 6 and 7. Complete immobility, ice, and other remedies removed any immediate danger. On the evening of July 8, the patient was taken down to the infirmary on the ground floor.*

*The hemoptyses began again very soon. Doctor de Cornière no longer had any hope of a cure. On July 29, her condition worsened to such an extent that she was anointed the following day. They thought she would not pass the night.*

*At the beginning of the month, Thérèse had to abandon the writing of her manuscript. Her task was completed, and that of Mother Agnes of Jesus was about to begin. At the bedside of her little sister, the future "historian" (see July 29, no. 7) questioned and received instructions. Through childhood memories evoked by the patient, reflections on her religious experience, reactions to her physical and spiritual sufferings, the real Thérèse expressed herself with great spontaneity. Her "little way" must be transmitted to as great a number of people as possible. July was the month of prophetic intuitions on her future mission.*

*Thérèse wrote thirteen letters (in pencil) during this month.*

July 2

*She went for the last time before the Blessed Sacrament in the oratory in the afternoon; but she was at the end of her strength. I saw her look at the Host for a long time and I guessed it was without any consolation but with much peace in her heart.*

*I recall that in the morning after the Mass, when the community was going to the oratory to make thanksgiving, no one thought of helping her. She walked very quietly close to the wall. I didn't dare offer her my arm.*

\* \* \*

July 3.

1.   *One of our friends had died,*[1] *and Dr. de Cornière had spoken about her illness in the presence of Thérèse; she had a tumor that he was not able to define exactly. This case interested him very much from the medical viewpoint. "What a pity I was unable to make an autopsy," he said. She said later:*

"Ah! it's in this way that we are indifferent towards one another on earth! Would he say the same thing if it were a question of his own mother or sister? Oh! how I would love to leave this sad world!"

\* \* \*

2.   *I was confiding to her my thoughts of sorrow and discouragement after having committed a fault:*

"You don't act like me. When I commit a fault that makes me sad, I know very well that this sadness is a consequence of my infidelity, but do you believe I remain there? Oh! no, I'm not so foolish! I hasten to say to God: My God, I know I have merited this feeling of sadness, but let me offer it up to You just the same as a trial that You sent me through love. I'm sorry for my sin, but I'm happy to have this suffering to offer to You."

\* \* \*

3.   *"How is it that you want to die with your trial against faith that*

Jeanne-Marie Primois.

*doesn't come to an end?'' I asked:*
"Ah! but I really believe in the Thief! It's upon heaven that everything bears. How strange and incomprehensible it is!''

* * *

4.   *Since milk made her sick and since she was unable to take anything else at this time, Dr. de Cornière had prescribed a kind of condensed milk that was to be obtained at the pharmacists's under the name of "lait maternisé." This prescription, for various reasons, caused her pain, and when she saw the bottles arrive, she began to shed warm tears.*
*In the afternoon, she felt the need of going out of herself, and she said to us with a sad and gentle look:*
"I need some food for my soul; read a life of a saint to me.''
*"Do you want the life of St. Francis of Assisi? This will distract you when he speaks of the little birds.''*
"No, not to distract me, but to see some samples of humility.''

* * *

5.   *"When you are dead, they will place a palm in your hand,'' I said:*
"Yes, but I'll have to let it go whenever I want to, in order to give graces by the handful to my little Mother. I will have to do everything that will be pleasing to me.''

* * *

6.   *In the evening:*
"Even the saints are abandoning me! I was begging St. Anthony during Matins to find our handkerchief that I lost. Do you think he answered me? He did no such thing![2] But it doesn't make any difference; I told him I loved him just the same.''

* * *

7.   "During Matins I saw the stars twinkling, and then I heard the

---

[2]   The Norman expression for "bien gardé."

Divine Office, and this pleased me."
*The window of her cell was open.*

\* \* \*

July 4.
1. "God has helped me, and I have gained the upper hand over the matter of the milk."

\* \* \*

2. *In the evening:*
"Our Lord died on the Cross in agony, and yet this is the most beautiful death of love. This is the only one that was seen; no one saw that of the Blessed Virgin. To die of love is not to die in transports. I tell you frankly, it seems to me that this is what I am experiencing."

\* \* \*

3. *I exclaimed: "Oh, what a feeling I have that you're going to suffer!"*
"What does it matter! Suffering can attain extreme limits, but I'm sure God will never abandon me."

\* \* \*

4. "I'm very grateful to Father Alexis;[3] he did me much good. Father Pichon[4] treated me too much like a child; however, he did me much good also by telling me I'd not committed a mortal sin."

\* \* \*

July 5.
1. *I was talking to her about my weak points, and she said:*
"I have my weaknesses also, but I rejoice in them. I don't always succeed either in rising above the nothings of this earth; for example, I

---

[3]   See *Story of a Soul,* p. 173.
[4]   Ibid., p. 149.

will be tormented by a foolish thing I said or did. Then I enter into myself, and I say: Alas, I'm still at the same place as I was formerly! But I tell myself this with great gentleness and without any sadness! It's so good to feel that one is weak and little!''

\* \* \*

2. ''Don't be sad about seeing me sick, little Mother, for you can see how happy God makes me. I'm always cheerful and content.''

\* \* \*

3. *After looking at a picture representing Our Lord with two little children, the smaller one having climbed up on His lap, the other, standing at His feet, kissing His hand:*
''I'm this very little one who has climbed up on His lap, who is lifting his little head and is caressing Jesus without any fear. The other little one doesn't please me as much; he's acting like an adult. He's been told something, and he knows he must have respect for Jesus.''

\* \* \*

July 6.
1. *She had just coughed up some blood; I said: "You're going to leave us then?"*
''I am not. Father⁵ said to Me: 'You're going to have to perform a great sacrifice in leaving your sisters.' I answered: 'But, Father, I find I'm not leaving them; on the contrary, I'll be closer to them after my death.' ''

\* \* \*

2. ''I think that as far as my death is concerned I'll have to have the same patience regarding it as I had to have in the other great events of my life. Look: I entered Carmel when I was young, and yet, after everything had been decided, I had to wait three months; for my taking of the Habit, the same thing; for my Profession, the same thing

⁵ Fr. Louis Youf, see p. 309.

again. Well, for my death, it will be the same thing; it will come soon, but I'll still have to wait for it.''

\* \* \*

3. "When I'm in heaven, I'll advance towards God like Sister Elizabeth's[6] little niece, standing in front of the parlor grilles. You know how, when she recited her piece, and finished with a curtsy, she raised her arms, and said: 'Happiness to all those whom I love.'

"God will say to me: 'What do you want, my little child?' And I'll answer: 'Happiness for all those whom I love.' Then I'll do the same thing before all the saints."

*I said to her: "You're really happy today; I feel you've seen the Thief."*

"Yes, each time I am sicker I see Him again. But even though I were not to see Him, I love Him so much that I'm always content with what He does. I wouldn't love Him less if He were not to come and steal me away; it's just the opposite. When He misleads me, I pay Him all sorts of compliments, and He doesn't know what to do with me."

\* \* \*

4. "I read a beautiful passage in the Reflections of the Imitation.[7] It was a thought from Father de Lamennais, but it is still very beautiful. *(She believed, and we did too, that this Father de Lamennais had died impenitent.)*

"Our Lord enjoyed all the delights of the Trinity when He was in the garden of Olives, and still His agony was none the less cruel. It's a mystery, but I assure you that I understand something about it by what I'm experiencing myself."

\* \* \*

5. *I had placed a vigil light before the Virgin of the Smile[8] in order to receive the favor that Thérèse stop coughing up blood.*

---

[6]   See p. 305.
[7]   *The Imitation of Christ,* II, 9, Reflections.
[8]   Statue which Thérèse saw smile upon her when she was seriously ill, May 13, 1883. See *Story of a Soul,* p. 64.

"You're not rejoicing then that I'm dying! Ah, for me to rejoice, it's necessary that I continue to cough up blood. However, it's ended for today!"

\* \* \*

6.   *It was 8:15 in the evening, and I brought her lamp which they had forgotten to bring up to her; I also did a few other little services for her. She was very much touched and said:*
"You've always acted this way towards me. I cannot express my gratitude to you."
*Then drying her tears:*
"I'm crying because I'm so touched by everything you've done for me since my childhood. Ah, what I owe you! But when I'm in heaven, I'll tell the truth; I'll tell all the saints: It's my little Mother who gave me all that pleases you in me."

\* \* \*

7.   "When will the Last Judgment take place? Oh, I wish it were at this very moment! And what will happen afterwards?"

\* \* \*

8.   "I'm making very many little sacrifices."

\* \* \*

July 7.
1.   *After she had coughed up blood once more:*
"Baby is going to go to see God very soon."
*I asked: "Are you afraid of death now that you see it so close?"*
"Ah, less and less?"
*"Do you fear the Thief? This time He's at the door."*
"No, He's not at the door; He's inside! But what are you saying, little Mother! Do I fear the Thief! How can I fear one whom I love so much!"

2. *I asked her to explain what happened when she made her Act of Oblation to Merciful Love.*[9] *First she said:*

"Little Mother, I told you this when it took place, but you paid no attention to me."

*This was true; I'd given her the impression that I placed no importance on what she was saying.*

"Well, I was beginning the Way of the Cross; suddenly, I was seized with such a violent love for God that I can't explain it except by saying it felt as though I were totally plunged into fire. Oh! What fire and what sweetness at one and the same time! I was on fire with love, and I felt that one minute more, one second more, and I wouldn't be able to sustain this ardor without dying. I understood, then, what the saints were saying about these states which they experienced so often. As for me, I experienced it only once and for one single instant, falling back immediately into my habitual state of dryness."

*And later on:*

"At the age of fourteen, I also experienced transports of love. Ah! how I loved God! But it wasn't at all as it was after my Oblation to Love; it wasn't a real flame that was burning me."

\* \* \*

3. "This saying of Job: 'Although he should kill me, I will trust in him,'[10] has fascinated me from my childhood. But it took me a long time before I was established in this degree of abandonment. Now I am there; God has placed me there. He took me into His arms and placed me there."

\* \* \*

4. *I begged her to say a few edifying and friendly words to Dr. de Cornière:*

"Ah! little Mother, this isn't my little style. Let Doctor de Cornière think what he wants. I love only simplicity; I have a horror for 'pretense.' I assure you that to do what you want would be bad on my part."

[9]   June 9. 1895. See *Story of a Soul*, p. 180.
[10]   Job 13:15.

5.   "In fact, I could give him the impression that I'm really sick. Never shall I forget the scene this morning[11] when I was coughing up blood; Doctor de Cornière had a puzzled look."

* * *

6.   "See, it's for your sake that God treats me so sweetly. No more vesicatories, nothing but gentle remedies. I am suffering, but not enough to make me cry."

*After a moment, with a mischievous look:*

"However, He did send us trials that could have caused us to cry and still we didn't cry."

*She was referring to our great family trial.[12] As for the "gentle remedies," these weren't long lasting, and her sufferings were terrible.*

* * *

7.   "I'm just like a poor 'little gray wolf' that really wants to go back into the forest, but he is forced to live in houses."

*Our father, at Les Buissonnets, used to call her sometimes "my little gray wolf."*

* * *

8.   "I just saw a little sparrow on the garden wall, waiting patiently for its parents; from time to time, it gave forth its little chirp, calling them to come and give it a mouthful of food. I thought it was like me."

* * *

9.   *I told her that I enjoyed compliments:*

"I'll remember that when I'm in heaven."

[11]   See pp. 272-275.
[12]   M. Martin's illness.

July 8.

1. *She was so sick there was talk of giving her Extreme Unction. That day, she was taken down from her cell to the infirmary; she was no longer able to stand up, and she had to be carried down. While still in her cell, and knowing they were thinking of anointing her, she said in a tone of joy:*

"It seems to me that I'm dreaming! However, they aren't fools."
*She meant Father Youf, the chaplain, and Doctor de Cornière.*
"I fear only one thing: that all this will change."

\* \* \*

2. *She was trying to recall sins she could have committed through her senses in order to confess them before being anointed; we were considering the sense of smell, and she said:*

"I remember during my last trip from Alençon to Lisieux that I used a bottle of *eau de Cologne* which was given to me by Mme. Tifenne (a friend of the family), and I did this with pleasure."

\* \* \*

3. *We all wanted to talk to her at once:*
"Lots of people who have something to say!"

\* \* \*

4. *She was overflowing with joy and was trying to communicate it to us:*

"If, when I am in heaven, I can't come and play little games with you on earth, I will go and cry in a little corner."[13]

\* \* \*

5. *To me:*
"You have a long nose; it will serve you well later on."[14]

---

[13] Thérèse used the word *"toin"* for the correct word *"coin."*

[14] Mother Agnes states: "Papa used to say this at times; it was a well-known expression."

6.  *Looking at her emaciated hands:*
   "I'm becoming a skeleton already, and that pleases me."

* * *

7.  "I will tell you something: very soon I'm going to be dying. . . .
It reminds me of a greased pole; I've made more than one slip, then,
all of a sudden there I am at the top!"

* * *

8.  "I would rather be reduced to ashes than to be preserved like St.
Catherine of Bologna.[15] I know only St. Crispino, who came forth
from the tomb with honor."
   *The body of this Saint is admirably preserved in the Franciscan
monastery at Rome.*

* * *

9.  *Speaking to herself:*
   "It's really something to be in one's agony! But what does it matter
after all! I have sometimes agonized over foolish things."

* * *

10. *With a serious and gentle look, I don't recall any longer the occasion, but she had been misunderstood:*
   "The Blessed Virgin did well to keep all these things in her 'little'
heart. . . .[16] They can't be angry with me for doing as she did."

* * *

11. "The little angels amused themselves very much by playing little
tricks on me. They all tried to hide from me the light which was
showing me my approaching end."

---

[15] See *Story of a Soul,* p. 128.
[16] Luke 2:19 and 51.

*I asked: "Did they hide the Blessed Virgin from you?"*

"No, the Blessed Virgin will never be hidden from me, for I love her too much."

\* \* \*

12. "I want to be anointed very much; let them laugh at me afterwards if they want to."

*She meant that the Sisters could laugh if she were restored to health, for she knew that some of them didn't think she was in danger of death.*

\* \* \*

13. "Oh, certainly, I shall cry when I see God! No, we can't cry in heaven. Yes, we can, since it is said: 'And God will wipe away every tear from their eyes.' "[17]

\* \* \*

14. "I'll offer you my little fruits of joy such as God gives them to me.

"In heaven, I shall obtain many graces for those who did good to me. For my little Mother, everything. You won't even be able to make use of them all, there will be so many for you to enjoy."[18]

\* \* \*

15. "If you only knew how gentle God will be with me! But if He is the least bit not gentle, I'll still find Him gentle. . . . If I go to purgatory, I'll be very content, I'll do like the three Hebrews in the furnace,[19] I'll walk around in the flames singing the canticle of Love. Oh, how happy I will be, if when going to purgatory I can deliver other souls, suffering in their place, for then I would be doing good, I would be delivering captives."

---

[17] Apocalypse 21:4.

[18] Thérèse used the word *"éjouir"* instead of the correct word *"réjouir."*

[19] Daniel 3:51.

16. *She warned me that later on a great number of young priests,
knowing she had been given as spiritual sister to two missionaries,*[20]
*will ask the same favor from the Carmel. She told me that this could
become a great danger:*

"Any Sister could write what I have written and would receive the
same compliments, the same confidence. But it's only through prayer
and sacrifice that we can be useful to the Church. Correspondence
should be very rare, and it mustn't be permitted at all for certain
religious who would be preoccupied with it, believing they're doing
marvels, and would be doing nothing really but harming themselves
and perhaps falling into the devil's subtle traps."

*With further insistence:*

"Mother, what I've just told you is very important; I beg you not to
forget it later on. At Carmel, we should never make any false currency
in order to redeem souls. And often the beautiful words we write and
the beautiful words we receive are an exchange of false money."

* * *

17. *To make us laugh:*

"I would rather be placed in a little Gennin box, not in a coffin."

*Someone had sent the Carmel some beautiful artificial flowers in
long, well-seasoned wooden boxes from "Maison Gennin" at Paris.*

* * *

18. "It makes us so good when we suffer something; it leads to more
regular observance and charity."

* * *

July 9.

1. *She didn't want any sadness around her, nor at Uncle's home:*

"I want them all to have a 'good time' at La Musse. I'm having a
spiritually good time all day long."

*"This 'good time' can't be very happy," I said:*

"I find it very happy."

---

[20] Fathers Bellière and Roulland; see pp. 297 and 307.

2. "Sister Geneviève will need me. . . . However, I will come back."

\* \* \*

3. *After the Father Superior's*[21] *visit, I made the remark that she didn't know how to use the proper tactics to receive Extreme Unction, that she didn't appear to be sick in the least when receiving these visits:* "I don't know the trade!"[22]

\* \* \*

4. "I would love to go! . . ."

\* \* \*

5. *I said: "You will probably die on July 16, the feast of Our Lady of Mount Carmel, or on August 6, the feast of the Holy Face."*[23] "Eat 'dates' as much as you want; I myself no longer want to eat any. . . . I have been too much taken in by dates."\*

\* \* \*

6. "Why should I be protected more than anyone else from the fear of death? I won't say like St. Peter: 'I will never deny you.'"[24]

\* \* \*

7. *We were speaking about "holy poverty."* "Holy poverty! How funny to speak of a 'holy one' who will never enter heaven!"\*\*

---

(\*) "Mangez des 'dattes' tant que vous voudrez, moi je ne veux plus en manger. . . . J'ai été trop attrapée par les *dates.*"

(\*\*) "Sainte Pauvreté! Que c'est drôle une sainte qui n'ira pas dans le Ciel!"

[21] Canon Charles Maupas; see p. 306.
[22] Mother Agnes says elsewhere: "the trade of trickery."
[23] The custom of honoring the "Holy Face of Jesus" was restored at the Carmel during Mother Agnes' term as prioress, 1893-1896.
[24] Matthew 26:35.

8.  *I was somewhat troubled:*
"My love should be a consolation to you."
*To those who were present:*
"I'm going to manage everything for my little Mother."
*In the evening, to me alone:*
"Oh! then, I've not been mistaken; I know very well that everything you do for me is done through love. . . ."

\* \* \*

9.  *We had caught a mouse in the infirmary, and she made up a whole story about it, begging us to bring her the wounded mouse so that she could put it in bed by her side and have the doctor examine it. We laughed very much over this, and she was happy for having distracted us.*

\* \* \*

July 10.
1.  "Little children are not damned."

\* \* \*

2.  *"What you have written*[25] *could very well one day go to the Holy Father."*
*Laughing:*
*"Et nunc et semper!"**

\* \* \*

3.  *Showing me with a childish gesture the picture of the Blessed Virgin nursing the child Jesus, she said:*
"There's something that's good milk; you must tell Dr. de Cornière that."[26]

(*)   "Now and forever!"

[25] *Story of a Soul.*
[26] Thérèse was on a milk diet and found it very difficult.

4. *It was Saturday, and she had coughed up blood at midnight:*
"The Thief had made His mamma a thief. . . . So she came at midnight to force the Thief out of hiding; or else she came all alone because the Thief didn't want to come."

\* \* \*

5. "They will not make me last one minute longer than the Thief wants."

\* \* \*

6. *To me alone:*
"You go to too much trouble over things that aren't worth any trouble."

\* \* \*

7. *With a smile:*
"When you've done something like this, what is even much worse is that you fear the consequences too much. . . ."

\* \* \*

8. "You're like a timid little bird that hasn't lived among people; you're always afraid of being caught. I haven't any fear of anyone; I have always gone where I pleased. I always slipped by them."

\* \* \*

9. *Holding her Crucifix, after having kissed it at three in the afternoon,*[27] *she was acting as though she wanted to remove the crown and the nails.*

---

[27] It was customary in the monastery to ring the bell at three o'clock in the afternoon in memory of Christ's death; each nun kissed her crucifix.

10. *Returning to her accident during the night,*[28] *she said in a char-*
*ming way, looking at the picture of the Blessed Virgin attached to the*
*curtain of her bed:*
"The Blessed Virgin isn't a thief by nature. . . . But ever since she
had her Son, He taught her the trade. . . ."
*After a pause:*
"However, the Child Jesus is still too small to have ideas like that.
. . . He hardly thinks of stealing when on His Mother's breast. . . .
Yes! He's already thinking like this, He knows well enough He will
come to steal me."
"*At what age?*"
"At twenty-four."

\* \* \*

11. *We were speaking about death and the distortions brought upon*
*the features at the moment of death. She said:*
"If this happens for me, don't be sad, for immediately afterwards
I'll have nothing but smiles."
*Sister Geneviève was looking at the lid of a baptismal case, saying*
*that the beautiful head she saw there would serve her as a model for*
*the head of an angel. Our little Thérèse really wanted to see it, but no*
*one thought of showing it to her, and she didn't ask. I learned this*
*later on.*

\* \* \*

12. "*What will I have to think when I see the window of your cell*
*when you have already left this earth? My heart will be heavy.*"
"Ah! you will think that I'm very happy, that there I struggled and
suffered very much. . . . I would have been content to die there."

\* \* \*

13. *(During Matins)*
*It came into her head that she wasn't seriously ill, that the doctor*

---

[28] Thérèse's coughing up of blood.

*was mistaken about her state of health. She told me about these trials and added:*

"If my soul had not been filled in advance with abandonment to God's will, if it had been necessary that it let itself be submerged by these feelings of joy and sadness that succeed each other so quickly on this earth, this would have been a bitter pain, and I could not have borne it. But these changes only touch the surface of my soul. . . . Ah! nevertheless, they are great trials!"

\* \* \*

14. "I believe it isn't the blessed Virgin who is playing these tricks on me! . . . She is forced to do so by God! . . . He tells her to try me so that I give further proofs to Him of my abandonment and love."

\* \* \*

15. *To me alone:*

"You're always there to console me. . . . You fill my last days with sweetness."

\* \* \*

July 11.

1. *She recited the whole stanza:*

> Since the Son of God willed that His Mother
> Be subjected to the night, to anguish of heart,
> It is, then, a good thing to suffer on earth?[29]
> Etc. . . . . . . . . . . . . . . . . . . . . \*

*"You don't see her any longer, the thief?"*

"Yes, I see her! You don't understand! She is really free not to steal me. . . . Ah! 'I looked to the right, and there was no one who knew me.'[30] God alone can understand me."

> (\*) *Puisque le Fils de Dieu a voulu que sa Mère*
> *Fût soumise à la nuit, à l'angoisse de coeur*
> *Alors, c'est donc un bien de souffrir sur la terre?*[29]
> Etc. . . . .

[29] Thérèse's poem: *Pourquoi je t'aime, ô Marie.*
[30] Psalm 141:5.

2.  *During Matins. She spoke to me about her prayers of former days, in the summer evenings during the periods of silence, and she understood then by experience what a "flight of the spirit" was.*[31] *She spoke to me about another grace of this kind which she received in the grotto of St. Mary Magdalene,*[32] *in the month of July, 1889, a grace followed by several days of "quietude."*[33]

". . . It was as though a veil had been cast over all the things of this earth for me. . . . I was entirely hidden under the Blessed Virgin's veil. At this time, I was placed in charge of the refectory, and I recall doing things as though not doing them; it was as if someone had lent me a body. I remained that way for one whole week."

* * *

3.  *I was speaking to her about the manuscript of her Life, about the good it would do to souls.*

". . . But how well they will understand that everything comes from God; and what I shall have of glory from it will be a gratuitous gift from God that doesn't belong to me; everybody will see this clearly. . . ."

* * *

4.  *She spoke to me about the Communion of Saints, and she told me how the goods of one would be the goods of another:*

". . . Just as a mother is proud of her children, so also we shall be proud of each other, having not the least bit of jealousy."

* * *

5.  "Alas! how little I've lived! Life always appeared short to me. My childhood days, these seem but of yesterday!"

---

[31] Teresa of Avila, St., *The Interior Castle.* See *The Complete Works of St. Teresa,* 2:123.

[32] A hermitage in the garden.

[33] Teresa of Avila, St., *The Way of Perfection,* See *The Complete Works of St. Teresa,* 2:123

6. "One could believe that it is because I haven't sinned[34] that I have such great confidence in God. Really tell them, Mother, that if I had committed all possible crimes, I would always have the same confidence; I feel that this whole multitude of offenses would be like a drop of water thrown into a fiery furnace. You will then tell the story about the converted sinner who died of love; souls will understand immediately, for it's such a striking example of what I'm trying to say. However, these things cannot be expressed in words."*

\* \* \*

7. *In the evening, she quoted this stanza from "The Young Consumptive," I believe. She did it with great charm:*
    My day declines, earth's scene for me shall fade.
    A last farewell, my dear one, draweth near;
    Thy guarding glance through all shall be my aid,
    And Autumn's falling leaves call forth thy prayer.**

\* \* \*

8. ". . . There's great peace in my soul. . . . My little boat is sailing once again. I know I shall not return, but I am resigned to remain sick for several months, as long as God wills it."

(\*) *Novissima Verba adds:*
    This is the story exactly as she related it to me:
    "It is related in the *Lives of the Fathers of the Desert* that one of them converted a woman who was a public sinner, and whose evil life had scandalized the entire countryside. Touched by grace, that poor sinner followed the Saint into the desert, there to carry out rigorous penance. On the very first night of the journey, however, even before she had come to the place of her retreat, her earthly ties were snapped by the violence of her repentant love. At that very moment, the holy man saw her soul being carried by angels up to the very bosom of God. This is a striking example of what I mean but cannot express."

      (\*\*) *Mes jours sont condamnés, je vais quitter la terre,*
         *Je vais vous dire adieu sans espoir de retour:*
         *Vous qui m'avez aimé, bel Ange tutélaire,*
         *Laissez tomber sur moi vos doux regards d'amour.*
         *Quand vous verrez tomber, tomber les feuilles mortes*
         *Si vous m'avez aimé, vous prierez Dieu pour moi.*

[34] See *Story of a Soul*, pp. 149 and 258.

9.   *"How God has favored you! What do you think of this predilec-tion?"*
   "I think that 'the Spirit of God breathes where he wills.' "[35]

\* \* \*

July 12.
1.   *She told me that formerly she had to undergo a rough battle with regard to a lamp to be prepared for Mother Marie de Gonzague's family that arrived unexpectedly to spend the night in the extern Sisters' quarters. The struggle was so violent, there came such thoughts against authority into her mind, that, not to give in to them, she had to implore God's help with insistence. At the same time, she applied herself as well as she could to what had been demanded of her. It was during the night silence. She was portress, and Sister St. Raphael was first in charge:*
   "To conquer myself I imagined I was preparing the lamp for the Blessed Virgin and the Child Jesus; and then I did it with an incredible care, not leaving on it the least speck of dust, and, little by little, I felt a great appeasement and a great sweetness. Matins sounded, and I was not able to go to it immediately, but I experienced such a disposition of mind, I had received such a grace, that if Sister St. Raphael had come and had said, for example, that I was mistaken about the lamp, that I had to prepare another, I would have obeyed her happily. From that day, I made the resolution never to consider whether the things commanded me appeared useful or not."

\* \* \*

2.   *Sister Marie of the Eucharist*[36] *was saying that I was admirable:*
   "Admirable Mother! Oh! no, rather amiable Mother,[37] because love is worth more than admiration."

---

[35]   John 3:8.
[36]   See p. 303.
[37]   A reference to the Blessed Virgin's Litany.

3. *To Mother Marie de Gonzague:*
"I hold nothing in my hands. Everything I have, everything I merit is for the Church and for souls. If I were to live to eighty, I will always be as poor as I am now."

\* \* \*

July 13.
1. "I really see I will have to watch over the fruits when I am in heaven, but you must not kill the birds, or else people will not send you alms."
*Swinging her arms gently towards the picture of the Child Jesus:*
"Yes, yes!"

\* \* \*

2. "God will have to carry out my will in heaven because I have never done my own will here on earth."

\* \* \*

3. *"You will look down upon us from heaven, won't you?"*
"No, I will come down!"

\* \* \*

4. *During the night, she composed the couplet for Holy Communion:*
"You who know, etc."[a]

(a) *At the process of beatification and canonization, Mother Agnes stated: "During the night of July 12, she composed this couplet as a preparation for Holy communion:*

> You who know my extreme littleness,
> You don't hesitate to lower Yourself to me!
> Come into my heart, O white Host that I love,
> Come into my heart, for it longs for You!
> Ah, I desire that Your goodness would let me
> Die of Love after receiving this favor.
> Jesus! Listen to my tender cry.
> Come into my heart!

Toi qui connais ma petitesse extrême,
Tu ne crains pas de t'abaisser vers moi
Viens en mon coeur, Ô blanche Hostie qui j'aime,
Ah! je voudrais que ta bonté me laisse
Mourir d'amour après cette faveur.
Jésus! entends le cri de ma tendresse.
Viens en mon coeur!

*With reference to it, she said:*
"I composed it very easily; it's extraordinary. I believed I could no longer compose any verses."

\* \* \*

5.   "I don't say: 'Although it is hard to live in Carmel, it is sweet to die there,' but: 'Although it is sweet to live in Carmel, it is still sweeter to die there.' "

\* \* \*

6.   *The doctor had found her better than usual. Then holding her side from which she was suffering very much, she said:*
"Yes, yes, she's much better than usual! . . ."

\* \* \*

7.   *It seemed to me she was down-hearted in spite of her happy mood, and I said: "It's for our sake that you take on this happy mood and say these cheerful things, isn't it?"*
"I always act without any 'pretence.' "

\* \* \*

8.   *We offered her some Baudon wine.*[38]
"I don't want any earthly wine; I want to drink only the new wine in the kingdom of my Father."[39]

---

[38]   A strength-giving wine.
[39]   Matthew 26:29.

9. "When Sister Geneviève used to come to visit me, I wasn't able to say all I wanted to say in a half hour. Then, during the week, whenever I had a thought or else was sorry for having forgotten to tell her something, I would ask God to let her know and understand what I was thinking about, and in the next visit she'd speak to me exactly about the thing I had asked God to let her know.

"At the beginning, when she was really suffering and I was unable to console her, I would leave the visit with a heavy heart, but I soon understood it wasn't I who could console anyone; and then I was no longer troubled when she left very sad. I begged God to supply for my weakness, and I felt he answered me. I would see this in the following visit. Since that time, whenever I involuntarily caused anyone any trouble, I would beg God to repair it, and then I no longer tormented myself with the matter."*

\* \* \*

10. "I beg you to make an act of love to God and an invocation to all the saints; they're all my 'little' relatives up there."

\* \* \*

11. "I want them to buy three little pagans for me; a little Marie-Louis-Martin, a little Marie-Théophane; and a little girl in between the two called Marie-Cécile."
*A moment afterwards:*
"Rather, a little Marie-Thérèse."
*She wanted this in preference to money being spent for flowers after her death.*

\* \* \*

12. "With the virgins we shall be virgins; with the doctors, doctors; with the martyrs, martyrs, because all the saints are our relatives; but

---

(\*)   [She is speaking here of Céline, before her entrance, when she was taking care of her father during his illness.]

those who've followed the way of spiritual childhood will always retain the charms of childhood.''

*She developed these thoughts.*

\* \* \*

13. "Ever since I was young, God gave me the feeling that I would die young.''

\* \* \*

14. *Looking at me tenderly:*
"You really have a face! And[40] you will always have it. I'll recognize you, there!''

\* \* \*

15. "God made me always desire what He wanted to give me.''

\* \* \*

16. *To all three of us:*
"Don't believe that when I'm in heaven I'll let ripe plums fall into your mouths. This isn't what I had, nor what I desired. You will perhaps have great trials, but I'll send you lights which will make you appreciate and love them. You will be obliged to say like me: 'Lord, You fill us with joy with all the things You do for us.' ''[41]

\* \* \*

17. "Don't imagine that I'm experiencing, in dying, a living joy, such as, for example, I experienced formerly when I spent a month at Trouville or Alençon; I no longer know what living joys really are. I'm not expecting some kind of joyful feast; this isn't what attracts me. I can't think very much about the happiness of heaven; only one expectation makes my heart beat, and it is the love I shall receive and I

---

[40] Thérèse used the word "pis" for the correct word "puis."
[41] Psalm 91:5.

shall be able to give. And then I think of all the good I would like to do after my death: have little children baptized, help priests, missionaries, the whole Church.

"But first console my little sisters."

"This evening, I heard some music in the distance, and I was thinking that soon I would be listening to incomparable melodies, but this feeling of joy was only passing."

\* \* \*

18. *I asked her to point out her various assignments since she was in Carmel:*

"At my entrance into Carmel, I was placed in the linen-room, working with Mother Sub-prioress, Sister Marie of the Angels; besides, I had to sweep the staircase and the dormitory.

"I recall how much it cost me to ask our Mistress permission to perform acts of mortification in the refectory, but I never gave in to my repugnances; it seemed to me that the Crucifix in the courtyard, which I could see from the linen-room window, was turned towards me, begging this sacrifice.

"It was at this time that I was going out to weed the garden in the afternoon at 4:30; this displeased Mother Prioress very much.

"After I received the Habit, I was put in charge of the refectory until I was eighteen; I swept it and set out the water and the beer. During the Forty-Hours devotion in 1891,[42] I was assigned to the sacristy with Sister St. Stanislaus. From the month of June of the following year,[43] I went for two months without any assignment; during this time I was painting the angels in the oratory and was companion to the Procuratrix.[44] After these two months I was assigned to the Turn with Sister St. Raphael, while still being in charge of painting. I had these two assignments until the elections of 1896, when I asked if I could help Sister Marie of St. Joseph in the linen-room, under the circumstances about which you are aware."

*She then told me how others found her slow, little devoted to her duties, and how I myself believed it; and in fact, we both recalled how*

---

[42] The three days before Ash Wednesday.

[43] Actually, June, 1893.

[44] See note 5 for April.

*much I scolded her for a refectory tablecloth which she had kept in her basket for a long time without mending it. I accused her of negligence, and I was wrong, for she didn't actually have time to do it. On that occasion, without excusing herself, she had cried very much, when she saw that I was sad and very much displeased. Is this possible?*

*She told me, too, how she had suffered in the refectory with me (I was in charge), not being able to speak to me about her little affairs as she was formerly, because she didn't have permission and for other reasons.*

"You had come to the point where you no longer knew me," *she added.*

*She spoke to me, moreover, about the violence she had to do to herself to remove the spiders' webs from the alcove of St. Alexis under the stairs (she had a horror of spiders), and a thousand other details which proved to me how faithful she had been in her tasks, and what she had suffered from them without anyone's being aware of it.*

\* \* \*

July 14.
1.   "I read how the Israelites built the walls of Jerusalem, working with one hand and holding a sword in the other.[45] This is what we must do: never give ourselves over entirely to our tasks."

\* \* \*

2.   "If I had been rich, I would have found it impossible to see a poor person going hungry without giving him my possessions. And in the same way, when I gain any spiritual treasures, feeling that at this very moment there are souls in danger of being lost and falling into hell, I give them what I possess, and I have not yet found a moment when I can say: Now I'm going to work for myself."

\* \* \*

3.   *She began to recite with a heavenly expression in her voice the stanza in her poem "Rappelle-toi," which begins with these words:*

---

[45] Nehemias 4:11.

"Remember that Your holy will
Is my repose, my only happiness."[46]

* * *

4. "It is not the pain it appears to be (dying of love), provided it is really it!"

* * *

5. "What God has given me has always pleased me, even to the point that, if He had given me a choice in the matter, I would have chosen those things; even the things which appear to me less good and less beautiful than those which others had."

* * *

6. "Oh, what poisonous praises I've seen served up to Mother Prioress! How necessary it is for a person to be detached from and elevated above herself in order not to experience any harm!"

* * *

7. *In his visit, the doctor gave us renewed hope, but she experienced only pain and said to us:*
"I'm accustomed to it now! What does it matter if I remain sick for a long time! It was to spare you any anxiety that I wanted to have it over quickly."

* * *

8. "Oh, how I love you, little Mother!"

* * *

9. "My heart is filled with God's will, and when someone pours something on it, this doesn't penetrate its interior; it's a nothing which

---

[46] Thérèse's poem entitled: *Jésus, mon Bien-Aimé, rappelle-toi!*

glides off easily, just like oil which can't mix with water. I remain always at profound peace in the depths of my heart; nothing can disturb it.''

\* \* \*

10. *Looking at her emaciated hands:*
    "Oh, what joy I experience when seeing myself consumed!''

\* \* \*

July 15.
1. *I said: "Perhaps you'll die tomorrow (the feast of Our Lady of Mount Carmel) after you have received Holy Communion.''*
    "Oh, that wouldn't resemble my little way. Would you want me to leave this little way, then, in order to die? Dying after receiving Holy Communion would be too beautiful for me; little souls couldn't imitate this.

    "I only hope there will be no mishaps[47] tomorrow morning! It's things of this nature that can happen to me; for example, it's impossible to give me Communion; God is obliged to return to the tabernacle; understand?''

\* \* \*

2. *She spoke to me about Blessed Théophane Vénard, who had been unable to receive Holy Communion before his death, and she heaved a deep sigh.*

\* \* \*

3. *We had made preparations for her to receive Holy Communion the next day from Sister M. Philomena's[48] nephew who was coming to celebrate his first Mass at the Carmel and to bring her Communion afterwards. Seeing that she was sicker than usual, we feared she would cough up blood after midnight, and so we asked her to pray that no*

---

[47] Coughing up of blood.
[48] Fr. Paul Troude, see p. 308.

*such unfortunate incident take place to interfere with our plans. She
answered:*

"You know well that I cannot ask this myself, but you ask it for me
. . . . This evening, in spite of my feelings, I was asking God for this
favor in order to please my little sisters and so that the community
might not be disappointed; but in my heart I told Him just the contrary; I told Him to do just what He wanted."

\* \* \*

4.   *Seeing us decorating the infirmary:*

"Ah! what trouble we go to in order to get everything ready the way
it should be! How good earthly feasts really are! We bring beautiful
white dresses to the little communicants, and all these have to do is to
put them on; all the trouble we have gone to for their sake is hidden
from them, and all they have is joy. It's no longer the same thing when
we grow up."

\* \* \*

5.   *She told me about the following incident, the memory of which
was the source of a great grace to her:*

"Sister Marie of the Eucharist wanted to light the candles for a
procession; she had no matches; however, seeing the little lamp which
was burning in the front of the relics, she approached it. Alas, it was
half out; there remained only a feeble glimmer on its blackened wick.
She succeeded in lighting her candle from it, and with this candle, she
lighted those of the whole community. It was, therefore, the half-
extinguished little lamp which had produced all these beautiful flames
which, in their turn, could produce an infinity of others and even light
the whole universe. Nevertheless, it would always be the little lamp
which would be first cause of all this light. How could the beautiful
flames boast of having produced this fire, when they themselves were
lighted with such a small spark?

"It is the same with the Communion of Saints. Very often, without
our knowing it, the graces and lights that we receive are due to a hidden soul, for God wills that the saints communicate grace to each
other through prayer with great love, with a love much greater than
that of a family, and even the most perfect family on earth. How often

have I thought that I may owe all the graces I've received to the prayers of a person who begged them from God for me, and whom I shall know only in heaven.

"Yes, a very little spark will be capable of giving birth to great lights in the Church, like the Doctors and Martyrs, who will undoubtedly be higher in heaven that the spark; but how could anyone think that their glory will not become his?

"In heaven, we shall not meet with indifferent glances, because all the elect will discover that they owe to each other the graces that merited the crown for them.

*The conversation was too long, and I wasn't able to take it down entirely or word for word.*

* * *

July 16.

1.   *"I fear you will have to suffer very much to die," I said:*

"Why fear in advance? Wait at least for it to happen before having any distress. Don't you see that I would begin to torment myself by thinking that, if persecutions and massacres come, as they are predicted, someone will perhaps snatch out your eyes!"

* * *

2.   "I had made a complete sacrifice of Sister Geneviève,[49] but I can't say that I no longer desired her here. Very often in the summer, during the hour of silence before Matins, while I was seated on the terrace, I would say to myself: Ah! if only my Céline were near me! No! This would be too great a happiness for this earth!

"And this seemed to me an unrealizable dream. However, it wasn't through selfishness that I desired this happiness; it was for her soul, it was so that she walk our way. . . . And when I saw her enter here, and not only enter, but was given to me completely to be instructed in all things, when I saw that God was doing this, thus surpassing all my desires, I understood what an immensity of love He has for me.

"And so, little Mother, if a desire that is hardly expressed is answered in such a way, it is then impossible that all my great desires

---

[49]   See *Story of a Soul,* p. 177.

about which I've so frequently spoken to God will not be completely answered.''

\* \* \*

3. *She repeated with an air of conviction this statement of Father Bourb's which she had read in his book: "Petites Fleurs."*
"The saints of the latter days will surpass those of the first days just as the cedars surpass the other trees.''

\* \* \*

4. "You know all the inner recesses of my little soul."[a]

\* \* \*

5. *Like a little child with a bit of naughtiness in her head, she said:*
"I would like to give you a proof of love that nobody has ever before given you.''
*(I wondered what she was going to do, when . . .)*[50]

---

(a) *On August 28, 1940, at the end of her notebook, Mother Agnes of Jesus added this text:*
*Important remark:*
*When my saintly little sister told me on July 16, 1897, "You alone know all the inner recesses of my little soul," I am sure that she was not excluding from this complete knowledge of her soul, Sister Marie of the Sacred Heart and Sister Geneviève of the Holy Face. Sister Marie of the Sacred Heart, to whom she owed the Blessed Virgin's smile and who had prepared her for her First Communion, and to whom we ourselves owe her goddaughter's marvelous response in Manuscript B, Story of a Soul, on September 17, 1896. Sister Geneviève of the Holy Face, her Céline, whom she called: 'The sweet echo of my soul.' ''*
*"But she was inspired by God to tell me this in particular, so that, later on, because of the authority that would be given to me, others could place their trust entirely in what I said and wrote about her.''*

*Sister Agnes of Jesus*
*August 28, 1940.*

[50] The three lines following this are erased, illegible.

6. "If God were to say to me: If you die right now, you will have very great glory; if you die at eighty, your glory will not be as great, but it will please Me much more. I wouldn't hesitate to answer: 'My God, I want to die at eighty, for I'm not seeking my own glory but simply Your pleasure.'

"The great saints worked for the glory of God, but I'm only a little soul; I work simply for His pleasure, and I'd be glad to bear the greatest sufferings when this would be for the purpose of making Him smile only once."

\* \* \*

July 17.

*Saturday, at 2:00 in the morning, she coughed up blood:*

"I feel that I'm about to enter into my rest. But I feel especially that my mission is about to begin, my mission of making God loved as I love Him, of giving my little way to souls. If God answers my desires, my heaven will be spent on earth until the end of the world. Yes, I want to spend my heaven in doing good on earth. This isn't impossible, since from the bosom of the beatific vision, the angels watch over us.

"I can't make heaven a feast of rejoicing; I can't rest as long as there are souls to be saved. But when the angel will have said: 'Time is no more!'[51] then I will take my rest; I'll be able to rejoice, because the number of the elect will be complete and because all will have entered into joy and repose. My heart beats with joy at this thought."

\* \* \*

July 18.

1. "God would not have given me the desire of doing good on earth after my death, if He didn't will to realize it; He would rather have given me the desire to rest in Him."

\* \* \*

2. "I have only inconveniences to put up with, not sufferings."

---

[51] Apocalypse 10:6.

July 19.

1.   *I said: "I'm going to water the garden this evening." (It was the beginning of recreation.)*

"But it would be much better to water me!"

*"What are you?" I asked.*

"I'm a little seed; no one knows yet what will develop."

\* \* \*

2.   "Just now I wanted to ask Sister Marie of the Sacred Heart, who had come back from a visit with Father Youf, what he had said about my condition after his visit to me. I was thinking to myself: This would perhaps do me some good; it would console me to know. When I thought the matter over further, I said: No, it's only curiosity; I don't want to do anything in order to learn what he said, and since God hasn't permitted her to tell me herself, this is a sign He doesn't want me to know. And I avoided bringing the conversation back to this subject lest Sister Marie be forced to tell me. I wouldn't have been happy."

\* \* \*

3.   *She told me she dried her face carefully, because Sister Marie of the Sacred Heart noticed she was perspiring a lot.*

\* \* \*

July 20.

1.   *She coughed up blood at three in the morning.*

*"What would you have done had one of us been sick instead of you? Would you have come to the infirmary during the recreation periods?" I asked.*

"I would have gone directly to recreation, without asking for any information. However, I'd have done this quite simply so that no one would notice the sacrifice I was making. If I had come to the infirmary, it would have been to please others and not to satisfy myself. I would do all this in order to accomplish my little task and to draw down grace upon you, which the seeking of myself would certainly not accomplish. I myself would have drawn great strength from this sacrifice. If at times through weakness, I would have acted otherwise, I would not have been discouraged. I would have been careful to make up for my failures by depriving myself still more, without allowing this to be seen by others.''

\* \* \*

2.   ''God allows Himself to be represented by whomever he wills, but this is of no importance. With you as Prioress now, there would have been the human element, and I prefer the divine. Yes, I say this from the bottom of my heart; I'm happy to die in the arms of Mother Prioress because she represents God for me.''

\* \* \*

3.   ''Mortal sin wouldn't withdraw my confidence from me; don't forget to tell the story of the sinful woman! This will prove that I'm not mistaken.''

\* \* \*

4.   *I was saying that I feared she would suffer death's agonies:*
   ''If by the agonies of death you mean the awful sufferings which manifest themselves at the last moment through sighs which are frightful to others, I've never seen them here in those who have died under my eyes. Mother Geneviève experienced them in her soul but not in her body.''

\* \* \*

5.   ''You don't know how much I love you, and I'll prove it to you.''

\* \* \*

6.   ''They plague me with questions; it reminds me of Joan of Arc before her judges. It seems to me I answer with the same sincerity.''

July 21.

1. "When I see you, little Mother, it gives me great pleasure. You never bore me; on the contrary. I was saying recently that while I'm obliged to give so often, you are the one who supports me."

\* \* \*

2. "If God should scold me, even only a little bit, I will not cry. However, if He doesn't scold me at all, if He welcomes me with a smile, I'll cry."

\* \* \*

3. "Oh, I would like to know the story of all the saints in heaven; however, nobody will have to tell it to me as it would take too long. When approaching a saint, I'll have to know his name and his whole life in one single glance."

\* \* \*

4. "I've never acted like Pilate, who refused to listen to the truth.[52] I've always said to God: O my God, I really want to listen to You; I beg You to answer me when I say humbly: What is truth? Make me see things as they really are. Let nothing cause me to be deceived."

\* \* \*

5. *We were telling her she was fortunate in having been chosen by God to tell souls about the way of confidence; she answered:*

"What does it matter whether it's I or someone else who gives this way to souls! as long as the way is pointed out; the instrument is unimportant."

\* \* \*

July 22.

1. *Sister Marie of the Sacred Heart said: "You are attended to with much love."*

[52] John 18:38.

"Yes, I see that. It's an image of God's love for me. I've never given Him anything else besides love, and so now He gives me love, and that's not all. Very soon He'll give me more love.

"I'm very much touched by this, for it's like a ray, or rather a flash of lightning in the midst of darkness; but only like a flash of lightning!"

\* \* \*

2.   *She repeated with a smile this remark of Father Youf after she had made her confession:*
"If the angels were to sweep heaven, the dust would be made of diamonds!"

\* \* \*

July 23.
1.   *We were speaking to her about Associations.*[53]
"I'm so close to heaven that all this seems sad."

\* \* \*

2.   *One of us had said and read something to her, thinking it had given her some consolation and joy in her great trial. "Did your trial cease for a moment?"*
"No, it was as though you were singing."

\* \* \*

3.   *I was always telling her of my fear that she'd have to suffer much more:*
"We who run in the way of love shouldn't be thinking of sufferings that can take place in the future; it's a lack of confidence, it's like meddling in the work of creation."

---

[53] Pious confraternities.

4. "At the time of Papa's trials, I had a violent desire to suffer. One night, knowing he was sicker than usual,[54] Sister Marie of the Angels[55] noticed I was very sad, and she consoled me as well as she could. I said: 'Oh, Sister Marie of the Angels, I feel I can suffer more!' She looked at me, surprised, and has often reminded me of it since."

*(Sister Marie of the Angels had never forgotten that night. Our little Saint was still a postulant and was ready to retire; she was sitting on her bed in her nightgown, her beautiful hair was falling over her shoulders. "Her appearance and her entire person had something about them so noble and so beautiful that I thought I was looking at a virgin from heaven.")*

\* \* \*

5. "I remember one day when we were at the height of our trials, I met Sister Marie of the Sacred Heart after I'd swept the dormitory staircase (on the linen-room side). We had permission to speak, and she stopped me. I told her I had a lot of strength, and that at the moment I was thinking of that statement of Mme. Swetchine. It had so penetrated my whole being that I seemed on fire with it: 'Resignation is still distinct from God's will; there is the same difference between the two as there is between union and unity. In union there are still two; in unity there is only one.' "

*(I'm not sure if I have quoted the text with total fidelity.)*

\* \* \*

6. "I was obliged to ask for Papa's cure on the day of my Profession;[56] however, it was impossible for me to say anything else but this: My God, I beg You, let it be Your will that Papa be cured!"

\* \* \*

7. "At the time of our great trial, how happy I was to say this verse in choir: *'In te, Domine, speravi!'* "[57]

---

[54] June, 1888. See *Story of a Soul,* p. 156.
[55] See p. 304.
[56] September 8, 1890.
[57] "In you, O Lord, I have hoped." Psalm 70:1.

July 24.

1.  *She had been sent some beautiful fruit but was unable to eat any of it. She took each one in her hands, one after the other, as though offering them to someone, and then she said:*

"The Holy Family has been well served. St. Joseph and the little Jesus have each received a peach and two prunes." *Then she asked in a low tone of voice:* "I've touched them with pleasure, and perhaps that's not good? I get so much pleasure out of touching fruit, especially peaches, and I like to see them near me." *After I had reassured her, she continued:*

"The Blessed Virgin had her share, too. When I'm given milk with rum, I offer it to St. Joseph; I say to myself: Oh, how much good this will do to St. Joseph!

"In the refectory, I always considered to whom I should offer the food. Sweets were for little Jesus; strong foods were for St. Joseph, and I didn't forget the Blessed Virgin either. But when I missed anything, for example, when they forgot to give me sauce or salad, I was very happy, for then I could really offer it to the Holy Family, being really deprived of what I was offering."

\* \* \*

2.  "When God wills that we be deprived of something, there is nothing we can do about it; we must be content to go this way. Sometimes Sister Marie of the Sacred Heart placed my bowl of salad so close to Sister Marie of the Incarnation, that I couldn't consider it my own, and I didn't touch it.

"Ah, little Mother, what 'poor' omelet they served me during my life! They were convinced I liked it when it was all dried up. You must pay particular attention after my death not to give bad fare to the poor Sisters."

\* \* \*

July 25.

1.  *I was telling her that I was coming to a point where I desired her death so that she wouldn't suffer any longer:*

"Yes, but you mustn't say that, little Mother, because suffering is exactly what attracts me in life."

2.   "Are peaches in season? Are they selling plums in the streets now? I don't know what's happening anymore.

> When we reach our declining years,
> We lose both our memory and our head.

* * *

3.   *Uncle sent her some grapes; she ate a few and said:*
"How good those grapes are! However, I don't like to eat what comes from my relatives. Formerly, when they brought me bouquets of flowers for my little Jesus,[58] I could never take them until Mother Prioress had said so."

* * *

4.   *Upon her request, I had her kiss her Crucifix, and I handed it to her in the customary way:[59]*
"Ah! but I kiss His face!"
*Then gazing at a picture of the Infant Jesus, which Sister Marie of the Trinity had brought from the Carmel at Paris,[60] she said:*
"It appears to me that this little Jesus here is saying: *'You will come to heaven very soon; I'm the one who is telling you!'* "

* * *

5.   *I asked: "Where's the Thief now? You don't speak of Him anymore." She placed her hand on her heart, saying:*
"He's there! He's in my heart!"

* * *

6.   *I was telling her that death was a sad affair, that I would suffer a lot when she died. She answered tenderly:*
"The Blessed Virgin held her dead Jesus on her knees, and He was disfigured, covered with blood! You will see something different! Ah!

---

[58] A statue she was in charge of decorating all through her religious life.
[59] "I offered her the feet of the crucifix to kiss."
[60] The Carmel on Avenue de Messine, Paris; today this community is at Boulogne-sur-Seine.

I don't know how she stood it! Imagine if they were to bring me to you in this state, what would become of you? 'Responde mihi!' "[61]

* * *

7.  *After she had confided several little faults for which she reproached herself, she asked me if she had offended God. I answered simply that these little sins were nothing and that she had done me a lot of good in telling me about them; she appeared very much touched and she said later:*
"When I was listening to you, I was reminded of Father Alexis; your own words penetrated my heart as much as his."
*Then she began to cry; I gathered up these tears, drying them with a little piece of linen, which Sister Geneviève keeps as a relic.*

* * *

8.  *Sister Geneviève gave her a little geranium which had been on the table for a long time so that she could cast it at her holy pictures pinned to the bedcurtains:*
"Never cast little faded flowers . . . only little flowers 'freshly blooming.'"

* * *

9.  *Someone suggested a rather noisy distraction; she answered with a smile:*
"No little boys' games! No little girls' games either! Just the games of little angels."

* * *

10.  "I look at the grapes, and I say to myself: They are beautiful, they look good. Then I eat one; I don't give this one to Jesus, because He's the one giving it to me."

[61] "Answer me!"

11. "I'm like a real little child during my sickness; I don't think of anything; I'm content to go to heaven, and that's it!"

* * *

12. "The first time I was given grapes in the infirmary, I said to Jesus: 'How good the grapes are! I can't understand why You are waiting so long to take me, since I am a little grape, and they tell me I'm so ripe!' "

* * *

13. *With reference to spiritual direction:*
   "I think we have to be very careful not to seek ourselves, for we can get a broken heart that way, and afterwards, it can be said of us in all truth: 'The keepers . . . wounded me; they took away my veil from me. . . . When I had passed by them a little, I found Him whom my soul loves.'[62]
   "I think that if this soul had humbly asked the keepers where her Beloved was, they would have shown her where He was to be found; however, because she wanted to be admired, she got into trouble, and she lost simplicity of heart."

* * *

14. "You are my light!"

* * *

15. "Listen to this little, very funny story: One day, after I received the Habit,[63] Sister St. Vincent de Paul saw me with Mother Prioress, and she exclaimed: 'Oh! how well she looks! Is this big girl strong! Is she plump!' I left, quite humbled by the compliment, when Sister Magdalene stopped me in front of the kitchen and said: 'But what is beoming of you, poor little Sister Thérèse of the Child Jesus! You are fading away before our eyes! If you continue at this pace, with an ap-

---

[62] The Canticle of Canticles 5:7; 3:4.
[63] Thursday, January 10, 1889.

pearance that makes one tremble, you won't observe the Rule very long!' I couldn't get over hearing, one after the other, two such contrary appraisals. Ever since that moment, I have never attached any importance to the opinion of creatures, and this impression has so developed in me that, at this present time, reproaches and compliments glide over me without leaving the slightest imprint.''

\* \* \*

July 26.
1.   "I dreamed last night that I was at a bazaar with Papa, and there I saw some pretty little white cushions that tempted me as a place to put my pins; but in the end I told myself that they made the same things in Carmel, and I asked for a little music box.''

\* \* \*

2.   *She was telling me that around December 8, 1892, she was occupied with Sister Martha; in 1893, she was helping Mother Marie de Gonzague in the novitiate, and after the election of 1896, she was placed in complete charge of the novices.*

\* \* \*

3.   "Virtue shines forth naturally, and as soon as it is no longer present, I can see this.''

\* \* \*

July27.
1.   *She didn't want me to forget to take some drops of a medicine which had been prescribed for me:*
    "Oh, you must strengthen yourself; thirty drops tonight, don't forget!''

\* \* \*

2.   *I asked: "Do we tire you out?''*
    "No, because you are very nice people.''

3. *She was telling us with a smile that she had a dream in which she was being carried to the heated room,*[64] *between two torches in order to celebrate the feast of our Father Superior.*[65]

\* \* \*

4. *The community was doing the laundry:*

"Around one o'clock in the afternoon, I said to myself: They're really tired out from doing the washing! And I prayed to God to console all of you, so that you would work in peace and love. When I saw how sick I was, I rejoiced at having to suffer like all of you."

\* \* \*

5. *In the evening, she recalled for me St. John of the Cross' words:*

" 'Tear through the veil of this sweet encounter!'[66] I've always applied these words to the death of love that I desire. Love will not wear out the veil of my life; it will tear it suddenly.

"With what longing and what consolation I repeated from the beginning of my religious life these other words of St. John of the Cross: 'It is of the highest importance that the soul practice love very much in order that, being consumed rapidly, she may be scarcely retained here on earth but promptly reach the vision of her God face to face.' "[67]

\* \* \*

6. *With reference to the difficulties I foresaw with regard to the publication of her Life:*

"Well, I say with Joan of Arc: 'And the will of God will be carried out in spite of the envy of men!' "

---

[64] Recreation room.

[65] Canon Charles Maupas; see p. 306.

[66] John of the Cross, St., *The Living Flame of Love,* st. 1, v. 6. See *The Collected Works of St. John of the Cross,* trans. Kieran Kavanaugh, O.C.D. and Otilio Rodriquez, O.C.D. (Washington, D. C.: ICS Publications, Institute of Carmelite Studies, 1973), p. 578.

[67] Ibid., st. 1, explanation of v. 6. See *Collected Works,* p. 591.

7.   *I said: "Soon I will see your beloved little face no more; I'll see
only your little soul."*
   "It's much more beautiful."

\* \* \*

8.   *I said to her: "When I think that we are about to lose you."*
   "But you will not lose me . . . not smart! . . ."[68]

\* \* \*

9.   *She said to Sister Geneviève, who was crying:*
   "And she really sees that the same thing will happen to her *(death),*
and see how she's seized with fear now!"

\* \* \*

10.   *After she had offered a cluster of grapes to the Infant Jesus:*
   "I offered Him these grapes to give Him the desire to take me
because I believe I'm this type."
   *The skin wasn't hard and it was very golden; tasting one grape:*
   "Yes, this is my type."

\* \* \*

11.   "Little Mother is my telephone; I've only to cock my little ear
when she comes, and I know everything."

\* \* \*

12.   "I'm no egoist; it's God whom I love, not myself!"

\* \* \*

13.   "According to my natural inclinations, I prefer to die, but I
rejoice in death only because it's God's will for me."

---

   [68] "You are not smart!"

14. "I've never asked God for the favor of dying young; I'm sure, then, that at this moment He's accomplishing His own will."

\* \* \*

15. *She was having difficulty breathing, and I showed my sympathy and sorrow for her:*
"Don't be disturbed; if I can't breathe, God will give me the strength to bear it. I love Him! He'll never abandon me."

\* \* \*

16. *She told me how she'd worn her little iron cross for a long time and that it made her sick. She told me, too, that it wasn't God's will for her, nor for us to throw ourselves into great mortifications; this sickness was proof of it.*

\* \* \*

17. *With reference to some massages prescribed for her by the doctor:*
"Ah, to be 'trounced' as I was, it's worse than anything!"

\* \* \*

18. "From June 9 onward, I was sure I would die very soon."

\* \* \*

July 29.
1. "I would like to go!"
*I asked: "Where?"*
"Above, in the blue heavens!"[69]

\* \* \*

2. *A Sister reported this reflection made during recreation: "Why are they talking of Sister Thérèse as though she were a saint? She prac-*

---

[69] A poem Thérèse had learned as a child. See *Story of a Soul*, p. 29.

ticed virtue, true, but it wasn't a virtue acquired through humiliations and especially sufferings." She said to me afterwards:

"And I who suffered so much from my most tender childhood! Ah, how much good it does me to see the opinion of creatures, especially at the moment of my death!"

\* \* \*

3.   *One of the Sisters thought she was pleasing Thérèse by bringing her a certain object,[70] but it had just the opposite effect. She showed her displeasure, thinking someone had been deprived of the object in question, but she was sorry immediately and begged pardon with tears in her eyes:*

"Oh, I really beg pardon; I've acted through selfishness. Please pray for me!"

*A little later:*

"Oh, how happy I am to see myself imperfect and to have such need of God's mercy at the moment of my death!"

\* \* \*

4.   *She coughed up blood in the morning and at three o'clock in the afternoon.*

\* \* \*

5.   *We expressed our fears that she'd die during the night:*

"I'll not die during the night, believe me; I have had the desire not to die at night."

\* \* \*

6.   "Two days after the entrance of Sister Marie of the Trinity[71] I had to be taken care of for a sore throat. God permitted that the novices should exhaust me. Sister Marie of the Eucharist told me that the same thing happened to me as happens to preachers."

---

[70]   This was a little music box.
[71]   Sister Marie of the Trinity entered Carmel of Lisieux on June 16, 1894.

7. "To be my historian, you'll have to spare yourself."

\* \* \*

8. "Well, 'baby' is about to die! For the last three days, it's true that I've suffered very much; tonight, it's as though I were in purgatory."

\* \* \*

9. "Very often, when I'm able to do so, I repeat my Act of Oblation."[72]

\* \* \*

10. *I confided some trouble I was having:*
"It's you who sowed in my little soul the seed of confidence; you don't remember that?"

\* \* \*

11. *I was holding her up while they were arranging her pillows:*
"I'm resting my head on the heart of my little Mother."

\* \* \*

12. *She hadn't asked for a certain remedy, and we believed it was done out of virtue; however, she hadn't thought of mortifying herself in the matter. When we were admiring her action, she said:*
"I'm tired of this earth! We receive compliments when we don't merit them and reproaches when we don't merit them either. All that! . . . All that! . . ."

\* \* \*

13. "What is our humiliation at the moment is our glory later on, even in this life."

---

[72] This was made on June 9, 1895. See *Story of a Soul,* p. 180.

14. "I haven't the capacity for enjoyment; I've always been like that; but I have a great capacity for suffering. Formerly, when I had a lot of trouble, I experienced a big appetite in the refectory, but when I had joy, it was just the contrary: impossible to eat."

\* \* \*

July 30.
1. " . . . My body has always embarrassed me; I've never been at ease in it . . . even when very small, I was ashamed of it."

\* \* \*

2. *For having rendered her a little service:*
   "Thanks, Mamma!"

\* \* \*

3. "I would not want to have picked up a pin to avoid purgatory. Everything I did was done to please God, to save souls for Him."

\* \* \*

4. *"Looking at a picture of Fathers Bellière and Roulland:*
   "I'm much prettier than they are!"

\* \* \*

5. *Someone had promised to buy some Chinese babies for her.* \*
   "It's not Chinese babies I want, it's black ones!"

\* \* \*

6. "It's bitter for me when you don't look at me."

_____

(\*)  [This is a reference to the custom of aiding the foreign missions by small contributions made for abandoned children.]

7.  *The flies tormented her, but she wouldn't kill them:*

"I always give them freedom. They alone have caused me misery during my sickness. I have no enemies, and since God recommends that we pardon our enemies, I'm happy to find this opportunity for doing so."

\* \* \*

8.  *"It's very hard to suffer so much; this must prevent you from thinking?"*

"No, it still allows me to tell God that I love Him; I find that this is enough."

\* \* \*

9.  *Pointing to a glass containing a very distasteful medicine that looked like a delicious red-currant liqueur:*

"This glass is an image of my whole life. Yesterday, Sister Thérèse of St. Augustine said: 'I hope you're drinking some good liqueur!' I answered: 'O Sister Thérèse, it's the worst possible thing to drink!' Well, little Mother, this is what happens in the eyes of creatures. It has always seemed to them I was drinking exquisite liqueurs, and it was bitterness. But no! My life hasn't been bitter, because I knew how to turn all bitterness into something joyful and sweet."

\* \* \*

10.  "If you want to give Doctor de Cornière a souvenir of me, give him a picture with the words: 'What you have done to the least of my brethren, that you have done to me.' "[73]

\* \* \*

11.  *Someone had given her a fan from the Carmel of Saigon; she used it to shoo away the flies. When it became very hot, she began fanning her holy pictures pinned to her bedcurtains, and she fanned us, too:*

---

[73] Matthew 25:40.

"I'm fanning the saints instead of myself; I'm fanning you to do you some good because you, too, are saints!"

\* \* \*

12. *Doctor de Cornière told us to give her five or six spoonfuls of Tisserand water, and she begged Sister Geneviève to give her five; turning to me, she said:*
"Always the least; right, Mamma?"

\* \* \*

13. "Don't tell Father Ducellier[74] that I've only a few more days to live; I'm still not weak enough to die, and after these visits when I continue living, others are 'kaput.' "[75]

\* \* \*

14. *She was smiling at me, after a visit from one of the nuns. I said: "Rest now; close your eyes!" (Four o'clock.)*
"No, I just love looking at you!"

\* \* \*

15. *I was trying to catch a fly that was bothering her:*
"What will you do to it?"
*"I'll kill it."*
"Oh! no, I beg you!"

\* \* \*

16. "Want to prepare me for extreme Unction?"
*Looking at me with a smile:*
"I'm not thinking of anything! Pray to God so that I receive it as well as it can be received."

---

[74] See p. 298.
[75] This has the meaning of "confused," "puzzled," "embarrassed."

17. *She told me what Father Superior had said to her before the ceremony:*

" 'You're going to be like a little child who has just received baptism.' Then, he spoke to me only about love. Oh! how touched I was!''

\* \* \*

18. *She was showing us her hands with reverence after the Extreme Unction. I was collecting as usual the little pieces of skin from her desiccated lips, but that day she said to me:*

"I am swallowing my little skins today because I've received Extreme Unction and Holy Viaticum."

*It was afternoon. She had hardly any time to make her thanksgiving when some Sisters came to see her. She told me in the evening:*

"How they came to disturb me after Communion! They stared me in the face . . . but in order not to be provoked, I thought of Our Lord, who retreated into solitude and was unable to prevent the people from following Him there. And He didn't want to send them away.[76] I wanted to imitate Him by receiving the Sisters kindly."

\* \* \*

July 31.

1. *We were still imagining a date on which she would die, for instance, August 6, the Transfiguration of Our Lord, or August 15, the Assumption of Our Lady, and she said:*

"Don't talk of a date; it will always be a feast day!"

\* \* \*

2. *After telling us La Fontaine's fable:* \* *"The Miller and his three Sons," she said:*

"I have two boots, but I have no bag! This means I'm not near to dying."

---

(\*) *This is the story of "Puss in Boots," and not a La Fontaine fable.*

[76] Mark 3:7.

3.  *They had brought down her paillasse to lay her body out after her death. She noticed it when someone opened the door of the cell adjoining the infirmary, and she cried out with joy:*

"Ah! there's our paillasse! It's going to be very close to place my corpse on. . . . My little nose was always good!"

\* \* \*

4.  "What is baby to do in order to die? But what shall I die from?"

\* \* \*

5.  "Yes, I'll steal. . . . Many things will disappear from heaven because I'll bring them to you. I'll be a little thief; I'll take whatever I please."

\* \* \*

6.  *Looking at the Blessed Virgin's statue and pointing to her little cup[77] with her finger:*

"When it happened last night *(a great coughing up of blood),* I believed you were coming to take me away!"

\* \* \*

7.  *We all fell asleep while watching by her bedside:*

"Peter, James, and John!"[78]

\* \* \*

8.  "I tell you that I'll have this for a long time if the Blessed Virgin does not intervene."

\* \* \*

9.  *Lovingly:*

"Let's not chat together; it's really enough to peep at each other!"[79]

---

[77] A little cup used as a spittoon.

[78] Reference to garden of Gethsemani, Matthew 26:36-46.

[79] Thérèse uses the French verb "guigner" which really has the meaning of "looking at a person out of the corner of one's eye, with the eyes closed slightly."

10.                              The Thief will come
                                 And carry me off
                                 Alleluia!

* * *

11. *We were discussing the few days of life she had left:*
   "It's still the patient who knows best! And I feel I still have a long time."

* * *

12. "I thought that I should be very good and should wait for the Thief very nicely."

* * *

13. "I have found happiness and joy on earth, but solely in suffering, for I've suffered very much here below; you must make it known to souls. . . .

   "Since my First Communion, since the time I asked Jesus to change all the consolations of this earth[80] into bitterness for me, I had a perpetual desire to suffer. I wasn't thinking, however, of making suffering my joy; this is a grace that was given to me later on. Up until then, it was like a spark hidden beneath the ashes, and like blossoms on a tree that must become fruit in time. But seeing my blossoms always falling, that is, allowing myself to fall into tears whenever I suffered, I said to myself with astonishment and sadness: But I will never go beyond the stage of desires!"

* * *

14. "This evening, when you told me that Dr. de Cornière believed I still had a month or more to live, I couldn't get over it! It was so different from yesterday when he was saying that I had to be anointed that very day! However, it left me in deep peace. What does it matter if I remain a long time on earth? If I suffer very much and always

---

[80] *The Imitation of Christ,* III, 26:3.

more, I will not fear, for God will give me strength; He'll never abandon me.''

* * *

15. *I said: ''If you live a long time now, no one will understand anything.''*

''What does it matter! Everybody can misunderstand me, that's what I've always desired; and I shall have these misunderstandings till the end of my life.''

* * *

16. ''God has done what He willed to do, He has misled everybody. He will come like a thief at an hour when no one is thinking of Him; that's my idea.''

* * *

# AUGUST

*The daily hemoptyses ceased August 5. Her physical condition became stable, but she had great difficulty in breathing. Sunday, August 15, marked a new stage in her illness; she experienced very sharp pains in her left side. In the absence of her own doctor, Doctor La Néele was called in and stated that "the tuberculosis had reached its final stage." On August 22, her condition worsened.*

*The medical report for this month is reflected in the notes taken down by Mother Agnes of Jesus. The first half of the month is the same as that of July: references to the manuscripts and the young Carmelite's future mission, biographical reminiscences, reflections of a doctrinal nature on her "little way." Then from August 15 on Thérèse's resistance declines noticeably. Henceforth, the "Last Conversations" describe a great patient, an heroic patient.*

*Her sisters must now witness Thérèse suffering, smiling, suffocating, and crying. In every gesture and word, however, she rises to a full measure of love. The final days of the month are punctuated by admissions of physical distress which reveal extreme sufferings. At the same time, her spiritual trial against faith has not ceased.*

*In this context, we can appreciate the strength of will of a little Thérèse, who has left us five letters written in pencil, among which is a long letter to Father Bellière, dated August 10.*

August 1.

1. *With reference to the great grace she had received formerly[1] when she looked at the pierced hand of Jesus in a picture which had accidentally slipped from her missal:*

"Oh! I don't want this Precious Blood to be lost. I shall spend my life gathering it up for the good of souls."

\* \* \*

2. *During Matins, with a reference to her autobiographical manuscripts:*

"After my death, you mustn't speak to anyone about my manuscript before it is published; you must speak about it only to Mother Prioress. If you act otherwise, the devil will make use of more than one trap to hinder the work of God, a very important work!"\*

\* \* \*

3. "I shall write no more now!"

\* \* \*

4. "Oh, how sick I really am! . . . For you know . . . with you!"
*She was unable to speak because of her poor breathing.*

\* \* \*

5. "I'm really abandoned; I shall wait as long as He wills."

(\* *Novissima Verba adds (the authenticity of this text is questionable):*

*A few days later, having asked her to read again a passage of her manuscript which seemed incomplete to me, I found her crying. When I asked her why, she answered with angelic simplicity:*

"What I am reading in this copybook reflects my soul so well! Mother, these pages will do much good to souls. They will understand God's gentleness much better."

*And she added:*

"Ah, I know it; everybody will love me!"

[1]  In July, 1887, in the Cathedral of St. Pierre where she was attending Mass. See *Story of a Soul,* p. 99.

6. "How well God did to say: 'In My Father's house there are many mansions.' "[2]

*(She said this because of a priest who was doing unusual mortifications.)*

"As for me, I prefer to practice mortifications in other ways, and not in such irritating things; I can't control myself in that way."

\* \* \*

7. *There was question of some ice which had made me cry; I asked her if I was wrong, and to console me she said:*

"You're always so gracious!"

\* \* \*

8. *I asked: "Are you thinking of your missionary brothers?"*

"I was thinking of them very often; but ever since my sickness, I don't think of anything much."

\* \* \*

9. *One of these missionaries[3] had promised her a Mass for Christmas, 1896. She was telling me about her disappointment when he was unable to fulfill his promise:*

"And I who was united with this Mass with such great joy at this very hour! Ah! Everything on this earth is uncertain!"

\* \* \*

August 2.

1. *I said: "I'd like to preserve your heart as we did that of Mother Geneviève."*

"Do whatever you wish!"

*I changed my mind because even the thought repelled me, and I told her this. She appeared to be sad about it. I guessed at what she was thinking: We would be depriving ourselves of a consolation which she*

---

[2]   John 14:2.

[3]   Fr. Adolphe Roulland.

*wouldn't grant us through a miracle, for we knew she would not be preserved after death. Then she said:*

"You waver too much, little Mother; I've noticed that many times in my life."

\* \* \*

2. *We were speaking together about the little attention that was paid to the practice of hidden virtues:*

"This struck me in the life of St. John of the Cross, about whom they said: 'Brother John of the Cross! He's a religious who is less than ordinary!'"

\* \* \*

3. "I have no great desires for heaven; I'll be content to go there, and that's it!"

\* \* \*

4. "They won't be able to say of me: 'She died because she couldn't die.'[4] I've already told you: as far as nature is concerned, yes, heaven! But grace has taken over control of nature in my soul, and now I can only repeat to God:

> I want to live for a long time still,\*
> Lord, if this be Your desire.
> I would like to follow You in heaven,
> If this would please You.

> (\*)   *Longtemps encore, je veux bien vivre*
> *Seigneur, si c'est là ton désir.*
> *Dans le Ciel, je voudrais te suivre,*
> *si cela te faisait plaisir.*
> *L'Amour, ce feu de la Patrie,*
> *Ne cesse de me consumer*
> *Que fait la mort ou la vie?*
> *Mon seul bonheur, c'est de t'aimer.*[5]

---

[4]   Teresa of Avila, St., *Poems, Muero porque no muero.* See *The Complete Works of St. Teresa,* 3:277.

> Love, that fire of our Fatherland,
> Never ceases to consume me.
> What matters life or death to me?
> My sole happiness is to love You only.[5]

\* \* \*

5.  *To Sister Geneviève:*
"Everything passes away in this world, even 'baby,' but she will come back."
*Sister Geneviève was kissing the feet of her Crucifix:*
"You're not following 'baby's teaching! Kiss Him quickly on both cheeks, and make Him embrace you."

\* \* \*

6.  "I experience a very living joy not only when I discover I'm imperfect, but especially when I feel I am. All this surpasses all praise, which only bores me."

\* \* \*

August 3.
1.  *I asked: "What did you do to reach such unchangeable peace?"*
"I forgot self, and I was careful to seek myself in nothing."

\* \* \*

2.  *I was telling her that she must have had to struggle a lot in order to become perfect:*
"Oh, it's not that!"\*

---

(\*) *Novissima Verba adds (The authenticity of this text is questionable):*
*And a little later she said:*
"Sanctity does not consist in this or that practice; it consists in a disposition of heart which makes us humble and little in the arms of God, conscious of our weakness, and confident to the point of audacity in the goodness of our Father."

[5] Poem written by Thérèse and entitled: *Ma Joie!*

3. *She was having trouble with a Sister, and she said to me very seriously but tenderly:*
"I tell you frankly: I have to see you close to me in the last days of my life."

\* \* \*

4. "Little sisters, pray for the poor sick who are dying. If you only knew what happens! How little it takes to lose one's patience! You must be kind towards all of them without exception. I would not have believed this formerly."

\* \* \*

5. *I was talking to her about mortifications under the form of penitential instruments:*
"We must be very restrained on this point, for often nature is involved in this matter more than anything else."\*

\* \* \*

6. *To the three of us:*
"You must pay attention to regular observance. After a visit, don't stop to talk among yourselves, because then it's like being at home, and we deprive ourselves of nothing."
*Turning to me:*
"This, Mother, is the most useful of all."

(\*)   *Novissima verba adds:*
   *She had told me on another occasion:*
"A passage in the life of Blessed Henry Suso struck me with regard to corporal penances. He had performed frightful penances which had destroyed his health; an angel appeared to him, telling him to stop. Then he added: 'You are no longer to fight as a simple soldier; from this moment I shall arm you as a knight.' And he made the Saint understand the superiority of the spiritual combat over corporal mortifications.
   "Well, little Mother, God didn't want me to be a simple soldier; I was armed from the beginning as a knight, and I went out to war against self in the spiritual domain, through self-denial in hidden sacrifices. I discovered peace and humility in this obscure struggle in which nature finds nothing for self."

7.  "Oh, how sore my little shoulder is! If you only knew!"
*When we tried to place a padding on it:*
"No, you mustn't take away my little cross."

* * *

8.  "It's a long time since I've been suffering, but only little sufferings. Ever since July 28, these are big sufferings."

* * *

9.  *We no longer understood the progress of the sickness, and one of us said: "What are you dying from?"*
"I'm dying from death! Didn't God tell Adam what he would die of in these words: 'You will die the death.'[6] That's it in simple words."

* * *

August 4.
1.  "I had a lot of nightmares last night, very frightful ones, but at the worst moment, you came to me and then I wasn't afraid."

* * *

2.  "No, I don't believe I'm a great saint; I believe I'm a very little saint; but I think God has been pleased to place things in me which will do good to me and to others."

* * *

3.  *Someone brought her a sheaf of corn; she detached the most beautiful one and said to me:*
"Mother, this ear of corn is the image of my soul: God has entrusted me with graces for myself and for many others."
*Then fearing she had entertained a proud thought, she said:*
"Oh, how I want to be humiliated and mistreated in order to see if I

---

[6] Genesis 2:17.

have humility of heart! However, when I was humbled on former occasions, I was very happy. Yes, it seems to me I am humble. God
shows me truth; I feel so much that everything comes from Him.''

\* \* \*

4. ''How easy it is to become discouraged when we are very sick!
Oh, how I sense that I'd become discouraged if I didn't have any
faith! Or at least if I didn't love God.''

\* \* \*

5. ''It's only in heaven that we'll see the whole truth about
everything. This is impossible on earth. Thus, even regarding Holy
Scripture, isn't it sad to see so many different translations! Had I been
a priest, I would have learned Hebrew and Greek, and wouldn't have
been satisfied with Latin. In this way, I would have known the real
text dictated by the Holy Spirit.''

\* \* \*

6. ''I fell asleep for a second during prayer. I dreamed that they
needed soldiers for a war. You said: 'You must send Sister Thérèse of
the Child Jesus.' I replied that I would have preferred this to be a holy
war. Finally, I left just the same.

   ''Oh, no, I would not have been afraid to go to war. With what happiness, for example, during the time of the Crusades, would I have left
to fight against the heretics. I would not have been afraid to get a
bullet in me!''

\* \* \*

7. ''And I who desired martyrdom,[7] is it possible that I should die in
bed!''

---

[7]   See *Story of a Soul,* p. 193.

8. *I asked: "What are you doing about your little life now?"*

"My little life is to suffer, and that's it! Otherwise, I wouldn't be able to say: My God, this is for the Church; my God, this is for France, etc. God knows best what to do with these sufferings; I've given them all to Him to do with as He pleases. Besides, it would tire me out to tell Him: Give this to Peter, that to Paul. When a Sister asks me for anything, I do it right away and then give it no further thought. When I pray for my brother missionaries, I don't offer my sufferings. I say simply: My God, give them everything I desire for myself."

\* \* \*

August 5.

1. *It was very warm, and the sacristan was pitying us for having to wear such heavy habits:*

"Ah, in heaven, God will reward us for having worn heavy habits here on earth out of love for Him."

\* \* \*

2. *Aware that she was unable to move by herself, she said:*

"David says in the psalms: 'I'm like the grasshopper which continually changes its place.'[8] As for myself, I can't say the same thing! I would like to walk, but my feet are tied with a rope!"

\* \* \*

3. "When the saints have closed the gates of heaven on me, they will sing:

> At last, we have you,
> Little gray mouse,
> At last, we have you
> And we won't let you go!\*

*This was a little childhood song that had come back into her mind.*

(\*) *Enfin nous te tenons,*
*Petite souris grise,*
*Enfin nous te tenons*
*Et nous te garderons!*

[8] Psalm 108:23.

4.  *Sister Marie of the Sacred Heart told her that when she died the
angels would come to her in the company of Our Lord, that she would
see them resplendent with light and beauty:*

"All these images do me no good; I can nourish myself on nothing
but the truth. This is why I've never wanted any visions. We can't see,
here on earth, heaven, the angels, etc., just as they are. I prefer to wait
until after my death."

\* \* \*

5.  "During Vespers, little Mother, I was thinking you're my sun."

\* \* \*

6.  "I fell asleep and I dreamed you were bending over me to kiss me;
I wanted to return the kiss, but all of a sudden I came awake, totally
surprised that my kiss fell into the void."

\* \* \*

7.  *Her bed was no longer in the center of the infirmary, but at the
end of the room in a corner. To celebrate the feast of the following
day, August 6, feast of the Transfiguration, we took from the choir the
picture of the Holy Face she so much loved and hung it on the wall to
the right, decorating it with flowers and lights. She said, looking at the
picture:*

"How well Our Lord did to lower His eyes when He gave us His
portrait! Since the eyes are the mirror of the soul, if we had seen His
soul, we would have died from joy.

"Oh! how much good that Holy Face has done me in my life! When
I was composing my canticle: *'Vivre d'armour,'* it helped me to do it
with great ease. I wrote from memory, during my night silence, the fifteen couplets that I had composed during the day without a rough
draft. That same day, when going to the refectory after the
examination of conscience, I had just composed the stanza:

>           To live from love is to dry Your Face,
>           It's to obtain pardon for sinners.\*

>    (\*)    *Vivre d'amour c'est essuyer ta Face,*
>            *C'est obtenir des pécheurs le pardon.*

"I repeated this to Him while passing by, doing so with great love. When looking at the picture, I cried out of love."

* * *

8. "I repeat like Job: 'In the morning, I hope I'll not see the night; in the evening, I hope no longer to see the morning.' "[9]

* * *

9. "These words of Isaias: 'Who has believed our report? . . . There is no beauty in him, no comeliness, etc.,'[10] have made the whole foundation of my devotion to the Holy Face, or, to express it better, the foundation of all my piety. I, too, have desired to be without beauty, alone in treading the winepress, unknown to everyone."

* * *

10. *With reference to a certain confidence I had entrusted to her:*
"A Mother Prioress must always allow others to believe she is without any sufferings. This does us so much good, and it gives us so much strength not to speak of our troubles. For example, she should avoid expressing herself like this: 'You have your trials and difficulties, but I have the same and many others, etc.' "

* * *

August 6.
1. *She had hoped she would die during the night, and she told me:*
"I watched all through the night like the little girl in the song about the Christmas slipper.[11]

"I never ceased looking at the Holy Face. I repelled many temptations. Ah! how many acts of faith I made!

"I can also say: 'I looked to my right hand and considered, and I found none who understood me.'[12] By this I mean that nobody knows

---

[9]   Job 7:4.
[10]  Isaias 53:1-2.
[11]  Song of L. Amat.
[12]  Psalm 141:5.

the moment of my death. The right is the side on which you are for
me.''

*She looked at the statue of the Blessed Virgin, and she sang sweetly:*
When will it come, O tender Mother,
When will that beautiful day come,
That day on which from this earthly exile,
I shall fly to my eternal repose?*

\* \* \*

2.  *Her violent pain in the side had ceased during the night. Upon
examination, Doctor de Cornière found her still very sick; however,
she herself doubted that death was close:*

"I'm like a little Robinson Crusoe on his island. As long as no one
made any promises, I was exiled, true; however, I never thought of
leaving my island. But behold they told me of the certain arrival of a
ship that was to bring me back soon to my country. Then I stayed on
the shore, looking into the distance, always looking . . . and seeing
nothing appearing on the horizon, I said to myself: They've deceived
me! I'm not going to be leaving!''

\* \* \*

3.  *She showed me in the little breviary of the Sacred Heart, the
words of Our Lord to Blessed Margaret Mary, which she had drawn
out on the feast of the Ascension:*

"The cross is the bed of my spouses; it's there that I have them taste
the delights of my love.''

*She told me, too, that one day one of the Sisters drew out from this
same book a passage that was very severe; this Sister asked her to draw
one, and her eyes fell upon these words:*

"Trust in me.''

(\*)   *Quand viendra-t-il, ma tendre Mère,
Quand viendra-t-il ce beau jour,
Où, de l'exil de la terre
Je volerai dans l'éternel Séjour?*

4.   "I can depend on nothing, on no good works of my own in order
to have confidence. For example, I'd like to be able to say that I've
carried out all my obligations of reciting my prayers for the dead. This
poverty, however, was a real light and a grace for me. I was thinking
that never in my life would I be able to pay my debts to God; this was
real riches, real strength for me, if I wanted to take it in this way.

"Then I made this prayer to God: O my God, I beg You, pay the
debt that I have acquired with regard to the souls in purgatory, but do
it as God, so that it be infinitely better than if I had said my Offices
for the Dead. And then I remembered with great consolation these
words of St. John of the Cross' canticle: 'Pay all debts.'[13] I had
always applied this to Love. I felt this grace can't be expressed in
words; it's far too sweet! We experience such great peace when we're
totally poor, when we depend upon no one except God."

* * *

5.   "Oh! How few perfect religious there are, who do nothing, or
next to nothing, saying: I'm not obliged to do that, after all. There's
no great harm in speaking here, in satisfying myself there. How few
there are who do everything in the best way possible! And still these
are the most happy religious. Take silence for example, what good it
does to the soul, what failures in charity it prevents, and so many
other troubles of all kinds. I speak especially about silence because it's
on this point that we fail the most."

* * *

6.   "How proud I was when I was hebdomadarian[14] during the
recitation of the Divine Office, reciting the prayers out loud in the cen-
tre of the Choir! I was proud because I remembered that the priest
said the same prayers during Mass, and I had the right, like him, to
pray aloud before the Blessed Sacrament, giving the blessings and the
absolutions, reading the Gospel when I was first chantress.

---

[13] John of the Cross, St., *The Living Flame of Love,* st. II, v. 5. See *Collected
Words,* p. 579.

[14] The nun who presides at the Divine Office during the week, leading in the prayers,
etc.

"However, I must also admit that this Office was at once my happiness and my martyrdom. I had a great desire to recite it well, without making any mistakes. Sometimes, even after being aware only a minute before of what I was supposed to say, I would let it pass without opening my mouth because of a totally involuntary distraction. I don't believe that one could have had a greater desire to recite the Office more perfectly than I and to be present in Choir.

"I excuse very much those Sisters who forget or make mistakes during the Office."

\* \* \*

7.   *Sister St. Stanislaus, the main infirmarian, had left Sister Thérèse by herself all through Vespers, forgetting to close the infirmary door and window; there was a very strong draft, as a consequence, and Mother Prioress demanded an explanation when she found her in this condition; she told me later:*

"I told Mother Prioress the truth, but while I was speaking, there came to my mind a more charitable way of expressing it than the one I was going to use, and still it wasn't wrong, certainly. I followed my inspiration, and God rewarded me for it with a great interior peace.''\*

\* \* \*

8.   *I asked her to explain what she meant by "remaining a little child before God." She said:*

"It is to recognize our nothingness, to expect everything from God as a little child expects everything from its father; it is to be disquieted about nothing, and not to be set on gaining our living. Even among

(\*)   *Mother Agnes further explains:*

     *"One of the infirmarians (an old Sister) had left her in a draft all through Vespers. Before she had left, Sister Thérèse had made a sign for her to close the door. Thinking she was asking for a blanket, she placed one at her feet; she tried to speak, but because of her difficulty in breathing, she was unable to make herself understood, and the good Sister brought her another blanket, a pillow, etc., believing she was cold. The poor patient was suffocating, but no longer tried to explain herself.*

     *"Returning from Vespers, Sister X, taking note of the draft and all the blankets, expressed her discontent rather loudly; the Prioress came and asked for an explanation from Sister Thérèse, who gave evidence of both charity and patience in the circumstances."*

the poor, they give the child what is necessary, but as soon as he grows up, his father no longer wants to feed him and says: 'Work now, you can take care of yourself.'

"It was so as not to hear this that I never wanted to grow up, feeling that I was incapable of making my living, the eternal life of heaven. I've always remained little, therefore, having no other occupation but to gather flowers,[15] the flowers of love and sacrifice, and of offering them to God in order to please Him.

"To be little is not attributing to oneself the virtues that one practices, believing oneself capable of anything, but to recognize that God places this treasure in the hands of His little child to be used when necessary; but it remains always God's treasure. Finally, it is not to become discouraged over one's faults, for children fall often, but they are too little to hurt themselves very much."

\* \* \*

August 7.
1. *Sister X, who has left our monastery,*[16] *wanted to confide in me even though I was no longer prioress:*

"Don't ever listen to her, even though she be an angel; you would be unfortunate to do so because you wouldn't be doing your duty; it would be a weakness which would surely displease God."

\* \* \*

2. "Oh, how little God is loved on this earth, even by priests and religious! No, God isn't loved very much."

\* \* \*

3. *She was showing me the picture of Our Lady of Victories, to which she had pasted the little flower Papa had given her on the day she had confided her vocation to him;*[17] *the root was detached from it, and the Infant Jesus seemed to be holding it, while He and the Blessed Virgin smiled at her:*

---

[15] See *Story of a Soul*, p. 196.
[16] Sister Marie of St. Joseph.
[17] See *Story of a Soul*, p. 107.

"The little flower has lost its root; this will tell you I'm on my way to heaven. It's because of this that they are so nice to me." *(The Blessed Virgin and the Child Jesus.)*

\* \* \*

4. "Oh! If I were unfaithful, if I committed only the slightest infidelity, I feel that I would pay for it with frightful troubles, and I would no longer be able to accept death. Thus I never cease to say to God: 'O my God, I beg You, preserve me from the misfortune of being unfaithful.'"

*I asked: "What infidelity are you speaking about?"*

"A proud thought voluntarily entertained. For example, if I were to say to myself: I have acquired a certain virtue, and I am certain I can practice it. For then, this would be relying upon my own strength, and when we do this, we run the risk of falling into the abyss. However, I will have the right of doing stupid things up until my death, if I am humble and if I remain little. Look at little children: they never stop breaking things, tearing things, falling down, and they do this even while loving their parents very, very much. When I fall in this way, it makes me realize my nothingness more, and I say to myself: What would I do, and what would I become, if I were to rely upon my own strength?

"I understand very well why St. Peter fell.[18] Poor Peter, he was relying upon himself instead of relying only upon God's strength. I conclude from this experience that if I said to myself: "O my God, You know very well I love You too much to dwell upon one single thought against the faith," my temptations would become more violent and I would certainly succumb to them.

"I'm very sure that if St. Peter had said humbly to Jesus: 'Give me the grace, I beg You, to follow You even to death,' he would have received it immediately.

"I'm very certain that Our Lord didn't say anymore to His Apostles through His instructions and His physical presence than He says to us through His good inspirations and His grace. He could have said to St. Peter: "Ask me for the strength to accomplish what you want." But no, He didn't because He wanted to show him his weakness, and

[18] Matthew 26:69-75.

because, before ruling the Church that is filled with sinners, he had to experience for himself what man is able to do without God's help.

"Before Peter fell, Our Lord had said to him: 'And once you are converted, strengthen your brethren.'[19] This means: Convince them of the weakness of human strength through your own experience."

\* \* \*

5.   "I would like you to be always with me; you're my sun!"

\* \* \*

August 8.
1.   *I was telling her I'd make her virtues valued later on; she answered:*

"It is to God alone that all value must be attributed; there's nothing of value in my little nothingness."

\* \* \*

2.   *She was gazing at the sky through the window of the infirmary, and Sister Marie of the Sacred Heart said: "You look up at the heavens with so much love!" She was very tired at the moment, and she answered simply with a smile; later on she confided what she was thinking to me:*

"Ah! she believed I was looking at the sky and thinking of the real heavens! No, it was simply because I admire the material heavens; the other is closed against me more and more. Then immediately I said to myself with great gentleness: Oh, certainly, it's really through love that I'm looking up at the sky; yes, it's through love for God, since everything that I do, my actions, my looks, everything, since my Offering,[20] is done through love."

---

[19]  Luke 22:32.
[20]  Thérèse's "Act of Offering to Merciful Love," made on June 9, 1895.

3. "Today, I was thinking of my past life, about the courageous act I performed formerly at Christmas,[21] and the praise directed to Judith came into my mind: 'You have acted with manly courage, and your heart has been strengthened.'[22] Many souls say: I don't have the strength to accomplish this sacrifice. Let them do, then, what I did: exert a great effort. God never refuses that first grace that gives one the courage to act; afterwards, the heart is strengthened and one advances from victory to victory."

\* \* \*

4. "If Our Lord and the Blessed Virgin had not themselves gone to banquets, never would I have understood the custom of inviting one's friends to meals. It seemed to me that in order to nourish ourselves we would have to hide ourselves, or, at least, stay at home. Accept invitations, yes, but only for the purpose of conversing together, recounting one's trips, memories, and for things of a spiritual nature.

"I had great sympathy for persons who served at large banquets. If, unfortunately, they let some drops fall on the tablecloth or on one of the guests, I saw the mistress of the house looking at them severely, and then these poor people blushed with shame, and I said to myself, with great interior revulsion: Oh! how this difference that exists here on earth between masters and servants proves so well that there is a heaven where each one will be placed according to his interior merit, where all will be seated at the heavenly Father's banquet. But, then, what a Servant we shall have, since Jesus has said: 'He will come and serve them!'[23] This will be the moment for the poor, and especially for the little ones to be recompensed amply for their humiliations."

\* \* \*

August 9.

1. *I was saying about her: "Our warrior is down."*

"I'm not a warrior who fought with earthly arms but with 'the sword of the spirit which is the word of God.'[24] And this sickness

---

[21] In 1886. On the importance of this grace, see *Story of a Soul,* p. 97.

[22] Judith 15:11.

[23] Luke 12:37.

[24] Ephesians 6:17; quoted in Carmelite Rule.

hasn't been able to put me down, and no later than yesterday evening, I made use of my sword with a novice. I told her: I'll die with my weapons in my hands.''

\* \* \*

2. *With reference to her manuscript:*
"There will be something in it for all tastes, except for those in extraordinary ways.''

\* \* \*

3. "You have become again for me what you were during my childhood. I cannot express what you mean to me!''

\* \* \*

4. *They told her she was a saint:*
"No, I'm not a saint; I've never performed the actions of a saint. I'm a very little soul upon whom God has bestowed graces; that's what I am. What I say is the truth; you'll see this in heaven.''

\* \* \*

August 10.
1. *She was looking at the picture of Théophane Vénard pinned to the curtain of her bed. The picture represented the missionary pointing to heaven:*
"Do you believe he knows me? Look at what he's pointing to. He would not have been able to take that pose.''

\* \* \*

2. *They were saying that souls who reached perfect love like her, saw their beauty,*[25] *and that she was among their number:*

---

[25] John of the Cross, St., *The Living Flames of Love,* explanation of st. I, v. 6. See *Collected Words,* p. 592.

"What beauty? I don't see my beauty at all; I see only the graces I've received from God. You always misunderstand me; you don't know, then, that I'm only a little seedling, a little almond."

*(I was distracted and was unable to write down the explanation which followed.)*

\* \* \*

3.   *With a happy and a very beautiful look when gazing at the picture of Théophane Vénard:*
"Ah! but! . . . "
*Sister Geneviève asked: "Why do you say: 'Ah! but!'? "*
"It's because each time I look at him, he looks at me, too, and then he seems to look at me out of the corner of his eye with a kind of mischievous look."

\* \* \*

4.   *We were showing her a picture of Joan of Arc in her prison:*
"The saints encourage me, too, in my prison. They tell me: As long as you are in irons, you cannot carry out your mission; but later on, after your death, this will be the time for your works and your conquests."

\* \* \*

5.   "I'm thinking of the words of St. Ignatius of Antioch: 'I, too, must be ground down through suffering in order to become the wheat of God.' "[26]

\* \* \*

6.   *During Matins:*
"If you knew what you were for me! But I'm always telling you the same thing."

---

[26] Romans 4:1.

7. *I was talking to her about heaven, Our Lord, and the Blessed Virgin, who are there in body and soul; she heaved a deep sigh with this exclamation:*

"Ah!"

*I said: "You're making me understand that you are suffering very much because of your interior trial?"*[27]

"Yes! Must one love God and the Blessed Virgin so much and have these thoughts! However, I don't dwell on them."

\* \* \*

August 11.
1. "I've always found, Mother, that you put too much ardor into your work." *(I was doing some washing.)*

\* \* \*

2. *I was telling her that after her death, we would become very good and that the community would be renewed:*

"Amen, amen, I say to you, unless the grain of wheat falls into the ground and dies, it remains alone; but if it dies, it produces much fruit."[28]

\* \* \*

3. "I didn't expect to suffer like this; I'm suffering like a little child.

"I would never want to ask God for greater sufferings. If He increases them, I will bear them with pleasure and with joy because they will be coming from Him. But I'm too little to have any strength through myself. If I were to ask for sufferings, these would be mine, and I would have to bear them alone, and I've never been able to do anything alone."

---

[27] Mother Agnes of Jesus in her "Preparatory Notes for the Apostolic Process" explains Thérèse's "trial of faith." See p. 257.

[28] John 12:24-25.

4.   "The Blessed Virgin doesn't have a Blessed Virgin to love, and so she's less happy than we are."
*(She once said this to me during recreation.)*

* * *

5.   "I often pray to the saints without receiving any answers; but the more deaf they are to my prayers, the more I love them."
*I asked: "Why?"*
"Because I've had a greater desire not to see God and the saints, and to remain in the night of faith, than others have desired to see and understand."

* * *

6.   *She told us all sorts of things about the time of the influenza epidemic.*[29] *I said to her: "What fatigue you underwent! And how nice and amiable you were! Certainly, all that cheerfulness was not sincere; you were suffering too much in both body and soul." With a smile, she said:*
"I never 'pretend,' I'm not like Jeroboam's wife."[30]

* * *

August 12.
1.   *She had received Holy Communion:*
"Adieu, sisters, I'm going on a long journey."
*She was alluding to my departure for my retreat.*

* * *

2.   *Looking at the picture of Father Bellière, dressed as a soldier:*
"To this soldier, cutting such a dashing figure, I'm giving advice as to a little girl! I'm pointing out to him the way of confidence and love."

---

[29]   Winter, 1891-92. See *Story of a Soul,* p. 171.
[30]   A reference to I Kings 14, where Jeroboam's wife disguises herself to consult the prophet Ahijah.

3. "Ever since the ear of corn,* my sentiments regarding myself are even lower. But how great the grace is that I received this morning when the priest began the Confiteor before giving me Communion, and all the Sisters continued. I saw Jesus very close to giving Himself to me, and this confession appears to me as such a necessary humiliation. 'I confess to Almighty God, to Blessed Virgin Mary, to all the saints, that I have sinned exceedingly . . . .' Oh! yes, I said to myself, they do well to beg pardon from God and all the saints for me at this moment. . . . Like the publican, I felt I was a great sinner. I found God to be so merciful! I found it so touching to address oneself to the whole heavenly court to obtain God's pardon through its intercession. Ah! I could hardly keep from crying, and when the Sacred Host touched my lips, I was really moved.

"How extraordinary it is to have experienced this at the Confiteor! I believe it's because of my present disposition; I feel so miserable! My confidence is not lessened, on the contrary; and the word 'miserable' is not exact, because I am rich with all the divine treasures; but it's exactly because of this that I humble myself even more. When I think of all the graces God gave me, I restrain myself so as not to shed tears of gratitude continually.

"I believe the tears I shed this morning were tears of perfect contrition. Ah! how impossible it is to give oneself such sentiments! It is the Holy Spirit, who gives them, He who 'breathes where he wills.' "[31]

\* \* \*

4. *We were speaking to her of her resistance when we told her to take care of her health, not to rise at the hour when the community arose, not to attend Matins. She said:*

"You didn't understand when I insisted, but it was because I felt that you would try to influence Reverend Mother. I wanted to tell the whole truth to Reverend Mother in order that she would decide herself. I assure you that if she herself had asked me to stay away from Mass, Communion, the Divine Office, I would have obeyed with a great docility."

(\*) See August 4, no. 3.

[31] John 3:8.

5.  "It's quite unbelievable! Now that I can no longer eat, I have a desire for all sorts of things, for example, chicken, cutlets, rice, tuna fish!"

* * *

6.  "You will be able to say of me: 'It wasn't in this world that she lived but in heaven, there where her treasure was.' "

* * *

August 13.

*I was telling her about a thought I had during Compline about heaven:*

"As for me, I have lights only to see my little nothingness. This does me more good than all the lights on the faith."

* * *

August 14.

*(Communion)*

"Lots of little troubles all through the day. Ah! how much trouble I cause!"

*During Matins I said to her: "You had a lot of trouble today."*

"Yes, but since I love it . . . I love everything that God gives me."

* * *

August 15.

1.  *(Communion)*

*I was recalling for her what St. John of the Cross said on the death of those who were consumed by love.*[32] *She sighed and said:*

"I shall have to say that 'joy and transports' are at the bottom of my heart. But it wouldn't be so encouraging to souls if they didn't believe I suffered very much."

*I said: "How I sense your agony! And yet it's a month ago that you were saying such beautiful things about the death of love."*

"What I was saying then, I would say right now."

[32] John of the Cross, st., *The Living Flame of Love, st. I, v. 6. See Collected Works,* p. 592.

2. *She was having much trouble with her breathing and as this continued to increase each day, she said:*

"I don't know what I shall become!"

*I asked: "Does what you will become disturb you?" With an indescribable tone and a smile:*

"Oh! no."

\* \* \*

3. "I dreamed during the silence[33] that you were saying to me: 'You will get very tired when the community comes, and you are looked at by all the Sisters, and you are obliged to speak a little to them.' I answered: 'Yes, but when I am up in heaven, I shall take a rest from it all.' "

\* \* \*

4. "I was asking the Blessed Virgin yesterday evening to stop me from coughing in order that Sister Geneviève would be able to sleep,[34] but I added: If you don't do it, I'll love you even more."

\* \* \*

5. *Our new bells rang for Vespers; I opened the door so that she could hear them well, and I said: "Listen to the bells ringing." After listening:*

"Not yet[35] very beautiful!"

\* \* \*

6. "God gives me courage in proportion to my sufferings. I feel at this moment I couldn't suffer any more, but I'm not afraid, since if they increase, He will increase my courage at the same time."

---

[33] The afternoon silence at one o'clock, during which the nuns could rest.

[34] Sister Geneviève was sleeping in a room adjoining the infirmary.

[35] Norman for "pas encore."

7. "I wonder how God can hold Himself back for such a long time from taking me. . . . And then, one would say that He wants to make me 'believe' that there is no heaven! . . . And all the saints whom I love so much, where are they 'hanging out'? . . .

"Ah! I'm not pretending, it's very true that I don't see a thing. But I must sing very strongly in my heart: 'After death life is immortal,'[36] or without this, things would turn out badly. . . ."

\* \* \*

8. *After Matins, she was exhausted and when we came to arrange her pillows, she said:*
"Now do with me what you will."

\* \* \*

August 16.
1. *She could scarcely speak so weak and breathless was she:*
"I . . . can . . . no longer . . . even . . . speak . . . to you! Oh! if one only knew! . . . If I didn't love God! . . . Yes, but. . . ."

\* \* \*

2. "In the speakroom, you must not speak on any subject you please, for example, speaking about the fashions."

\* \* \*

3. "You will not have any 'little Thérèse' to come looking for you."
*She smiled, and looking at the Statue of the Blessed Virgin and the picture of Théophane Vénard, she pointed out each of them with her finger.*

\* \* \*

4. "The angels can't suffer; therefore, they are not as fortunate as I am. How astonished they would be if they suffered and felt what I feel! Yes, they'd be very surprised because so am I myself."

---

[36] From Herculanum's "Credo" in the opera of F. David.

5. *During Matins, she woke up suddenly, and looking at me with a sweet smile, she said:*
   "Beautiful little Mother!"

* * *

August 17.
1. *(Communion)*
   "I really feel that God wants me to suffer. The remedies which should be doing me some good and which comfort other patients, do me harm."

* * *

2. *We had just raised her, and someone bumped against her while arranging the bed; besides this, she had to suffer from certain remedies that were applied. She asked for a little piece of linen; we hesitated to give it to her as we didn't know what she wanted it for, and she said gently:*
   "You should believe me when I ask for something, because I'm a very good 'little girl.' *(She meant that she asked only for what was necessary.)*
   *After she was once again in bed, feeling she was at the end of her strength, she said:*
   "I'm a very sick 'little girl,' yes, very sick!"

* * *

3. *She touched a periwinkle to the picture of Théophane Vénard; I have kept this periwinkle.*

* * *

4. *I told her: "I'm going to pray that the Blessed Virgin relieve your breathing difficulties."*
   "No, we must leave them alone up there!"

5. *During Matins, looking at the picture of Théophane Vénard:*
"I don't know what is the matter with me; I can't look at him without crying."

* * *

6. *She was having less trouble with her breathing after Matins, and she said to Sister Geneviève, pointing to me:*
"She prayed to Mary, and I am no longer hiccupping."
*(She used this word only as a joke, and she said it in such a nice way when she meant actually that she was coughing, even to the point of suffocating.)*

* * *

August 18.
1. "I'm suffering very much, but am I suffering very well? That's the point!"

* * *

2. " 'Baby' is exhausted!"
*During the afternoon silence, I was hiding in back of the bed in order to write something down:*
"Turn to the side so that I can see you."

* * *

3. "Mamma, you must read the letter you received for me.[37] I deprived myself of asking this from you during prayer, in order to prepare myself for Communion tomorrow and because it isn't permitted."
*(This was during the recreation period.)*
*Seeing me take my pencil to write this down, she said:*
"Perhaps my merit will be lost, since I've told you and you are writing it down."

[37] Undoubtedly Fr. Bellière's letter of August 17, 1897.

*I asked: "You want to acquire merits?"*

"Yes, but not for myself; for poor sinners, for the needs of the whole Church; finally, to cast flowers upon everybody, the just and the sinners."

* * *

4.   *I was telling her she was very patient:*

"I haven't even one minute of patience. It's not my patience! You're always wrong!"

* * *

5.   "Since they say that all souls are tempted by the devil at the moment of death, I'll have to pass this way, too. But perhaps not, I'm too little. With the very little, he cannot do anything."

* * *

6.   *I was saying: "It would really be something for you if you were to regain your health."*

"If this were the will of God, I would be very happy to make this sacrifice. But I assure you, this would be no small thing, for to go so far and then return! Listen!"

* * *

7.   "In the state of weakness in which I actually am, I wonder what would become of me if I were to see a huge spider on our bed. Well, I still want to accept this fear for the sake of God.

"But would you ask the Blessed Virgin not to allow this to happen?"

* * *

August 19.

1.   *She must have felt bad before Holy Communion when hearing the Sisters reciting the "Miserere" in a low tone of voice. She told me afterwards, shedding huge tears:*

"I'm perhaps losing my wits. Oh! If they only knew the weakness I'm experiencing.

"Last night, I couldn't take anymore; I begged the Blessed Virgin to hold my head in her hands so that I could take my sufferings."

\* \* \*

2.   "Remain with me, little Mother; it's like a support to have you."

\* \* \*

3.   *Sister Geneviève handed her the Crucifix; she kissed it on the face with great tenderness. She was as beautiful as an angel at that moment. This particular Crucifix had the head of Our Lord inclined, and looking at it, she said:*
"He is dead! I prefer when they represent Him as dead, because then I think He is no longer suffering."

\* \* \*

4.   *She was asking for certain remedies which cost her quite a bit of pain; however, they were prescribed by the doctor and Mother Prioress. Sister Geneviève said to her as though speaking to a little child: "Who has asked this from 'bobonne'?"[38]*
" 'Baby', through fidelity."

\* \* \*

5.   *She stroked Théophane Vénard on the cheeks. (His picture was pinned to the curtain of her bed, at a little distance from her.)*
*I asked: "Why are you stroking him like that?"*
"Because I can't reach him to kiss him."

\* \* \*

6.   *To Sister Marie of the Eucharist:*
"You shouldn't sit sideways in the chair; it's forbidden."

---

[38] A nickname given by Thérèse to Sister Geneviève when they were together in the infirmary.

7. *To Sister Geneviève, who was arranging her pillows without taking any care of her pictures on the curtains:*
   "Be careful of little Théophane!"

* * *

8. *We were talking too much when all three of us were gathered around her; this tired her out, because we were asking her too many questions at the same time:*
   *"What do you want us to talk about today?"*
   "In order to do some good, it would be necessary to say nothing at all because to tell the truth, there is nothing to say."
   *I said: "Everything is said, right?"*
   *With a pretty little nod of her head:*
   "Yes!"

* * *

9. "No matter what you say, even the most unimportant things, you remind me of a gracious troubador who is always singing his songs in new melodies."
   *And then she pretended to be taking little sips to make me see that she was drinking in my words.*

* * *

10. "I'm suffering only for an instant. It's because we think of the past and the future that we become discouraged and fall into despair."

* * *

August 20.
1. *To Sister Geneviève, like a little child:*
   "You know that you're taking care of a 'baby' who is dying. And (pointing to her glass) you must put something good in the glass, because 'baby' has a very rotten taste in her mouth."

2.   *She had asked us to kiss her only a little because our breath offended her, she was so weak:*
   *I asked: "Can we give you just a little caress?"*
   "Yes, because hands don't breathe."

* * *

3.   *We were speaking to her about the troubles given to the infirmarians by Mother Heart of Jesus:*
   "Oh! How I wish I had been infirmarian, not by natural inclination but 'through the attraction of grace.' And it seems to me that I would have made Mother Heart of Jesus happy! Yes, I would have had an inclination for all that. And I'd have put so much love into the work, thinking of God's words: 'I was sick and you visited me.'[39] It's very rare to find this beautiful opportunity in Carmel."

* * *

4.   *With a happy and mischievous air:*
   "I shall soon be in the horrors of the tomb! And you will one day be there also, little Mother! And when I see you arrive next to me, 'my humbled bones will leap with gladness.'"[40]

* * *

5.   "As soon as I go to drink, this does this to me."
   *She coughs and says to her glass of Bottot water:*
"It's not for drinking!" *Aside:* "It doesn't understand!" *Then louder:* "It's not for drinking, I tell you!"

* * *

6.   *She was no longer able to see the milk which she had never taken with pleasure and which caused her much repugnance. I said to her:*
*"Would you drink this cup to save my life?"*
   "Oh! yes! . . . So, look, and I wouldn't take it for love of God."
   *And she drank the cup in one gulp.*

[39] Matthew 25:36.
[40] Psalm 50:10.

7. *We were making some reflections on the markings on the in-firmary mantle. + .F.*

"No, it doesn't mean what you say. It means that we must carry the cross ( + ), in order to go afterwards higher than the firmament (F)."

\* \* \*

8. "When I suffer very much, I'm happy it's I; I am happy it isn't one of you."

\* \* \*

9. "It's in your company that I'm the most contented, my good Clarisse."
*Words addressed to Mother Genevieve[41] by her little brother.*

\* \* \*

10. *With reference to Communion which she felt she could no longer receive in the future, and as a consequence of many reflections she had heard on the subject, this day was one of intense agony for her and of temptations, too, which I imagine were terrible.* \* *She begged me in the*

(\*)   *The green copybooks explain:*
*She had terrible agonies to suffer that day. This is the reason for them: Holy Communion, so much desired by her, became a source of torment during her illness. Because of her vomiting, her breathing difficulties, her weakness, she feared accidents and she would have preferred that we tell her not to receive. She did not want to take this responsibility upon herself, but since she had said nothing, we believed she was in agreement with us when we insisted that she receive Communion. She continued to be silent, but that day she was unable to restrain herself any longer, and she fell into tears.*
*We didn't know to what we should attribute her sadness, and we begged her to tell us. However, the choking produced by her sobs was so violent that, not only was she unable to answer us, but she made a sign to us not to say a word, not even to look at her.*
*At the end of several hours, having remained alone with her, I dared to approach her and tell her that I had guessed the source of her tears. I consoled her as well as I could, and she seemed close to dying of sorrow. Never had I seen her in such agony.*
*She did not receive Communion from then on right up to her death, August 19, the day of her last Communion, and the feast of St. Hyacinthe; she offered it up for the conversion of the unfortunate Father Hyacinthe. This conversion had preoccupied her all through her life.*

[41] Mother Geneviève of St. Teresa, foundress of the Lisieux Carmel, had the name Claire.

*afternoon to keep silent and not even to look at her. She whispered:*

"I would cry too much if I were to tell you my troubles right now, and I'm having such difficulty in breathing that I would certainly suffocate."

*She spoke to me after a silence of at least an hour, but she was so much disturbed that she held before her eyes the fan she had been given to chase away the flies.*

* * *

11. *She spoke to me about the letter of a priest who said the Blessed Virgin didn't know physical sufferings from actual experience:*

"When I was looking at the statue of the Blessed Virgin this evening, I understood this wasn't true. I understood that she suffered not only in soul but also in body. She suffered a lot on her journeys from the cold, the heat, and from fatigue. She fasted very frequently.

"Yes, she knew what it was to suffer.

"But it's bad perhaps to wish that the Blessed Virgin suffered? I, especially, who love her so much!"

* * *

12. *She was having great difficulty with her breathing. For some time now she found some sort of relief in these painful situations by making little cries like: "Oh! là là!" or "Agne! Agne!"*

"It's when the breathing difficulties come from below that I say: 'Agne! Agne! However, this isn't nice; it displeases me, and so now I'll say: Anne! Anne!' "

*"We'll place this in your circular letter," I said:*

"You'll make it sound like a recipe!"

* * *

13. "It's you who have given me the consolation of having Théophane Vénard's portrait; it's an extremely great consolation. But what he would have been able to do very well doesn't please me! . . . But he is 'very pleasant,' he is 'very lovable.' "

*(These were expressions she'd heard and they amused her.)*

14. "How charming it will be in heaven to know everything that took place in the Holy Family! When little Jesus began to grow up, perhaps when He saw the Blessed Virgin fasting, He said to her: 'I would really like to fast, too.' And the Blessed Virgin answered: 'No, little Jesus, You are still too little, You haven't the strength.' Or else perhaps she didn't dare hinder Him from doing this.

"And good St. Joseph! Oh! how I love him! He wasn't able to fast because of his work.

"I can see him planing, then drying his forehead from time to time. Oh! how I pity him! It seems to me that their life was simple.

"The country women came to speak familiarly with the Blessed Virgin. Sometimes they asked her to entrust her little Jesus to them so that He would go and play with their children. And little Jesus looked at the Blessed Virgin to see if He should go and play. At times, the good women went directly to the Child Jesus and said to Him quite simply: 'Come and play with my little boy.'

"What does me a lot of good when I think of the Holy Family is to imagine a life that was very ordinary. It wasn't everything that they have told us or imagined. For example, that the Child Jesus, after having formed some birds out of clay, breathed upon them and gave them life. Ah! no! little Jesus didn't perform useless miracles like that, even to please His Mother. Why weren't they transported into Egypt by a miracle which would have been necessary and so easy for God. In the twinkling of an eye, they could have been brought there. No, everything in their life was done just as in our own.

"How many troubles, disappointments! How many times did others make complaints to good St. Joseph! How many times did they refuse to pay him for his work! Oh! How astonished we would be if we only knew how much they had to suffer!"

*She spoke to me a long time about this subject, and I was not able to write it all down.*

* * *

15. "I would like to be sure that she loves me; I mean the Blessed Virgin."

16. "When I think of how much trouble I've had all my life trying to recite the rosary!"[42]

* * *

17. "When I received absolution, instead of losing myself in prayers of thanksgiving to God, I thought very simply with gratitude that He had put a little white dress on me and had changed my smock. Neither had been very soiled, but that doesn't matter; my little clothes were brighter, and I was better seen by everybody in heaven."

* * *

18. "No one suspects that Sister Marie of the Sacred Heart, when she was acting as provisor, made me do many mortifications. She loves me so much that I appeared to be spoiled; and mortification is greater in this case.

"She took care of me according to her own taste, which was absolutely opposed to mine."

* * *

August 21.
1. *She was suffering very much, and I was gazing at her on my knees, my heart filled with sadness:*
   "Little sad eyes, why?"
   *I answered: "Because you're suffering so much!"*
   "Yes, but peace, too, peace!"

* * *

2. "There's no longer anything but bed for baby! . . . Everything, everything makes her suffer!"
   *Almost immediately she began to cough and was unable to fall asleep:*
   "Now there's not even bed for baby! It's finished! I'll suffocate one night, I feel it!"

[42] See *Story of a Soul*, p. 242.

3. "How I would have loved to be a priest in order to preach about the Blessed Virgin! One sermon would be sufficient to say everything I think about this subject.

"I'd first make people understand how little is known by us about her life.

"We shouldn't say unlikely things or things we don't know anything about! For example, that when she was very little, at the age of three, the Blessed Virgin went up to the Temple to offer herself to God, burning with sentiments of love and extraordinary fervor. While perhaps she went there very simply out of obedience to her parents.

"Again, why say, with reference to the aged Simeon's prophetic words, that the Blessed Virgin had the Passion of Jesus constantly before her mind from that moment onward? 'And a sword will pierce through your soul also,' the old man said.[43] It wasn't for the present, you see, little Mother; it was a general prediction for the future.

"For a sermon on the Blessed Virgin to please me and do me any good, I must see her real life, not her imagined life. I'm sure that her real life was very simple. They show her to us as unapproachable, but they should present her as imitable, bringing out her virtues, saying that she lived by faith just like ourselves, giving proofs of this from the Gospel, where we read: 'And they did not understand the words which He spoke to them.'[44] And that other no less mysterious statement: 'His father and mother marveled at what was said about him.'[45] This admiration presupposes a certain surprise, don't you think so, little Mother?

"We know very well that the Blessed Virgin is Queen of heaven and earth, but she is more Mother than Queen; and we should not say, on account of her prerogatives, that she surpasses all the saints in glory just as the sun at its rising makes the stars disappear from sight. My God! How strange that would be! A mother who makes her children's glory vanish! I myself think just the contrary. I believe she'll increase the splendor of the elect very much.

"It's good to speak about her prerogatives, but we should not stop at this, and if, in a sermon, we are obliged from beginning to end to exclaim and say: Ah! Ah!, we would grow tired! Who knows whether

---

[43] Luke 2:35.
[44] Ibid., 2:50.
[45] Ibid., 2:33.

some soul would not reach the point of feeling a certain estrangement from a creature so superior and would not say: If things are such, it's better to go and shine as well as one is able in some little corner!

What the Blessed Virgin has more than we have is the privilege of not being able to sin, she was exempt from the stain of original sin; but on the other hand, she wasn't as fortunate as we are, since she didn't have a Blessed Virgin to love. And this is one more sweetness for us and one less sweetness for her!

"Finally, in my poem: *Pourquoi je t'aime, ô Marie,* I have said everything I would preach about her.

\* \* \*

August 22.
1.   "It's grandpapa's feast today." (St. Joachim)

\* \* \*

2.   "Oh! little Mother, what would happen to me if God didn't give me courage? I have only the use of my hands now![46] We don't realize what it is to suffer like this. No, we must experience it."

\* \* \*

3.   *"Someone found you imperfect on a certain occasion,"* I said: "Oh, well, so much the better!"

\* \* \*

4.   *With regard to her intestines and elsewhere, she was suffering violent pains, and we even feared gangrene:* \*

(\*)   *The green copybooks add:*
    *She was seized with terrible intestinal pains and her stomach was as hard as a rock. She was no longer able to perform bodily functions except with terrible pains. If we placed her in a seated position to ease the suffocation after a long coughing spell, she thought she was sitting "on iron spikes." She begged prayers because, she said, the pain was enough "to make her lose her reason." She asked that we not leave poisonous*

[46] Elsewhere Mother Agnes adds the word: "free."

"Well, it's better to have several sicknesses together as long as one has to suffer very much and in all parts. It's like a journey on which we bear with all sorts of inconveniences, knowing very well that these will end promptly, and that once the goal is attained, we will enjoy ourselves all the more."

\* \* \*

5.   *Upon a reflection someone made to her (I don't recall what it was):*

"Do you believe the Blessed Virgin went through the same contortions as St. Mary Magdalene![47] Ah! no, this would not have been nice. It's all right for me to hiccup!"

\* \* \*

6.   *She had spilt some tea on her bed; and to console her, we said it didn't matter. With a gesture which said she had to suffer in all sorts of ways:*

"Ah! it doesn't matter, no!"

\* \* \*

7.   *She was looking at me during prayer, then at her picture of Théophane Vénard with a look that was so gentle and so profound.*

*A little later, she wanted to talk to me in order to please me; she could hardly breathe. I told her to keep silent.*

"No, I mustn't talk? . . . But . . . I believed. . . . I love you so much! . . . I'm going to be good. . . . Oh, little Mother!"

---

*medicines for external use within her reach and advised us never to leave them near patients suffering the same tortures, always for the same reason, the pain "is enough to make one lose one's reason," and, no longer knowing what one is doing, one could easily take one's life. Besides, she added, if she hadn't had any faith, she would not have hesitated for one instant to take her life.*

---

[47] There is reference here to the tortured poses attributed so often to St. Mary Magdalene in art.

8. *We wanted to stop her from taking the initiative in order to console us:*
   "You must let me perform my little 'monkey tricks.' "

\* \* \*

9. "I have experienced pleasure at the thought that they are praying for me; then I told God that I wanted all these prayers applied to sinners."
   *I asked: "You don't want them for your own consolation?"*
   "No!"

\* \* \*

10. *She was suffering much and she groaned:*
    "Little Mother! . . . Yes! . . . I want it!
    "I must no longer complain; this is useless. Pray for me, little sisters, but not on your knees, seated."
    *(We were on our knees.)*

\* \* \*

August 23.
1. "I have not yet spent a night so bad. Oh! How good God will have to be so that I can bear all I'm suffering. Never would I believe I could suffer so much. And yet I believe I'm not at the end of my pains; but He will not abandon me."

\* \* \*

2. *I said: You have sung to the Blessed Virgin:*
   *'All He has given to me, Jesus can take back,*
   *Tell Him not to be shy with me.'*[48]
   "She has told Him this, and He's taking you at your word."
   "I'm content and I do not repent."

---

[48] Thérèse's poem: *Pourquoi je t'aime, ô Marie.*"

3. "No, God gives me no premonition of an approaching death, but of much greater sufferings. . . . But I don't torment myself, I don't want to think of anything but the present moment."

\* \* \*

4. *I was telling her I'd been given a large blanket for the winter but that it was really too large:*
"Oh! no, one can never be too warm in the winter. . . . You will be cold, while I shall not be cold! I pity you."

\* \* \*

5. "Kiss me on the forehead."
*To Sister Geneviève:*
"Pray very much to the Blessed Virgin for me, you who are my little infirmarian, for if you were sick, I'd pray so much for you! But when it comes to praying for oneself, one doesn't dare."

\* \* \*

6. *She had offered her sufferings for Fr. de Cornière, then a seminarian, very much tempted. He learned of this and wrote her one of the most humble and touching letters:*
"Oh, what consolation this letter brought to me! I saw that my sufferings were bearing fruit. Did you notice the sentiments of humility the letter expresses? It's exactly what I wanted.

"And what good it did me to see how in such a short time we can have so much love and gratitude for a soul who has done us some good and whom we didn't know until then. What will it be then in heaven when souls will know those who saved them?"

\* \* \*

7. *In the midst of very great sufferings:*
"Little Mother! . . . Little Mother! . . . Oh! . . . Oh! . . . Yes! . . . Mamma! Mamma! Mamma!"

8. "When we pray to the Blessed Virgin and she doesn't answer, that's a sign she doesn't want to. Then it's better to leave her alone and not torment ourselves."

\* \* \*

9. *She was telling me that all she had heard preached on the Blessed Virgin hadn't touched her:*

"Let the priests, then, show us practicable virtues! It's good to speak of her privileges, but it's necessary above all that we can imitate her. She prefers imitation to admiration, and her life was so simple! However good a sermon is on the Blessed Virgin, if we are obliged all the time to say: Ah! . . . Ah! . . . we grow tired. How I like singing to her:

> ı The narrow road to heaven you have made
> visible *(she said: easy)*
> When practising always the most humble virtues."[49]

\* \* \*

10. ". . . Mamma! . . . Ah! I'm always complaining! . . . See, but! . . . Nevertheless, I want to be sick . . . but it's when I cough all the time and I can't . . ."
*(We stopped the milk diet today.)*
*I was patting her forehead after Matins:*
"Oh! how gentle that is!"

\* \* \*

August 24.
1. *"Are you discouraged?" I asked:*
"No! . . . however, everything is for the worst! At each breath I suffer violently. But not to the point of crying."
*(That morning, she was especially sweet and peaceful.)*

\* \* \*

2. ". . . I would so much like to talk! . . . What a mortification! . . . Well, this really costs me something."

---

[49] Ibid.

3. "Little Mother, do you want me to talk just the same?"
*I had kept her in silence for a long time. A half-hour afterwards, during recreation:*
"Little Mother! . . . ah! I who love you so much!"
*Waking up during Matins:*
". . . Alas, what a long time I've been talking with you! And I see now that you don't know the first word of the conversation!"
*(She explained her trouble in a nightmare.)*
". . . And now I feel a cough threatening to come on! Finally! . . ."
*"Everything is for the worst, isn't it?" I asked:*
"No, for the best."

\* \* \*

4. *I had expressed sympathy for her, and upon Sister Geneviève's reflection that this didn't accomplish great things, she said:*
"But yes, this is exactly what consoles the sick."

\* \* \*

August 25.
1. *I was telling her my desire to know the date of her death:*
"Ah! I myself don't want to know it! In what peace I am! This hardly disturbs me!"
*The door of the infirmary was left open during the silence, and Sister St. John of the Cross used to enter every evening, place herself at the foot of the bed and laugh for a long time.*
*"How indiscreet this visit is and how tiring it must be for you," I said:*
"Yes, it's painful to be looked at and laughed at when one is suffering. But I think how Our Lord on the Cross was looked at in the same way in the midst of His sufferings. It was even worse, for they were really mocking Him; isn't it said in the Gospels that they looked at him, shaking their heads?[50] This thought aids me in offering Him this sacrifice in the right spirit."

[50] Mark 15:29.

2.   *"How you are suffering! Oh! it's hard! Are you sad?" I said:*
"Oh, no, I'm not unhappy in the least; God gives me exactly what I can bear."

\* \* \*

3.   *Aunt sent her some pretty branches of artificial forget-me-nots. These were used to decorate her pictures.*
   *During the silence, with a very childlike and gracious air, she said:*
"I had a desire that someone give me something; I didn't analyse too much what or why. But I had the desire; then, they gave me this."

\* \* \*

4.   *"Alas, my poor little child, you can really say: 'My exile is long!' "*[51]
"But I don't find it long; it's not because I'm suffering that it's longer."

\* \* \*

5.   *She sighed gently:*
". . . Oh! how I complain! However, I wouldn't want to suffer less."

\* \* \*

6.   *She begged us to pray and have others pray for her:*
"Oh! how necessary it is to pray for the dying! If you only knew!
"I believe the demon has asked God permission to tempt me with an extreme suffering, to make me fail in patience and faith."
   *It's to Sister Marie of the Sacred Heart that she spoke about the Hymn in Compline pertaining to the temptations of the spirit of darkness and the phantoms of the night.*[52]

---

[51] Psalm 119:6.
[52] Sister Geneviève relates this scene to August 16, 1897; see pp. 223-224.

7. *It was the feast of St. Louis; she had prayed fervently to Papa, without being heard:*
"In spite of what I felt at the first moment, I repeated to God that I loved Him even more and all His saints, too."

\* \* \*

8. *I shared my sorrow with her, thinking over what she was still to suffer:*
"I'm ready for everything. . . . You see, however, that up to the present, I haven't had any sufferings beyond my control.
". . . We must abandon ourselves. I would like you to rejoice."

\* \* \*

9. ". . . Oh! yes, I wish it! yes, but it's good! . . ."
*"What?" I asked:*
"I shall suffocate!"

\* \* \*

August 26.
1. *We had left her all through the night with the blessed candle lighted:*
"It's because of the blessed candle that I didn't spend too bad a night."

\* \* \*

2. *To Mother Prioress, during prayer:*
"I'm very happy for not having asked anything from God; that way, He is forced to give me courage."[53]

\* \* \*

3. *I was telling her that she was made to suffer much, that her soul was tempered for it:*

---

[53] See p. 290.
[53] See p. 290.

"Ah! to suffer in my soul, yes, I can suffer much. . . . But as to suffering of body, I'm like a little child, very little. I'm without any thought, I suffer from minute to minute."

\* \* \*

4.  *She had to go to confession:*
"Little Mother, I would really like to talk to you, if I may. I don't know if I should tell Father Youf that I had thoughts of gluttony, because I thought of things I like, but I offer them to God."

\* \* \*

5.  *She was suffocating.*
"Ah! I'm choking! . . . Yes!"
*(With a sweet and plaintive voice, the 'yes' was like a little cry.)*

\* \* \*

6.  *During Matins, I was telling her to move at her ease in order to find a little relief:*
"How difficult it is with what I have wrong with me to find relief!"

\* \* \*

7.  *Some lace had come unravelled in the linen trimming her tunic; I was trying to repair it, but it was very difficult to do so and I went about it clumsily. I tired her very much, and when she was unable to take it any more, she said:*
"O little Mother, we mustn't be surprised when the poor infirmarian gets angry at times with her patients. . . . You see how difficult I am! How I love you! . . . You're so gentle. I'm so grateful to you, I could even cry."

\* \* \*

8.  *"How prolonged is your sickness, little one!" I said:*
"Oh, no, I don't find it long; when it is all over, you will see that it didn't appear long."

9.   "Oh, little Mother, how necessary it is for God to help us when we're suffering so much!"

\* \* \*

August 27.
1.   *"Oh! how unfortunate it is when one is sick!" I exclaimed:*
"Oh, no, we are *not* unfortunate when we're dying from our sickness. How strange it is to fear death! . . . But when we're married, when we have a husband and children, this is understandable; but I who haven't anything!"

\* \* \*

2.   "How I wish the Bishop wouldn't come to see me. . . . However, a bishop's blessing is a grace."
*With a laugh:*
"If it were only St. Nicholas, who raised three little children."
*(Bishop Hogonin was at Lisieux.)*

\* \* \*

3.   "Aren't you surprised, little Mother, at the way I'm suffering? . . . But I have great peace in my heart."

\* \* \*

4.   *I complained: "You've taken nothing since this morning!"*
"Taken nothing! But I took two cups of milk; I'm stuffed."\*

---

(\*)   *Thérèse's full statement in French is untranslatable because of the play on words:*
"Rien pris! mais j'ai pris deux tasses de lait, je suis bourrée. Je suis une bourrée, y a pas besoin d'en acheter."[54]
*The word "bourrée" has the meaning also of a "bundle of sticks," for firewood. Thérèse uses "y a pas" for "il n'y a pas." Translator's note.*

[54]   This is a "Bundle of wood made from the thinnest and poorest branches."

5. "I make this poor little Sister Geneviève spend sleepless nights!"

\* \* \*

6. *During the noon recreation: "You told me this morning that you had nothing, and you have little sisters, a little Mother:*
"No, I have nothing, because I'm not leaving them!
*With a mischievous air:*
"Now! if I were to think of leaving them!"

\* \* \*

7. *"Alas, if you were going to be sick until next spring! I fear it, and then what would you say?"*
"I would say so much the better!"

\* \* \*

8. *She had a moment of great relief in the afternoon, and she showed us little signs of affection.*

\* \* \*

9. *She was suffering continually from thirst.\* Sister Marie of the Sacred Heart said: "Do you want some ice water?"*
"Oh! I'd love it!"
*"Mother Prioress obliged you to ask for everything necessary."*
"I do ask for everything that I need."
*"You ask only for what is necessary? Never for what could give you any relief?"*
"No, what's necessary only. Thus when I don't have any grapes, I don't ask for any."
*A few moments after she had taken a drink, she was looking at her glass of water:*

---

(\*) *The green copybooks add: She was still suffering extremely from thirst.* "My thirst is never quenched; if I drink, the thirst increases. It's as though I were on fire inside." *Every morning her tongue was dried out so much it looked like a file, a piece of wood.*

*We said: "Drink some more!"*
"No, my tongue isn't dry enough."

\* \* \*

August 28.
1.  *We had turned her bed towards the window:*
"Oh! how happy I am! Place yourself in front of me, little Mother, so that I can see you well."

\* \* \*

2.  *Mother Prioress and other Sisters said she was pretty and we told her so:*
"Ah! what does that matter to me! It means less than nothing, it annoys me. When one is close to death, one can't take any joy out of that."

\* \* \*

3.  *During the noon silence:*
"Look! Do you see the black hole *(she was pointing to the chestnut trees near the cemetery)* where we can see nothing; it's in a similar hole that I am as far as body and soul are concerned. Ah! what darkness! But I am in peace."

\* \* \*

4.  *She wasn't able to stand the pain, and she groaned:*
"I believe God would be more content if I were to say nothing."

\* \* \*

5.  "Little Mother, catch me that pretty little white thing."
*"What is it?" I asked.*
"It's gone! It's a pretty little thing that flies around during the summer."
*(A seed.)*

6.  *Looking through an opening in her bedcurtain at the statue of the Blessed Virgin which was facing her:*[55]
   "Look! She's lying in wait for me!"

\* \* \*

7.  "I love very much flowers and roses, red flowers, and beautiful pink daisies."

\* \* \*

8.  *When she coughed and made the slightest movement in her bed, the branches of forget-me-nots swayed around her pictures:*
   "The little flowers tremble with me; that pleases me."

\* \* \*

9.  "My good Blessed Virgin, here is what gives me the desire to leave: I tire out my little sisters, and then I give them pain when being so sick. . . . Yes, I would like to go."

\* \* \*

10. *After Matins:*
   "O my good Blessed Virgin, take pity on me . . . 'this time!'"

\* \* \*

August 29.
1.  *I was reading the Sunday Gospel to her: the parable of the Good Samaritan:*[56]
   "I'm like this 'half-dead' traveller, half-dead, half-alive."

\* \* \*

2.  *I exclaimed: "It's very hard to suffer without any interior consolation."*

---

[55] The Virgin of the Smile.
[56] Luke 10:30-37.

"Yes, but it's a suffering without any disquietude. I am content to suffer since God wills it."

* * *

3.   "Little Mother."
*(She called me.)*
*"What do you want?"*
"I just counted nine pears on the pear tree near the window. There must be many others. I'm happy; you will eat some. Fruit is very good!"

* * *

4.   *She gave us a little kiss this evening.*

* * *

August 30.
1.   *She spent the night very peacefully, like the night of August 7: very happy to think she was going to die perhaps:*
"I joined my hands very nicely, expecting death."

* * *

2.   *"Would you be happy if you were told you would die in a few days at the latest? You would prefer this to being told that you will suffer more and more for months and years?"*
"Oh! no, I wouldn't be at all happier. What makes me happy is only to do the will of God."

* * *

3.   *We placed her on a folding bed and rolled her out onto the cloister walk up to the choir door. We left her there alone for a good length of time. She was praying with her eyes facing the grille. Then she cast some rose petals towards it.*
*We photographed her before bringing her in.*[57]

---

[57] See p. 269. Sister Marie of the Angels recalls an interesting incident regarding Thérèse.

*Doctor La Néele came and he said to her: "It will be soon, little Sister, I'm sure of it." She looked at him with a smile of happiness.*

*Fr. Youf came also, and he said these words which she reported to me:*

*"You have suffered more than you are suffering now. . . . We are finishing our ministry together, you as a Carmelite nun, I as a priest."*

\* \* \*

August 31.
1.   *Another visit from Dr. La Néele.*

\* \* \*

2.   *"If you were to die tomorrow, wouldn't you be afraid? It would be so close!"*
Ah! even this evening, I wouldn't be afraid; I would only be filled with joy."

\* \* \*

3.   "What courage I need in order to make the sign of the cross! . . . Ah! little sisters! Ah! my God! my God! . . . My God, have pity on me! . . . I have only this to say!"

\* \* \*

4.   *"Very soon we'll see this bed empty; what sadness for us!" I said:*
"Ah! were I in your place, I'd be happy!"

\* \* \*

5.   "I have an appetite that's making up for my whole life. I always ate like a martyr, and now I could devour everything. It seems to me I'm dying of hunger.

"How St. Veronica must have suffered!"
*(She had read that this Saint died from hunger.)*

6.  *One of us said: "How she's suffocating! She could very well die today."*
   "What happiness!"

* * *

7.  *In the afternoon. They told me she was sleeping, but she opened her eyes and said:*
   "No, advance, it gives me such pleasure to see you!"

* * *

8.  "How I need to see the marvels of heaven! Nothing touches me here on earth."

* * *

9.  *During Matins:*
   "Ah! it is incredible how all my hopes have been fulfilled. When I used to read St. John of the Cross,[58] I begged God to work out in me what he wrote, that is, the same thing as though I were to live to be very old; to consume me rapidly in Love, and I have been answered!"

* * *

10.  *After gazing a long time on the statue of the Blessed Virgin:*
   "Who could ever invent the Blessed Virgin?"

* * *

11.  *To me:*
   "Ah! if you love me, how I love you also!"

---

[58] John of the Cross, St., *The Living Flame of Love,* st. 1, explanation of v. 6. See *Collected Works,* p. 592.

12. *She told me that formerly in order to mortify herself she would think of unpleasant things when she was eating:*

   "But afterwards, I found it very simple to offer to God whatever appealed to my taste."

* * *

13. "Sometimes I wanted to have a real dinner, and I took a grape, then a mouthful of wine, and these I offered to the Blessed Virgin. Then I did the same thing for the Child Jesus, and my little dinner was finished."

* * *

# SEPTEMBER

*The beginning of this month saw the continuation of the relative calm which had succeeded the terrible sufferings of August 22 to 27. Thérèse was eating a little now, and the Guérins were trying to tempt her appetite with certain types of food. However, all the other symptoms did not leave any hope of a recovery. She had grown terribly thin and her weakness was extreme. She was no longer able to move her hands, and no one could touch her without causing her much pain. Her feet began to swell on September 12, and two days later, the doctor gave her no more than two weeks to live. From September 21, Thérèse said she felt she was always in her agony. She actually entered into this only on September 29, the eve of her death.*

*The content of the Yellow Notebook for this month is equally valuable for the actions it describes as for the words it reports. Thérèse is more than ever in control. The brief words that she pronounces have about them the stamp of authenticity and literalness. The dominant themes are her sickness, her suffering, and her death. The trial of faith is always present. The patient's prayer is supported by the holy pictures pinned to the curtains of her bed, and by the statue of the Blessed Virgin. Thérèse still looks with delight upon nature, and she continues to make joking remarks. She is also able to celebrate two anniversaries: September 8, that of her Profession (on that day she writes for the last time), and September 24, her reception of the Veil.*

*Since the Guérin family was still at Lisieux, we have only seven letters written to them, instructing us about the last days that mark out Thérèse's ascent of Calvary. To make up for this, we have the great number of testimonies on September 30 that permit us to reconstruct hour by hour Thérèse's last agony.*

September 2.
1.   *"Surely, you will die on a feast day,"* I said:
   "It will be a beautiful enough feast day in itself! I have never had
any desire to die on a feast day."

\* \* \*

2.   "It was perhaps two years after I was here that God brought an
end to my trial with regard to Sister Marie of the Angels,[1] and I was
able to open my soul to her; in the end, she consoled me very much."

\* \* \*

3.   "It cost me very much to ask permission to perform acts of mortification* in the refectory because I was timid and I blushed; but I
was faithful to my two weekly mortifications. When this trial of
timidity passed away, I paid less attention to them, and I must have
forgotten my two mortifications more than once."

\* \* \*

4.   *We were telling her that she was the head of the group, (i.e., her
own blood sisters), and that she had conquered all enemies; all we had
to do now was to follow her example. She made a gesture, very
familiar to us, by placing her two hands, one on top the other, at a little distance apart, saying:*
   "This big, in the family!"
   *Then pretending to be strewing pebbles:*
   "Little Tom Thumb!"

\* \* \*

5.   *Sister Geneviève said to her: "When I think they are still awaiting
you at the Carmel of Saigon!"*

---

(\*)   *It was customary for the Carmelite nuns to make these acts of mortification in
the refectory each week, for example, standing in the center of the refectory with arms
extended in the form of a cross, begging one's food, asking pardon for faults, etc.*

She was Thérèse's Mistress of Novices. See *Story of a Soul,* p. 151.

"I shall go; I shall go very soon; if you only knew how quickly I will make my journey!"

\* \* \*

6. "When we accept our disappointment at our failures, God immediately returns to us."

\* \* \*

7. "I've offered up my trial against faith especially for a member united to our family, who has lost the faith."
*(This was a M. Tostain.)*

\* \* \*

8. "Oh! yes, I desire heaven! 'Tear the veil of this sweet encounter,'[2] Oh, my God!"

\* \* \*

September 3.
1. *I was reporting what had been told me about the honors given to the Czar of Russia in France:*
"Ah! this doesn't dazzle me at all! Speak to me about God, the example of the saints, about everything that is the truth."

\* \* \*

2. *I said: "When I think we are taking care of a little saint!"*
"Well, so much the better! However, I would want God to say it."

\* \* \*

3. *Poor Mother C. of J.[3] was becoming more and more demanding,*

---

[2]  John of the Cross, St., *The Living Flame of Love,* st. I, v. 6. See *Collected Works,* p. 578.
[3]  Mother Hermance of the Heart of Jesus.

*and the infirmarians were complaining because they had to give in to her whims:*

"Ah! what an attraction I would have for all that!"

* * *

*September 4.*
*1.   Some said that Sister St. Stanislaus called her an angel because of the smiles and signs of affection*[4] *Thérèse showed her for the least service:*

"It's in this way that I've taken God in, and it's because of this that I'll be so well received by Him at the hour of my death."

* * *

2.   "I'm very happy that meat disgusts me because then I find no pleasure in it."

*(They were serving her a little meat.)*

* * *

3.   *At the moment when I was leaving the infirmary to go the refectory:*

"I love you!"

* * *

4.   *When the Angelus was ringing:*
"Must I extend my little hands?"

*I answered: "No, you're even too weak to recite the Angelus. Call upon the Blessed Virgin by simply saying: 'Virgin Mary!'" She said:*

"Virgin Mary, I love you with all my heart."

*Sister Geneviève said: "Tell her that you love her for me, too."*
*Then she added in a whisper:*

---

[4]   Sister Stanislaus was a little deaf and Thérèse used to thank her by pressing her hand.

"For 'Mlle. Lili,' for Mamma, for godmother, for Léonie, for little Marie, Uncle, Aunt, Jeanne, Francis, 'Maurice,' 'little Roulland,' and all whom I love."[5]

\* \* \*

5.   *She had a desire for a certain type of food, a very simple one, and one of us told our Uncle about it:*
"It's very strange that we make this known in the world! Well, I offered it up to God."
*I told her that it wasn't my fault, for in fact I had forbidden it. She replied by taking the little plate:*
"Ah! it's offered up to God. It no longer matters. Let them think what they want!"

\* \* \*

6.   *During Matins:*
"Little Mother, oh! how I love you!"
*With a pretty smile, trying to speak:*
"Let's say something, just the same; let's say . . . If you only knew how the thought of going soon to heaven leaves me calm. However, I'm very happy, but I can't say that I experiencing a living joy and transports of happiness, no!"

\* \* \*

7.   *I asked: "You prefer to die rather than to live?"*
"O little Mother, I don't love one thing more than another; I could not say like our holy Mother St. Teresa: 'I die because I cannot die.'[6] What God prefers and chooses for me, that is what pleases me more."

---

[5]   We can identify these persons easily: Sister Geneviève, Mother Agnes of Jesus, Sister Marie of the Sacred Heart, Léonie Martin, Sister Marie of the Eucharist, M. and Mme. Guérin, Mme. La Néele and Dr. La Néele, Fr. Bellière and Fr. Roulland.
[6]   Teresa of Avila, St., *Poems, Muero porque no muero*. See *The complete Works of St. Teresa,* 3:277.

September 5.

1.   *"You're not sorry, then, to leave 'Mamma?'" I asked:*

"No! . . . If there was no eternal life, oh, yes! . . . but there is one perhaps . . . and it's even certain!"

\* \* \*

2.   *If someone told you that you would die suddenly, at this instant, would you be afraid?"*

". . . Ah! what happiness! I would love to go!"

*"Then you prefer dying to living?"*

"No, not at all. If I were cured, the doctors would look at me in amazement, and I would say to them: 'Sirs, I am very happy to be cured to serve God still on earth, since it is His will. I suffered as if I had to die; well, I will begin this another time.' "

\* \* \*

3.   *Pointing to her glass of reddened water, with a nice little gesture, she said cheerfully:*

"Something to drink, little Mother, if you please. There is ice in it, that's good!"

*After drinking:*

"I drank without thirst! I'm a little 'drinker without thirst.'*

*I was telling her she suffered less during the silence:*

"Oh! just the opposite! I suffered very much, very much! But it's to the Blessed Virgin that I complained."

\* \* \*

4.   *A visit from Dr. La Néele, who after having told her after his last consultation that she was close to death, that she could die suddenly turning in her bed, now said: "You're like a ship that neither advances nor goes back." Surprised, she said:*

"You heard, you see how it changes! But I don't want to change, I want to continue abandoning myself entirely to God."

( \* )   "Je suis un petit 'boit sans soif.' "

September 6.
1. "Say a few sweet words to me, after what happened yesterday."[7]
*I said: "Ah! What could I say to console you, poor little one? I'm quite powerless."*
"I don't need any consolation."

\* \* \*

2. *In the afternoon, she cried with joy when someone brought her a relic of Blessed Théophane Vénard.*
*With great tenderness, she offered me a little daisy for my anniversary.*
*She was very demonstrative, all through the afternoon, in her affection for us, and was attractive in all sorts of ways. I said: "I've noticed that whenever you are able, you return to the way you were formerly."*
"Ah! That's very true! Yes, whenever I can, I do my very best to be cheerful in order to please you."

\* \* \*

3. *She was waiting for Father Youf to hear her confession; he was unable to come and this was a real disappointment. But immediately, she took on her beautiful peaceful expression.*

\* \* \*

4. *Someone brought her some nourishment because her stomach was very much improved:*
"Alas! Where am I in this sickness? Now I am eating!"

\* \* \*

September 7.
*She had not said a word about her day, and I was thinking in the afternoon: Today, I'll have nothing to write.*

---

[7] Undoubtedly she meant the disappointment caused by Dr. La Néele's diagnosis of her sickness.

*But almost immediately she said:*
"Ah! there isn't a soul like . . ."
*After this, she began to shed huge tears for fear that she had caused me trouble in a circumstance about which I wasn't even aware.*

\* \* \*

September 8.
*A little robin came and landed on her bed.*
*Léonie sent her the little music box we have preserved, and the tunes were so sweet, even though profane, that she listened to them with pleasure.*
*Finally, someone brought her a sheaf of wild flowers for the anniversary of her Profession. Seeing herself so loaded with gifts, she cried with gratitude and said:*
"It's all God's tenderness towards me: exteriorly, I'm loaded with gifts; interiorly, I'm always in my trial *(of faith)* . . . but also in peace."

\* \* \*

September 9.
1.   *The little music box had been wound up too tightly and appeared to be broken. Auguste[8] repaired it, but since then it missed (for one tune) the most beautiful note. I was rather disappointed, and I asked her if she was, too:*
"Oh! not at all! But I am simply because you are."

\* \* \*

2.   "Ah! I know what suffering really is!"

\* \* \*

September 10.
1.   *At Dr. de Cornière's consultation, the doctor seemed puzzled by her state.*

---

[8]   Auguste Acard; see p. 297.

*"Well, now, are you content?"* I asked after the doctor left:
"Yes, but I'm a little accustomed to it; they say and then they retract!"

\* \* \*

2.  *In the evening, when we were arranging her pillows, she leaned her head on me, looking at me tenderly. This reminded me of the Infant Jesus' look at the Blessed Virgin when He was listening to the angel's music in the picture where Thérèse said of the Blessed Virgin: "This is Pauline."*

\* \* \*

September 11.
1.  "Little Mother will be the last to die; we'll come looking for her with Théophane Vénard, when she will have finished working for me. . . . Unless little souls need her."

\* \* \*

2.  "I love you very much, but very much!

"When I hear the door open, I always believe it's you; and when you don't come, I'm very sad.

"Give me a kiss, a kiss that makes noise; so that the lips go 'smack!'

"Only in heaven will you know what you mean to me. . . . For me you're a lyre, a song . . . much more than a music box; even when you say nothing."

\* \* \*

3.  *She had made two crowns for the statue of the Blessed Virgin; these were made out of cornflowers, one to be placed at her feet, the other in her hands. I said:* "You no doubt think she will give you the one in her hands."

"Oh! no, it's as she herself wishes; what I give to her is only for her pleasure."

4.   "I'm afraid I've feared death, but I won't fear it after it takes place; I'm sure of this! And I'm not sorry for having lived; oh! no. It's only when I ask myself: What is this mysterious separation of the soul from the body? It's my first experience of this, but I abandon myself to God."

\* \* \*

5.   "Will you hand me my Crucifix so that I can kiss it after the Act of Contrition, in order to gain the plenary indulgence for the souls in purgatory; I can give them no more than that!

"Give me the holy water now; and bring close to me the relics of Blessed Anne of Jesus and Théophane Vénard; I want to kiss them."

*Afterwards she made a little sign of affection to her picture of the Virgin Mother, first to the Child Jesus, then to the Blessed Virgin. She wasn't able to fall asleep and she told me:*

"I know this, it's the devil's malice; he is furious because I didn't forget my little devotions. When, for one reason or another, I don't perform them, I fall asleep and awaken a few minutes after midnight. It's as though he were making fun of me because I missed out on my plenary indulgence."

\* \* \*

6.   "Should I fear the devil? It seems I should not, for I am doing everything out of obedience."

\* \* \*

7.   "Oh! no, I don't have any desire to see God here on earth. And yet I love Him! I also love the Blessed Virgin very much, and the saints, and I don't desire to see them."

\* \* \*

September 12.

*It was the feast of the Holy Name of Mary. She asked me to read her the Sunday Gospel. I didn't have the missal and told her simply:*

*"It's the Gospel where Our Lord warns us against serving two masters."*[9] *then, imitating the voice of a little child reciting her lesson, she said it from memory from beginning to end.*

\* \* \*

September 13.
1.   *She was much sicker and her feet were swollen since the evening before. We could not make the least movement around her, such as moving the bed slightly or touching her because it caused her much suffering, so great was her weakness. We were not aware of this at first, and both Sister Marie of the Sacred Heart and I took her pulse for a long period of time. She didn't show any sign of fatigue at first in order not to cause us any anguish, but finally, not being able to stand any more pain, she began to cry. And when we arranged her pillows and her bed cushion, she groaned, saying in a gentle tone of voice:*
   "I would like . . . I would like . . . "
   *"What would you like?" I asked:*
   "To cause my sisters no more pain; and in order to do this, that I go very quickly."
   *At this moment, she was looking at Sister Marie of the Sacred Heart, and gave her a ravishing smile; it was Marie especially to whom she feared causing any sorrow.*
   *Since we had not succeeded in arranging her bed cushion properly, for we dared not move her too much, she said gently, while supporting herself on her hands and attempting to do it herself:*
   "Wait, I'll push myself to the end of the bed, making movements like a little grasshopper."

\* \* \*

2.   *A Sister*[10] *had picked a violet for her in the garden; she offered it to her and then left. Our little Thérèse said to me, looking at the flower:*
   "Ah! the scent of violets!"
   *Then she made a sign to me to know if she could smell it without failing in mortification.*

---

⁹   Matthew 6:24-33.
¹⁰   Sister Marie of St. Joseph.

September 14.

1.   *Someone brought her a rose; she unpetalled it over her Crucifix with much piety and love, taking each petal and touching it to the wounds of Our Lord.*

"In the month of September, little Thérèse is still unpetalling 'the springtime rose.'

"When unpetalling for You the springtime rose,
I would love to dry Your tears!"[11]

*When the petals were slipping off her bed onto the floor, she said quite seriously:*

"Gather up these petals, little sisters, they will help you to perform favors later on. . . . Don't lose one of them."

\* \* \*

2.   "Ah! now . . .
"I have the hope that my exile will be short!"[12]

\* \* \*

3.   *Doctor La Néele had told her that she wouldn't have any agony, and when she still suffered more and more:*

"And yet they told me that I wouldn't have any agony! . . . But, after all, I do want to have one."

*I asked: "If you were made to choose one or the other, which would you choose?"*

"I would choose nothing!"

\* \* \*

September 15.

1.   *I said: "Today's great sufferings will appear to you as very small when you are in heaven."*

"Oh! even on earth, I find them already very small!"

---

[11]   A poem written by Thérèse and entitled: *Jeter des fleurs.*
[12]   A poem written by Thérèse and entitled: *Vivre d'amour.*

2. *In the evening, during recreation:*
"Just now when Sister Geneviève said to Sister Martha, who asked how I was: 'She is very tired!' I was thinking: That's really true, I am! Yes, I'm like a tired and harassed traveller, who reaches the end of his journey and falls over. Yes, but I'll be falling into God's arms!"

\* \* \*

3. "Mother Prioress told me that I have nothing to do in order to prepare for death because I was prepared in advance."

\* \* \*

September 16.
*To me alone in answer to some questions I'd asked:*
"What draws down God's lights and helps upon us when we are guiding and consoling souls is not the telling of our own troubles in order to receive consolation; besides, this is not a real consolation, it excites us rather than calms us down."

\* \* \*

September 17.
1. "When we are around the sick, we must be cheerful."
*She said this because we were telling her our troubles.*
"After all, we mustn't lament like those who have no hope."[13]
*Then with a mischievous look:*
"You'll end up by making me regret life."
*We said: "It would be hard for us to do that!"*
"That's true! I said it only to scare you a little."

\* \* \*

2. *When speaking to me about her childhood, she said we had given her a little basket and it made her cry with joy:*
"And now I desire nothing upon this earth!"
*She quickly changed her mind, saying:*
"Yes, I still desire something, and it's heaven!"

[13] 1 Thessalonians 4:13.

September 18.

1.   *I was telling her I feared tiring her out by speaking:*
"Little Mother, your conversation is so pleasing to me! Oh! no, it doesn't tire me out. It's just like music to me. There aren't two like you on earth. Oh! how I love you!"

\* \* \*

2.   *Gazing out the window at the very red Virginia vine that was creeping over the hermitage of the Holy Face:*
"The Holy Face is in all its splendor. See, there are some branches of the vine reaching above the chestnut trees."

\* \* \*

3.   "I'm feeling better this afternoon."
*As a matter of fact, she was interested in everything. She was looking with pleasure at an altar cloth Sister Geneviève was making for the altar in the Oratory and at the vestments she was making for Father Denis. In the morning, however, when Sister Aimée of Jesus had lifted her in her arms while we arranged her bed, I believed that she was going to die.*

\* \* \*

September 19.
*We had brought her a bouquet of dahlias from outside; she gazed at them with pleasure, running her fingers ever so gently through the petals!*
*After Father Denis' First Mass, she asked to see his chalice, and because she was looking for a long time at the bottom of the cup, someone asked: "Why are you looking so intently at the bottom of the chalice?"*
"Because my reflection is there; when I was Sacristan, I used to love doing this. I was happy to say to myself: My features are reflected in the place where the Blood of Jesus rested and where it will descend again.
"How many times, too, have I thought that at Rome, my face was reproduced in the eyes of the Holy Father."[14]

---

[14] At the time of her audience with Pope Leo XIII, November 20, 1887. See *Story of a Soul,* p. 134.

September 20.

1. *Doctor de Cornière paid her a visit, and he told us that she still had to suffer a real martyrdom. When leaving, he remarked on her heroic patience, and I told her this:*

"How can he say that I'm patient! It's not true! I never stop moaning and groaning; I'm crying all the time: Oh! là là! And: My God, I can't stand it anymore! Have pity, have pity on me!"

\* \* \*

2. *We changed her tunic in the afternoon and were struck by her extreme thinness because her face hadn't changed. I went to ask Mother Prioress to come and see her back. Mother was long in coming, and I had to admire the gentle and patient way in which Thérèse awaited her arrival. Mother was painfully surprised and said kindly: "What is this little girl who is so thin?"*

"A skeleton!"\*

\* \* \*

September 21.

1. *I'd just emptied her spittoon without saying a word, and I set it near her, thinking within myself: I'd be happy if she told me that she'd reward me in heaven for this. And instantly, turning to me, she said:*

"In heaven, I'll reward you for that."

\* \* \*

2. *Sister Geneviève said: "And when I think she's about to die!"*

"Ah! lady, yes; at last, I believe it!"

\* \* \*

3. *I said: "To say that she'll not have any little Thérèse to love!"*

"He calls me his little Thérèse!"

---

(\*) *There is a play on words here that can be readily appreciated by those who read French: The Prioress had said: "Qu'est-ce que c'est qu'une petite fille aussi maigre?" And Thérèse answered: "Un quelette!" (squelette)*

*"Who?"*

"Father Bellière!"

*He had just written her and I wanted to read his letter to her, believing she would be pleased when finding this passage again, but she was too tired and she said:*

"Oh! no, enough! I'm tired[15] of little Thérèse!"

*Then turning to me with a smile:*

"Not tired of little Pauline too! Oh! no!"

\* \* \*

4. *I was going to do the washing, having two turns to make up.*[16]

"Very hard for me, oh, yes!"

\* \* \*

5. *Sister Geneviève was asking for a pencil; I needed mine also, but I lent it to her just the same. Thérèse said in a low distinct tone:*

"That's nice."

\* \* \*

6. "Ah! what is the agony? It seems to me I'm in it all the time!"

\* \* \*

7. *When drying her eyes, a few eyelashes were detached from her eyelids:*

"Take these lashes, Sister Geneviève, for we must give as little as possible *to the earth." [à la terre]*

*(She was making a pun here upon the name Père Alaterre, a workman, and brother of Sister St. Vincent de Paul.)*

"Poor man, if this gives him any pleasure!"

*It was in this way that she was always cheerful in spite of her great sufferings of both body and soul.*

---

[15] Thérèse used the word "fûtée" instead of the correct word "fatiguée."

[16] Mother Agnes had to make up for two days of washing, thus she was unable to take recreation with Thérèse.

September 22.

1. *After having recalled several circumstances of her religious life in which she had been terribly humiliated, I added: "Oh! how many times I felt sorry for you!"*

"It wasn't necessary, I assure you, to be so sorry for me. If you only knew how I floated above all those things! I was going along strengthened by humiliations; there was no one as brave as I in the line of fire."

\* \* \*

2. *She wanted to talk to me but was unable to do so:*

"Ah! how hard it is to be in such a state of weakness! With you! It was so nice when I could talk to you! This is what is the most difficult to take."

\* \* \*

3. *I was saying when looking at the picture of Théophane Vénard: "There he is hat in hand, and to top it all, he doesn't come to get you!"*

*With a smile she said:*

"I myself don't make fun of the saints. . . . I love them so much! . . . They want to see . . ."

*"What?" I asked, "If you're going to lose patience?" With a mischievous but grave look, she said:*

"Yes. . . . But especially if I'm going to lose confidence. . . . and how far I'm going to push my confidence. . . ."

\* \* \*

4. *She called Sister Geneviève her "bobonne," Sister Marie of the Trinity, her "doll," and she did this simply to distract us, and not because of any dissipation or childishness on her part. We began going too far in this matter, and she said:*

"We should not call ourselves by all sorts of names. After all, it isn't being religious!"

5.  *"Time must seem long to you."*
"No, time doesn't seem long; it seems like yesterday that I was following community acts, writing my copybook." *(her Life)*

\* \* \*

6.  *"What a terrible sickness and how much you're suffering!"*
"Yes! What a grace it is to have faith! If I had not had any faith, I would have committed suicide without an instant's hesitation. . . ."

\* \* \*

September 23.
1.  "Oh! how much I owe you! . . . Also, how I love you! . . . but I don't want to talk about it anymore because I would cry. . . ."
*(It caused her great pain when she cried.)*

\* \* \*

2.  *"Tomorrow is the anniversary of your reception of the Veil, and it will undoubtedly be the day of your death," I said:*
"I don't know when; I expect it always, but I do know it won't be very long from now."

\* \* \*

3.  *She often smiled at us, but sometimes we didn't notice it, and she said:*
"Very often I give beautiful smiles that are lost on 'Bobonne' and the others."

\* \* \*

4.  *In the evening we heard the cooing of a bird at the closed window, and we asked what this could mean. One said: "It's a turtledove," another: "It's probably a bird of prey."*
"Well, if it's a bird of prey, so much the better! Birds of prey come to eat the flesh of the martyrs."

5. *With reference to an unimportant confidence a Sister had made to her, when she was asked about it:*
"If the Sisters forbid it, it's a sacred trust. . . . Even when this is for the least thing, we must not tell it."

\* \* \*

6. *After a very long silence, when gazing upon Sister Marie of the Sacred Heart and myself, who were alone with her:*
"Little sisters, it's you who raised me! . . ."
*And her eyes filled with tears.*

\* \* \*

September 24.
1. *For the anniversary of her reception of the Veil, I had a Mass offered for her:*
"Thanks for the Mass!"
*When I saw her suffering so much, I answered sadly: "Ah! you see, you haven't received any relief!"*
"It was to obtain relief for me that you received permission for the Mass?"
*I answered: "It was for your good."*
"My good, then, is to suffer, no doubt. . . ."

\* \* \*

2. *She was telling me about some suffering she experienced, when, much too late in the year, the chestnut trees were pruned:*
"At first, it was a bitter sadness and great interior struggles that I experienced at one and the same time. I so loved the shadows cast by the branches, and there were none that year. The branches, already green, were lying in bundles on the ground, and all that remained were the trunks of the trees! Then, all of a sudden, I got control over myself by saying: If I were in another Carmel, what difference would it make to me if they cut down entirely all the chestnut trees in the Carmel of Lisieux! And then I experienced a great peace and a heavenly joy."

3.  *She had a visit from Doctor de Cornière, who was more edified than ever. He said to Mother Prioress: "She's an angel! She has the face of an angel; her face hasn't changed, in spite of her great sufferings. I've never seen that in others before. With her general state of getting thinner, it's supernatural."*

\* \* \*

4.  "I would like to run through the fields of heaven. . . . I would like to run in its fields where the grass doesn't crumble, where there are beautiful flowers which don't fade, and beautiful children who would be little angels."

  *I said: "You never seem to be tired of suffering. Are you tired of it?"*

  "No! when I can't take it anymore, I can't take it, and that's it!"

\* \* \*

5.  "I had the desire to say to Doctor de Cornière: I'm laughing because you were not able to prevent me from going to heaven; but, for all your trouble, when I am there, I will prevent you from coming there so soon."[17]

\* \* \*

6.  "Soon I shall speak only the language of the angels."

\* \* \*

7.  *"You will go to heaven among the Seraphim."*

  "Ah! but if I go among the Seraphim, I *shall not do* as they do! All of them cover themselves with their wings before God; I will be very careful not to cover myself with my wings."[18]

\* \* \*

8.  ". . . My God! . . . have pity on Your little . . . girl!
  *(Turning over with very much pain.)*

---

[17] Dr. de Cornière died at the age of eighty, June 25, 1922.
[18] Isaias 6:2.

9. *As she was caressing her "Théophane," I said: "He is very much honored."*
"These are not honors. . . ."
*"What are they?"*
"Caresses, that's all!"
*(She hugged the picture of Théophane Vénard.)*

\* \* \*

10. *"You don't have any intuition about the day of your death?"*
"Ah! Mother, intuitions! If you only knew the poverty I'm in! I know nothing except what you know; I understand nothing except through what I see and feel. But my soul, in spite of this darkness, is in an astonishing peace."

\* \* \*

11. "Whom do you love the most on this earth? . . ."

\* \* \*

September 25.
1. *I had told her what was said in recreation regarding Father Youf (the Chaplain), who had a great fear of death. The Sisters were speaking about the responsibility of those who were in charge of souls and those who lived a long life.*
"As far as little ones are concerned, they will be judged with great gentleness.[19] And one can remain little, even in the most formidable offices, even when living for a long time. If I were to die at the age of eighty, if I were in China, anywhere, I would still die, I feel, as little as I am today. And it is written: 'At the end, the Lord will rise up to save the gentle and the humble of the earth.'[20] It doesn't say 'to judge,' but 'to save.'"

\* \* \*

2. *She had said to me on one of those last days of suffering:*
"O Mother, it's very easy to write beautiful things about suffering,

[19] Wisdom 6:7.
[20] Psalm 75:10.

but writing is nothing, nothing! One must suffer in order to know!''

*I had retained a painful impression from this statement of hers, when, that same day, appearing to remember what she had told me, she looked at me in a very special and solemn way, and pronounced these words:*

"I really feel now that what I've said and written is true about everything. . . . It's true that I wanted to suffer much for God's sake, and it's true that I still desire this."

\* \* \*

3.   *Someone said: "Ah! it's frightful what you're suffering."*
"No, it isn't frightful. A little victim of love cannot find frightful what her Spouse sends her through love."

\* \* \*

September 26.
*She no longer had any strength:*
"Oh! how crushed I am!"
*Looking out the window at a dead leaf, detached from the tree and suspended in the air by a light thread:*
"See, it's a picture of myself; my life hangs only on a light thread."
*After her death, in the evening of September 30, the leaf, which until then was still swinging in the wind, fell to the ground. I picked it up along with the spider's web which was still attached to it.*

\* \* \*

September 27.
*Between two and three o'clock, we asked her if she wanted something to drink; she asked for some Lourdes water, saying:*
"Until three o'clock, I prefer Lourdes water; it's more devotional."

\* \* \*

September 28.
1.   "Mamma!²¹ . . . earth's air is denied to me, when will God grant

---

²¹ Mother Agnes of Jesus.

me the air of heaven? . . .

"Ah! never was it this short! . . ." *(her breathing)*

\* \* \*

2.   *I said: "My poor little child, you're like the martyrs in the amphitheatre; we can no longer do anything for you!"*

"Oh! you can; nothing but seeing you does me a lot of good."

*All through the afternoon, she smiled at us; she listened attentively when I read her these passages of the Office of St. Michael, the Archangel: "The Archangel Michael came with a multitude of angels. It is to him that God has entrusted the care of the souls of His saints, in order to bring them to the joys of heaven. He said: 'Archangel Michael, I have placed you as prince over all the souls that are to be received.'"*

*She made a sign to me with her hand extended towards me, then she placed it on her heart; this meant that I was in her heart.*

\* \* \*

September 29.

1.   *From early morning, she appeared to be in her agony; she had a very heavy rattle in her throat and was unable to breathe. The community was summoned and gathered round her bed to recite the prayers of the dying from the manual. At the end of an hour, Mother Prioress dismissed the Sisters.*

\* \* \*

2.   *At noon, she said to Mother Prioress:*

"Mother, is this the agony? . . . What must I do to die? Never will I know how to die!"

\* \* \*

3.   *I read again several passages from the Office of St. Michael and the prayers for the dying. When I came to the part concerning the demons, she made a childlike gesture as though threatening them, and she exclaimed with a smile:*

"Oh! Oh!" *(This was said in a tone which meant: I don't fear them.)*

\* \* \*

4.   *After the doctor's visit, she said to Mother Prioress:* "Is it today, Mother?"
  *She answered: "Yes, my little child."*
  *One of us said: "God is very joyful today."*
  'I, too!
  "If I were to die right now, what happiness!"

\* \* \*

5.   "When shall I be totally suffocated! . . . I can't stand any more! Ah! pray for me! Jesus! Mary! . . . Yes, I will it, I really will it. . . ."

\* \* \*

6.   *Sister Marie of the Trinity came to see her; after a few minutes, Thérèse told her very gently to leave. When she had gone, I said: "Poor little thing! She loves you so much."*
  "Was I wrong in sending her away?"
  *Her face took on an expression of sorrow, but I quickly reassured her.*

\* \* \*

7.   *Six o'clock. Some kind of insect got into her sleeve, and we tried to get it out:*
  "Leave it alone; it doesn't matter."
  *I said: "But you might be stung by it."*
  "No, leave it alone, leave it alone; I assure you, I know these little beasts!"

\* \* \*

8.   *I had a violent headache and I was closing my eyes in spite of myself when looking at her:*

"Go to bed. . . . I, too!"
*But she couldn't sleep, and she said to me:*
"O Mother, what harm this does to the nerves!"

\* \* \*

9. *During the evening recreation:*
"Ah! if you only knew!"
*(If you only knew what I was suffering.)*

\* \* \*

10. "I'd like to smile at you all the time, and I turn my back on you! Does this cause you any pain?"
*(This was during the silence.)*

\* \* \*

11. *After Matins, when Mother Prioress came to see her, her hands were joined, and she said in a gentle and resigned tone of voice:*
"Yes, my God, yes, my God, I want it all!"
*Mother said: "It's terrible, then, what you are suffering?"*
"No, Mother, not terrible, but much, much . . . just what I can bear."
*She asked to remain alone throughout the night, but Mother Prioress didn't want this. Sister Marie of the Sacred Heart and Sister Geneviève shared this great consolation.\* I remained in the cell, close to the infirmary.*

(\*) *The green copybooks add:*
*She had never wanted us to spend the night by her side during her illness. On the night of September 29 to the 30, which was the last night of her life, she begged that she be left alone. Finally, Sister Marie of the Sacred Heart and Sister Geneviève shared this consolation. They found her totally occupied with the idea of not disturbing the rest of the one who was watching over her. And yet what sufferings she was enduring!*
*Sister Marie of the Sacred Heart had fallen asleep after having given her a glass of water, and what was her distress when she awakened only to find the poor little patient still holding the glass in her trembling hand, waiting patiently for her sister to awaken in order to place it on the table.*

September 30.

*Thursday, the day of her holy death.*

*In the morning, I was with her during the Mass. She didn't speak a word to me. She was exhausted, gasping for breath; her sufferings, I thought, were indescribable. One moment she joined her hands and looked at the statue of the Blessed Virgin.*

"Oh! I prayed fervently to her! But it's the agony, really, without any mixture of consolation."

*I spoke a few words of sympathy and affection and I added that she had edified me very much all through her illness:*

"And you, the consolations you've given me! Ah! they are very great!"

*All through the day, without a moment's respite, she remained, we can say without any exaggeration, in veritable torments.*

*She appeared to be at the end of her strength and nevertheless, to our great surprise, she was able to move, to sit up in her bed.*

"You see the strength that I have today! No, I'm not going to die! I still have strength for months, perhaps years!"

*"And if God willed it," asked Mother Prioress, "would you accept it?" She began to answer in her agony:*

"It would really have to be . . ."

*But checking herself immediately, she said with a tone of sublime resignation, falling back on her pillows:*

"I really will it!"

*I was able to gather these exclamations, but it is impossible to express the tone in which they were said:*

"I no longer believe in death for me. . . . I believe only in suffering. . . . Well, so much the better! . . ."

"O my God! . . ."

"I love God!"

"O good Blessed Virgin, come to my aid!"

"If this is the agony, what is death?! . . ."

"Ah! my God! . . . Yes, He is very good, I find Him very good. . . ."

*Looking at the statue of the Blessed Virgin:*

"Oh! you know I'm suffocating!"

*"God is going to aid you, poor little one, and it will soon be all over."*

"Yes, but when?"

". . . My God, have pity on Your poor little child! Have pity on her!''

*To Mother Prioress:*

"O Mother, I assure you, the chalice is filled to the brim! . . .''

"But God is not going to abandon me, I'm sure. . . .''

"He has never abandoned me.''

"Yes, my God, everything that You will, but have pity on me!''

"Little sisters! little sisters! pray for me!''

"My God! my God! You who are so good!''

"Oh, yes, You are good! I know it. . . .''

*After Vespers, Mother Prioress placed a picture of Our Lady of Mount Carmel on her knees. She looked at it for a moment and said, when Mother Prioress assured her she'd be soon caressing the Blessed Virgin and the Child Jesus:*

"O Mother, present me quickly to the Blessed Virgin; I'm a baby who can't stand anymore! . . . Prepare me for death.''

*Mother Prioress told her that since she had always understood humility, her preparation was already made. She reflected a moment and spoke these words humbly:*

"Yes, it seems to me I never sought anything but the truth; yes, I have understood humility of heart. . . . It seems to me I'm humble.''

*She repeated once more:*

"All I wrote about my desires for suffering. Oh! it's true just the same!''

"And I am not sorry for delivering myself up to Love.''

*With insistence:*

"Oh! no, I'm not sorry; on the contrary!''

*A little later:*

"Never would I have believed it was possible to suffer so much!\* never! never! I cannot explain this except by the ardent desires I have had to save souls.''

*Towards five o'clock, I was alone by her side. Her face changed all of a sudden; I understood it was her last agony.*

*When the community entered the infirmary, she welcomed all the Sisters with a sweet smile. She was holding her Crucifix and looking at it constantly.*

---

(\*) *She didn't receive a single injection of morphine.*

*For more than two hours, a terrible rattle tore her chest. Her face was blue, her hands purplish, her feet were cold, and she shook in all her members. Perspiration stood out in enormous drops on her forehead and rolled down her cheeks. Her difficulties in breathing were always increasing, and in order to breathe she made little involuntary cries.*

*All during this time, so full of agony for us, we heard through the window—it made me suffer very much—the twittering of robins, and other little birds, but this twittering was so strong, so close, and so prolonged! I prayed to God to make them keep silent; this concert pierced my heart, and I feared it would tire out our poor little Thérèse.*

*At one moment, her mouth seemed to be so dry that Sister Geneviève, thinking to relieve her, placed on her lips a little piece of ice. She accepted it, giving her a smile which I'll never forget. It was like a last farewell.*

*At six o'clock, when the Angelus was ringing, she looked at the statue of the Blessed Virgin for a long time.*

*Finally, at a few minutes past seven, Mother Prioress dismissed the community, and she sighed:*

"Mother! Isn't this the agony! . . . Am I not going to die? . . ."

*"Yes, my poor little one, it's the agony, but God perhaps wills to prolong it for several hours."*

*She answered with courage:*

"Well . . . All right! . . . All right!"

"Oh! I would not want to suffer for a shorter time!"

*And looking at her Crucifix:*

"Oh! I love Him! . . .

"My God . . . I love you! . . ."

*Suddenly, after having pronounced these words, she fell back, her head leaning to the right. Mother Prioress had the infirmary bell rung very quickly to call back the community.*

*"Open all the doors," she said at the same time. These words had something solemn about them, and made me think that in heaven God was saying them also to His angels.*

*The Sisters had time to kneel down around her bed, and they were witnesses to the ecstasy of the little, dying saint. Her face had regained the lily-white complexion it always had in full health; her eyes were fixed above, brilliant with peace and joy. She made certain beautiful movements with her head as though someone had divinely wounded her with an arrow of love, then had withdrawn the arrow to wound her again. . . .*

*Sister Marie of the Eucharist approached with a candle to get a closer view of that sublime look. In the light of the candle, there didn't appear any movement in her eyelids. This ecstasy lasted almost the space of a Credo, and then she gave her last breath.*

*After her death, she had a heavenly smile. She was ravishingly beautiful. She was holding her Crucifix so tightly that we had to force it from her hands to prepare her for burial. Sister Marie of the Sacred Heart and I performed this office, along with Sister Aimée of Jesus, and we noticed she didn't seem any more than twelve or thirteen years old.*

*Her limbs were supple right up to her burial, on Monday, October 4, 1897.*

*Sister Agnes of Jesus*
*Carmelite.*

Les Buissonets, childhood home of Thérèse from age 4½ to 15, when she entered the Carmel of Lisieux.


Thérèse as she looked during her interview with the Bishop of Bayeux.

Mr. Louis Martin, father of Thérèse, in wheelchair after his paralytic stroke, surrounded by (l.r.) Marie Guérin, Léonie Martin, a servant, Céline Martin, a servant, Mr. Isidore Guérin, Mrs. Céline Guérin, a friend, *(foreground)* family dog "Tom"

Mr. Martin's wheelchair, used by Thérèse.

# LAST CONVERSATIONS WITH HER SISTER CÉLINE

## INTRODUCTORY REMARKS

We don't have to read much of the "Yellow Notebook" before discovering the truth that Thérèse's relationship to Mother Agnes of Jesus (her sister Pauline) is that of a child to a mother. She never forgets the debt she owes to Pauline, who raised her from the age of four and a half when the mother died on August 28, 1877. Thérèse refers to this several times in the "last conversations," and she goes out of her way to express verbally her deep affection for her older sister. She gives evidence, as we shall see, of this same affection for Céline (Sister Geneviève), whose "last conversations" with Thérèse we are about to read. However, her relationship with Céline is entirely different: it is that of two younger sisters (Céline is three years older than Thérèse) conversing together. They had grown up as childhood companions, playing the same games, reading the same fables, etc., and their conversations in the infirmary are sometimes filled with these childhood experiences.

When still very young, both Céline and Thérèse had decided to enter the religious life. Céline generously stepped aside to allow Thérèse to enter the Lisieux Carmel, April 9, 1888, where she was preceded by two older sisters, Pauline and Marie. Six years were to pass before Céline was to join them in the same monastery on September 14, 1894. During those six years, she grew into a mature woman of twenty-five, had grown accustomed to her independence, had refused several marriage proposals, and had taken excellent care of her father, M. Martin, who suffered a paralytic stroke shortly after Thérèse's entrance in 1888. His sickness was to last up to his death on July 29, 1894.

After her father's death, Céline seemed to be faced with no obstacles to her vocation. However, several things came up which almost resulted in her not entering the Carmel of Lisieux. The first was a missionary project in Canada, very much encouraged by Fr. Almire Pichon, S.J., the spiritual director of Thérèse's older sisters, Marie and Pauline.[1] The second was a very strong opposition from some of the nuns who were opposed to the entrance of one more member of

---

[1] See *Story of a Soul,* p. 177.

the same family. When the opposition was at its height, Thérèse began to pray for a solution to the problem. She writes:

> When the difficulties seemed insurmountable one day, I said to Jesus during my act of thanksgiving: "You know, my God, how much I want to know whether Papa went *straight to heaven; I am not asking You to speak to me, but give me a sign. If Sister A. of J.* consents to Céline's entrance or places no obstacles to it, this will be an answer that Papa went *straight to You.*" This Sister, as you are aware, dear Mother, found we were already too many with three, and she didn't want another member of our family to be admitted. But God, who holds the hearts of His creatures in His hand, inclining them to do His will, changed this Sister's dispositions. The first to meet me after my thanksgiving was Sister Aimée, and she called me over to her with a friendly smile and told me to come up with her to your cell. She spoke to me about Céline, and there were tears in her eyes. Ah! how many things I have to thank Jesus for; He answers all my requests![2]

Céline entered, then, the Carmel of Lisieux on September 14, 1894, and she was given the name of Sister Geneviève of St. Teresa. It was no easy matter for her to accept the rigid training required by her new life, and, we might add, this training was all the more difficult because it was entrusted to her sister Thérèse, three years younger than herself. Thérèse had been placed in charge of the novices when Mother Agnes of Jesus was made Prioress in February, 1893. Her task was to edify, instruct, and correct the novices. Although she found the last task extremely distasteful, she never shirked her duty. Naturally the novices resented some of her correction, and her sister Céline was no exception to this. When explaining her experiences in the novitiate, Thérèse wrote the following interesting incident. We have to keep in mind that the novice to whom she refers was her own sister Céline:

> One day when I particularly desired to be humiliated, a novice took it upon herself to satisfy me, and she did it so well that I was immediately reminded of Semei cursing David. (2 Samuel 16:10) I said to myself: Yes, the Lord has commanded her to say all these things to me. And my soul enjoyed the bitter food served up to it in such abundance.[3]

With reference to this same Sister Geneviève, Fr. Guy Gaucher, O.C.D., has this to say:

[2]  See *Story of a Soul*, p. 177.
[3]  Ibid., p. 244.

With beautiful frankness, Sister Geneviève will later on recount her weak points and her struggles.[4] She will not really enter into the spirit of her sister's "little way" until October 9, 1897, through a sudden grace of conversion which will finally open her eyes and transform her heart. Hardly a week after her death Thérèse carried out her promise and succeeded in doing in one instant what she was unable to do in three years.[5]

This observation by Fr. Gaucher is very interesting. It brings out the truth once again that St. Thérèse was really "unknown" during her life in Carmel. This makes her all the more attractive. The full significance of the above words will become clearer when we read the "conversations" between Céline and Thérèse. However, I would like to point out what took place on October 9, 1897. This is best understood when we read Céline's explanation. In the course of a conversation, Thérèse suddenly said to Céline:

"We will be like two little ducks; you know how closely they follow each other!"

"How sad I would be if I were to see anyone but you on God's other knee; I would cry all day long!"[6]

Very frequently in these "conversations" Thérèse will promise Céline that she will come to get her soon after her death. This is one of those promises, and she used the figure of two ducks following each other closely. It was a promise she was not going to be able to carry out, for Sister Geneviève was to outlive St. Thérèse by more than sixty years, dying on February 25, 1959. This, of course, made it possible for her to work hard all through those years in spreading devotion to her saintly sister. What is interesting about the above conversation is the second statement, which Céline comments on this way:

My little Thérèse was struck by the passage in the Gospel where Jesus refuses to the two sons of Zebedee the privilege of standing on His right and left hand in the kingdom of heaven. (Matt. 20:23) She said: "I think this place has been reserved to little children." She hoped that these two privileged little children would be herself and I. This explains my repeated fears of being unworthy of this favor.

The grace of *"Haec facta est mihi"* came about three weeks after her death in answer to a question I had interiorly formulated during the

---

[4]   See *A memoir of My Sister, St. Thérèse, passim.*
[5]   See *La Passion de Thérèse de Lisieux*, p. 31.
[6]   See p. 215.

recitation of Tierce: My little Thérèse hasn't told me whether she received the place she wanted, sitting on God's knees? At that precise moment, the choir was reciting: *"Haec facta est mihi . . ."* (Psalm 118:56) I did not understand what these words meant, and went in search of a translation immediately after the Divine Office was completed. *"Haec facta est mihi"* means: "This has been done to me." [7]

Sister Geneviève was to enter into the spirit of the "little way" after having received this particular grace, taking quite a firm stand on its importance when testifying at her sister's beatification process. She tells us:

When the promoter of the faith asked me at the canonical process: "Why do you desire the beatification of Sister Thérèse of the Child Jesus?" I answered that it was solely that her Little Way *might become known to the world.* I spoke of it as a "Little Way" because the saint had consistently used this expression when referring to that particular road along which she was travelling to union with God. It was, what we might call, the symbol of her school of spirituality.

The promoter of the faith warned me, however: "Once you begin to speak of a special *Way,* the Cause is infallibly doomed; innumerable cases on record bear abundant witness to that."

"That is indeed too bad," I replied, "but a fear of hindering the beatification of Sister Thérèse could never deter me from stressing the only important point that interests me—that her Little Way might be raised with her, so to speak, to the honors of the altar."

So I held out; nor did the cause suffer as a result. In fact, everything relating to the process began to move so rapidly that it was only a few years later that the decree on the heroicity of the virtues of Sister Thérèse was promulgated by the Sovereign Pontiff, Benedict XV. On that day, August 14, 1921, when His Holiness in his discourse officially raised *The Way of Spiritual Childhood* to its exalted rank in the life of the Church, my joy reached heights never again attained, not even on those other memorable days when my little sister Thérèse was first beatified and then canonized by Holy Mother Church. [8]

It required a great deal of courage on the part of Céline to take this stand, especially when it was pointed out to her that a cause could possibly be abandoned if there were any insistence on a special teaching. She took up the defense of the "little way" inspite of this and she won out. Let me quote just one more important observation made by her on the "little way":

---

[7] See p. 215.
[8] See *A Memoir of My Sister, St. Thérèse,* pp. 38-39.

Through that hidden wisdom which is revealed to little ones, Thérèse possessed a special faculty for discovering again this door to eternal life and of pointing it out to others. Her *Little Way* was, in practice, the virtue of *humility*. But it also established her, unmistakably in the *spirit of childhood*. She used to delight in pointing out to me various passages of the Gospel where there is reference to this spirit of childhood.[9]

She goes on to point out many passages which are not even referred to by St. Thérèse herself in the *Story of a Soul* when she is explaining her "little way." What is particularly interesting are the many passages from the Gospel, and, among those from the Old Testament, the following must have reminded Céline of her own grace of *"Haec facta est mihi"*:

"As one whom a mother caresses, so will I comfort you . . . I shall carry you at my breast, and on my knee I shall caress you."[10]

[9]  Ibid., p. 41.
[10]  Isaias 66:12-13.

July 12.
1. *In the middle of the conversation, little Thérèse stopped suddenly and looked at me with sympathy and tenderness, saying:*

"Ah! my little Sister Geneviève will feel my departure the most; certainly, she's the one I pity the most because as soon as she is in trouble she comes looking for me, and she will no longer find me. . . . Yes, God will give her strength . . . and besides, I'll come back!"

*Speaking to me directly:*

"I will come back to get you as soon as possible, and I'll have Papa join me; you know how he was always in a great hurry."*

\* \* \*

2. *Later on, while I was carrying out my duties as infirmarian, talking constantly about our coming separation, she hummed the following verse that she composed according to the tune of: "Il est à moi":*

"She is mine, she whom heaven itself,
The entire heaven has come to delight me.
She is mine, I love her, oh! yes, I love her
And nothing can ever separate us."**

\* \* \*

3. *I said: "God will not be able to take me immediately after your death because I won't be good enough." She replied:*

"It makes no difference; you remember St. Joseph Cupertino, his intelligence was mediocre, and he was uninstructed, knowing perfectly only this verse of the Gospel: *Beatus venter qui te portavit.*[1] Questioned precisely on this subject, he answered so well that all were in admiration, and he was received with great honors for the

---

(*) *She was referring to our father's character of not putting off until tomorrow what could be done today; his decision once made had to be carried out immediately.*

(**) *"Elle est à moi celle que le Ciel même*
*Le ciel entier est venu me ravir.*
*Elle est à moi, je l'aime, oh! oui, je l'aime*
*Rien ne pourra jamais nous désunir."*

[1] "Blessed is the womb that bore thee." Luke 11:27.

priesthood, along with his three companions, without any further examination. For they judged after hearing his sublime answers that his companions knew as perfectly as he did.

"Thus I will answer for you, and God will give you *gratis* all He will have already given to me."

\* \* \*

4. *That same day, while I was coming and going in the infirmary, she said:*

"My little Valerian."

*She sometimes compared our union to that of St. Cecilia and Valerian.*

\* \* \*

July

1. *Reflections like the following came spontaneously to her when she looked at me:*

"We will be like two little ducks; you know how closely they follow each other!"

"How sad I would be if I were to see anyone but you on God's other knee; I would cry all day long!"

*My little Thérèse was struck by the passage in the Gospel where Jesus refused to the two sons of Zebedee the privilege of standing at His right and left hand in the kingdom of heaven.*[2] *She said:* "I think that this place has been reserved to little children." *She hoped that these two privileged children would be herself and I. This explains my repeated fears of being unworthy of this favor.*

*The grace of "Haec facta est mihi . . . ." came about three weeks after her death in answer to a question I had interiorly formulated during the recitation of Tierce: My little Thérèse hasn't told me whether she received the place she wanted, sitting on God's knees? At that precise moment, the choir was reciting: "Haec facta est mihi . . . ."*[3] *I did not understand what these words meant, and I*

---

[2]  Matthew 20:23.
[3]  Psalm 118:56.

*went in search of a translation immediately after the Divine Office was completed. "Haec facta est mihi" means: "This has been done to me."*

\* \* \*

2.   *I told her I would go crazy after I lost her. She answered:*
"If you're crazy, Bobonne, the "Bon-Sauveur"[4] will come to get you!"
*Bobonne was a nickname she had given me with the Prioress' permission because I used it, and since she had to call upon me constantly, this was easier to pronounce than my own name.*

\* \* \*

3.   *Seeing Mother Agnes writing down all the beautiful words of our Angel, while I was hastily writing down only those pertaining to me personally, I expressed my regret at not writing everything: "I don't act like the others; I don't take any notes of what you're saying." She answered:*
"You won't need any; I'll come and get you."
*During the month of June, before she had been taken down to the infirmary, one day when she saw how sad I was over her approaching death, she addressed the Child Jesus, holding up her finger as though teaching Him a lesson, and she said:*
"Little Jesus, if You take me away, You must also take Mademoiselle Lili.\* This is my condition, so You must think over well what You are about to do. There's no middle course. Take it or leave it!"

*(\*)   A little familiar nickname dating from our childhood which she gave me when we were together. It was inspired by a story for children: "M. Toto and Mlle. Lili"—She was M. Toto, I, Mlle. Lili.*

⁴   This is a play on words, for *"Bon Sauveur"* was the name of the hospital where M. Martin, Thérèse's father, stayed at the beginning of his illness.

4. *On July 22, I wrote to Aunt, Mme. Guérin: "The other day I was reading a passage on the happiness of heaven to my little patient, and she interrupted me, saying:*

"That's not what attracts me. . . ."

*"What then?" I asked:*

"Oh! it's Love! To love, to be loved, and to return to the earth to make love loved. . . ."[5]

\* \* \*

5. *She had coughed up blood during the night. Very joyful, with her childish gestures, she was showing me the saucer[6] from time to time. Often she pointed to its rim with a sad little look that meant* "I would have liked it to be up to there!" *I answered:*

"Oh! it makes no difference whether it was little or much, the incident itself is a sign of your death," *and I added:* "You are more fortunate then I, I haven't any sign of my own!" *She said:*

"Oh! yes, you have a sign! My death is a sign of yours!"

\* \* \*

July 21.

*While I was carrying out my duties in the infirmary, tidying up the room, she was following me with her eyes, and she broke the silence suddenly by making this unexpected statement:*

"In heaven, you will take your place at my side!"

*Later on, quoting from a beautiful poem on Louis XVII:[7]*

> You will come very soon with me
> . . . to rock the child who is weeping
> And in their flaming abode
> To rejuvenate the stars with a luminous breath.\*

> (\*)  *"Vous viendrez bientôt avec moi*
> *. . . bercer l'enfant qui pleure*
> *Et dans leur brûlante demeure*
> *D'un souffle lumineux rajeunir les soleils."*

[5]  "*. . . pour faire aimer l'Amour.*" Sister Geneviève ran her pen through these four words, adding that they did not appear in the letter of July 22, 1897; see p. 282.

[6]  A little cup used by Thérèse.

[7]  A poem by Victor Hugo.

"And then I'll place on you the sky-blue wings of a rosy cherub. I'll attach them myself, for you will not know how; you would put them too low or too high!"

\* \* \*

July 24.
1.   *She knew a lot of little stories and remembered many little details which she made use of upon occasion, making her conversations both lively and imaginative:*
"You're a soul of good will, have no fear of anything, for you have a little 'dog' who will save you from all dangers."
*She was making reference here to something the devil had said to Father Surin during an exorcism: "I've reached the end of my rope, and there's only this dog of good will against whom I can do nothing."*

\* \* \*

2.   *I was telling her:* "You are my ideal, and this ideal I cannot attain. Oh! it's so cruel! It seems to me I don't have what it takes; I'm like a little child who has no idea of distance: in its mother's arms, it reaches out its hand to grab the curtain, some object . . . it doesn't realize these things are too far away!"
"Yes, but on the last day, Jesus will approach His little Céline with all she has desired, and then she'll seize everything."

\* \* \*

August 3.
"You are *very little;* remember that and when one is very little, one doesn't have beautiful thoughts."

\* \* \*

August 4.
1.   *The first years of my religious life made me witness a real destruction of my natural tendencies; I saw nothing but ruins around me, and*

*I frequently complained about it. During one of these sessions, I heard her sing:*
> Bobonne, imperfect on earth
> You will be perfect in heaven!*

*This was sung according to the tune of a hymn to St. Joseph:*
> Joseph, unknown on earth
> How great you are in heaven!**

* * *

2.   *To relieve a pain my sister was suffering in her right shoulder and arm, I devised a large sling from folded linen cloths, attaching it to the ceiling directly above her bed. Her arm was suspended in the air; she wasn't able to make much use of it, but she expressed her gratitude tenderly:*
> "God will also make slings for Bobonne!"

* * *

3.   *Interrupting a conversation, I said sadly, thinking of her death:*
> "I'll not be able to live without her!"

*She answered quickly:*
> "That's right; so I'll bring you two wings!"

*[Translator's note: There is a play on the two French words: "elle" and "ailes" which have exactly the same sound. Céline said: "Moi, je ne saurai pas vivre sans elle!" Thérèse answers: "Vous avez bien raison, aussi je vous en apporterai deux!" (ailes)]*

* * *

4.   *When I was alone with Thérèse one day, I said to her: "You expect a delightful little bird like you to develop from a sparrow's egg; it's impossible!"*

---

(*)    Bobonne, imparfaite sur la terre
       Vous serez parfaite dans les Cieux!

(**)    Joseph inconnu sur la terre
        Que vous êtes grand dans les Cieux!

"Yes, but I'll perform a trick to amuse the saints. I'll take the little egg and I'll say to the saints: 'Look, I'm going to do a magic trick.'

'Here is a little sparrow's egg; well, I'm going to make a pretty little bird like me come out of it!'

"Then I'll say in a whisper to God, presenting Him my little egg: 'Change the nature of the little bird by breathing over it.' Then, when He has returned it to me, I'll ask the Blessed Virgin to kiss it. Finally, I'll give it to St. Joseph and beg him to touch it. Then I'll say aloud to all the saints:

'All of you say that you love as much as I do the little bird that is about to come out of the egg!'

"Immediately all the saints will cry out: 'We love as much as you do the little bird that is about to come out of the egg!'

"Then, triumphantly, I will break the egg and a pretty little bird will come out and place itself at my side on God's knees, and all the saints will be filled with joy when they hear the two little birds singing."

\* \* \*

August 5.

1.  *On the passage of the Gospel: "Two women will be grinding at the mill; one is taken and one is left:"*[8]

"We carry out our little business together; I will see that you cannot grind the wheat all alone, and so I will come and get you. Watch, therefore, for you do not know on what day your Lord is coming."[9]

*She often reminded me that we were two partners. What does it matter if one is incapable? From the moment they decide not to separate from each other they will both one day share in the profits.*

*In her comparison of the little bird in the cloister awaiting the Divine Eagle,[10] never ceasing to look upon Him as a magnet, my dear little Thérèse always told me that she never imagined herself alone, but that there were two little birds.*

---

[8]   Matthew 24:41.
[9]   Matthew 24:42.
[10]  See *Story of a Soul,* p. 199.

2.  *She tried to teach me poverty of spirit and heart by words like this:*

"Bobonne must keep herself in her position; she must not try to be a great lady, never!"

*And because I still had to recite a Little Hour of my Office, she said:*

"Go and recite None. And remember that you are a very little none [nun], *the last of the nones!*"

\* \* \*

3.  *"You're going to leave me!" I said:*

"Oh! not for the space of an inch!"

*Resuming my usual theme, I said: "Do you believe I can still hope to be with you in heaven? This seems impossible to me. It's like expecting a cripple with one arm to climb to the top of a greased pole to fetch an object."*

"Yes, but if there's a giant there who picks up the little cripple in his arms, raises him high, and gives him the object desired!

"This is exactly what God will do for you, but you must not be preoccupied about the matter; you must say to God: 'I know very well that I'll never be worthy of what I hope for, but I hold out my hand to You like a beggar and I'm sure You will answer me fully, for You are so good!' "

\* \* \*

August 8.

*I said: "If when you are gone, they write your little life,[11] I myself would rather be gone before they do so. Do you believe it?"*

"Yes, I believe it, but you must not lose patience; look at how patient I am. You will have to act like that."

\* \* \*

August.

1.  *My little sister tried in our meetings with one another to detach me from myself, and she compared our life to that of two little children*

---

[11] Céline meant the publication of *Histoire d'une Ame (Story of a Soul)*.

*represented in a picture. She went along, detached from everything, wearing only a tunic and holding nothing in her hands except her little sister whom she was leading by the hand. The latter resisted; she wanted to gather flowers although she was already burdened with a huge bouquet.*

\* \* \*

2. *One day she told me this little story:*

"Once there was a 'demoiselle' who possessed the riches of this world and was greatly attached to them.

"She had a little brother who possessed nothing and yet had everything in abundance. This little child fell sick, and he said to his sister: 'Demoiselle, if you wish to cast into the fire all your riches which serve only to disturb you, you will become my 'bobonne,' casting aside your title of 'demoiselle'. And when I shall be in the delightful country to which I must soon go, I will return to get you because you will have lived poor like me, without worrying about tomorrow.

"The 'demoiselle' understood that her little brother was right. She became poor like him, made herself his servant and was no longer tormented by the desire for the perishable riches which she had cast into the fire.

"Her little brother kept his word: he came to get her when he was in the delightful country where God is King and the Blessed Virgin is Queen, and *both of them* will live eternally on God's knees; it's the place they chose because, being too poor, they had not been able to merit thrones."

\* \* \*

3. *On another occasion, making allusion again to the picture of the two children, along with the mistress of a home who was lacking in nothing, she said:*

'A very rich 'demoiselle': many rosebuds, many songbirds at her ear, a skirt, a set of kitchen utensils, little parcels."

*This was taken from a passage she had read where the author praised her hero, Théophane Vénard: "He had a rosebud on his lips and a songbird at his ear."*

4.  *One night when she saw me taking off my habit she was filled with pity at the shabbiness of our clothes and, using a comical expression she had heard, she exclaimed:*

"Pauvre-Pauvre! how poor you are! But you will not always be like this, let me assure you!"

*Pauvre-Pauvre (poor thing) was a nickname Thérèse had given her sister Céline.*

\* \* \*

5.  "When I am in heaven, I'll draw from God's treasures and I'll say:

'This is for Marie, this for Pauline, this for Léonie, and this for the very little Céline.' And making a sign to Papa: 'She's the littlest now, so we must hasten to get her!' "

\* \* \*

6.  *She told me this dream she had before her sickness:*

"You were at the seashore with two persons whom I didn't know. One of them suggested a ride, but they were very stingy, and they said they should rent a lamb instead of a donkey in order that all three get on it together. But when you saw it burdened with these two persons, you said you would walk.

"The poor lamb went all along the hedges until it could take no more, and soon it fell down exhausted by its burden.

"Then, at the turn in the road, a delightful little white lamb came to you and offered its services. You understood then that it would sustain you during life's journey; then the little lamb added: 'You know that I want to breathe within you.'

"Afterwards, I understood that this was a reward for the love you had for these two persons, supporting them without any complaint. It's because of this that Jesus Himself came and gave Himself to you."

\* \* \*

August 16.

*When I rose early this morning, I found my dear little sister pale and disfigured by suffering and anguish. She said:*

"The devil is around me; I don't see him but I feel him. He is tormenting me; he is holding me with an iron hand to prevent me from taking the slightest relief; he is increasing my pains in order to make me despair. And I can no longer pray! I can only look at the Blessed Virgin and say: 'Jesus!' How necessary is that prayer at Compline: *'Procul recedant omnia et noctium phantasmata!'* Deliver us from the phantoms of the night.

"I experience something mysterious. Until now, I've suffered especially in my right side, but God asked me if I wanted to suffer for you, and I immediately answered that I did. At the same instant, my left side was seized with an incredible pain. *I'm suffering for you,* and the devil doesn't want it!"

*Deeply moved, I lighted a blessed candle and calm was restored shortly afterward, without, however, her new physical suffering being taken away from her.*

*Since then she has called her right side:* "Thérèse's side," *and her left,* "Céline's side."

\* \* \*

August 20.
"Oh! yes, I'll come to get you, because you look so heavenly when you're good."

\* \* \*

August 21.
"When I say: 'I'm suffering,' you answer: 'All the better!' I don't have the strength, so you complete what I want to say."

*Her breathing at this moment was very bad, and to help her breathe, she was saying over and over again:* "I'm suffering, I'm suffering. . . ." *But soon she reproached herself as though it were a complaint, and she told me to say what I've written.*

\* \* \*

August 22.
"Little Demoiselle? I love you very much and it's very sweet for me to be taken care of by you."

*She had called me over to tell me this.*

August 24.

*We were talking a sort of childish prattle which the others were unable to grasp. Sister St. Stanislaus, the first infirmarian, said admiringly: "How charming these two little girls are with their unintelligible jargon!"*

*Later I said to Thérèse: "Yes, how charming we both are, but you're the only one that is charming; I am only charming when I'm in your company!"*

*She answered immediately:*

"That's exactly why I'll come and get you!"[12]

\* \* \*

August 31.

"Bobonne, I love you very much!"

\* \* \*

September 3.

1. *I was standing in front of the fireplace, busied about my housework, and I was disturbed about something that wasn't going the way I wanted. She said:*

"Bobonne, no restlessness of spirit!"

\* \* \*

2. *That same day, but not in the same circumstances, I said: "Creatures will not be able to know that we loved each other so much." She answered:*

"It's not worth desiring that creatures believe it; the important thing is that it's so."

*Taking on a tone of assurance:*

"Yes, but since both of us will be on God's two knees!" *She had a delightful way of saying this "Yes, but!"*

\* \* \*

September 5.

1. "I shall protect you!"

---

[12] Thérèse used the word "cri" for the correct word "chercher."

2.  *I was very stingy with my Sundays, my free time when I was permitted to arrange my notes taken down in haste on scraps of paper. I
said: "Today is a wasted Sunday; I've written nothing in our little
notebook."*[13]
     "That's Lili's measure of things, but not Jesus'!"

\* \* \*

September 11.
1.  "Bobonne, you're no longer bobonne, you are my nurse . . . and
you're taking care of a baby who is dying."
     *Turning towards the picture of her dear little Théophane Vénard,
she said to him:*
     "Bobonne is taking good care of me, and as soon as I'm up there,
we shall come looking for her together, right?"

\* \* \*

2.  "I love my Bobonne very much, but very much . . . and when I
am gone, I will come back to thank her for having taken good care of
me."

\* \* \*

3.  *Looking at me tenderly:*
     ". . . But I will see you again, and your heart will rejoice, and no
one will take your joy from you!"[14]

\* \* \*

September 16.
1.  *I had just committed an imperfection when she said to me, her
eyes wide open:*
     "You will be there at my side just the same!"[15]

---

[13] Céline writes elsewhere: "petit carnet."
[14] John 16:22.
[15] What is understood here is "on God's knees."

2. *Touched to tears because of the attention I was giving her, she said:*
"Oh, how grateful I am to my poor little Bobonne! You will see all I'll do for you!"

\* \* \*

3. *I feared she was cold, and I said: "I'm going to get you a little 'consolation.'" But she replied:*
"No, you are my consolation."
*The "consolations" were little pieces of wool which were given out with the winter clothing.*

\* \* \*

September 19.
"My Bobonne is sweet, she takes good care of me. . . . I will pay her back for all this!"

\* \* \*

September 21.
"To love you, you have me . . . and not to love you, it isn't God! . . . it's the devil."

\* \* \*

September 23.
"You don't have to understand, you're too little."
*She meant I didn't have to understand what God was doing in me.*

\* \* \*

September 25.
"I'm going to die, it's certain. . . . I don't know when, but it's certain!"

September 26.
1.  *I said to her one day: "You will look at us from up there in heaven, right?" She replied spontaneously:*
    "No, I shall come down!"

\* \* \*

2.  *I arose several times during the night, in spite of her objections. On one of these visits I saw my dear little sister with hands joined and eyes raised to heaven: "What are you doing? You should try to sleep."*
    "I can't sleep, I'm suffering too much, so I am praying."
    *"And what are you saying to Jesus?"*
    "I say nothing to Him, I love Him!"

\* \* \*

3.  *On one of the last days of her life, in a moment of great suffering, she begged me:*
    "Oh! little Sister Geneviève, pray to the Blessed Virgin for me. I would pray so much to her if you were sick! One dares not ask for oneself."
    *She sighed once more, saying:*
    "Oh! how necessary it is to pray for the agonizing! If you only knew!"
    *All these words and the greater part of those written down by Mother Agnes of Jesus I heard, and it was because I'd seen her take them down that I didn't do so myself. I was witness to everything, except the words spoken when I was at the Hours of the Divine Office. Mother Agnes was with her alone.*

\* \* \*

September 27.
    "O Bobonne! I have a great tenderness for you in my heart!"

September 30.

*This was the last day of my dear little Thérèse's exile. On the day of her death, in the afternoon, Mother Agnes of Jesus and I were with her, and our dear little Saint called us over to help her. She was suffering extremely in all her muscles, and, placing one arm on Mother Agnes' shoulder and the other on mine, she remained thus her arms in the form of a cross. At that very moment, three o'clock sounded, and the thought of Jesus on the Cross came to our mind: was not our poor little martyr a living image of Him?*

*We had asked her: "Who will receive your last look?" She had answered a few days before her death: "If God leaves me free, it will be for Mother Prioress." (Mother Marie de Gonzague.)*

*During her final agony, a few moments before she expired, I was passing a little piece of ice over her burning lips, and at this moment she lifted her eyes to me and looked at me with prophetic insistence. Her look was filled with tenderness, and there was in it a superhuman expression of encouragement and promise as though she were saying to me:*

"Go, go! Céline, I shall be with you!"

*Did God reveal to her the long and laborious career I was to carry out here on earth for her sake, and did He will through this look to console me in my exile? For the memory of that last look, so much desired by all and given to me, sustains me always and is an inexpressible strength for me.*

*The community was in suspense in the presence of this great scene; but suddenly our dear little Saint lowered her eyes in search of Mother Prioress, who was kneeling by her side, and her look took on again the expression of suffering it had before.*

\* \* \*

September 30, 1897.

*Last words of St. Thérèse.*

"Oh! it's pure suffering because there isn't any consolation in it. No, not one!

"O my God! I love God, however. . . . O good Blessed Virgin, come to my aid!

"If this is the agony, what is death? . . ."

"O Mother, I assure you, the cup is filled to the brim!"

"Yes, my God, as much as You will . . . but have pity on me! Little sisters . . . little sisters . . . My God, my God, have pity on me!"

"I am . . . I am reduced. . . . No, I would have never believed one could suffer so much . . . never, never!"

"O Mother, I no longer believe in death for me. . . . I believe only in suffering!"

"Tomorrow, it will be still worse! Well, so much the better!"

*In the evening, Mother Prioress had just dismissed the community, saying that the agony would be prolonged a little more, and the saintly little patient replied immediately:*

"Well, all right! all right! oh! I wouldn't want to suffer less! . . ."

"Oh! I love Him. . . ."

"My God . . . I . . . love You!"

* * *

Carmelite community at Lisieux

St. Thérèse of the Child Jesus

photo taken of Thérèse June 7, 1897.

# LAST CONVERSATIONS WITH SISTER MARIE

## INTRODUCTORY REMARKS

We come now to the "last conversations" recorded by St. Thérèse's oldest sister, Marie (Sister Marie of the Sacred Heart). Marie was unable, because of circumstances, to be present in the infirmary as frequently as were her two other sisters, and this accounts for the very small number of "conversations" entered in her notebook. She was, however, very much interested in what her youngest sister had to say, and she had given positive proof of this long before Thérèse entered the infirmary on July 8, 1897. We have so much to be thankful for, in fact, with regard to Marie's attitude towards her sister that I want to point out how she was responsible for St. Thérèse's famous manuscripts.

One of the questions Marie was asked at the beatification process was to explain the origin of St. Thérèse's *Histoire d'une Ame (Story of a Soul)*. Quite simply she told the judges that it was at her suggestion the "childhood memories" were written. Towards the end of December, 1894, on a cold winter's evening, she was speaking to Mother Agnes and Sister Thérèse, and the latter was entertaining them both by recalling a few incidents of her childhood. The thought struck Marie that these incidents should be written down for the sake of the family, and so later on she said to Mother Agnes of Jesus, who was Prioress:

> "Is it possible that you should permit her to compose little poems to please everybody, and that she should not write anything about all the memories of her childhood? You'll see that she is an angel who will not remain long on earth, and we shall have lost all these detailed accounts that we find so interesting." Mother Agnes hesitated at first; then, at our insistence, she told the Servant of God that it would give her much pleasure if she would give her an account of her childhood for her feast day. . . .[1]

The above testimony on Marie's part gives us some valuable information. As early as December, 1894, Marie seems to be aware that Thérèse will not live very long. Also, Thérèse had discovered in Carmel that she had a talent for writing poetry, and she was permitted to use it, writing as many as fifty poems before she died. Some of these

[1]   See St. Thérèse of Lisieux by those who knew her, p. 83.

were only a few verses, others, twenty-five and thirty verses. We learn, too, that Marie's line of reasoning convinced Mother Agnes there was no harm in her sister's writing her "childhood memories." This work was begun in early January, 1895, and the completed manuscript was handed to Mother Agnes in the following January, 1896, the day before her feast. (This does not mean that Thérèse took a year to write it; she confined herself to an hour or so of free time in the evenings.)

There is a second observation made by Marie at the beatification process which explains the existence of St. Thérèse's second manuscript, her "masterpiece," we might call it. Marie stated:

> " . . . I asked her myself during her last retreat (1896) to write down for me what I have described as her little doctrine. She did so, and these pages were added to form the third part when *Histoire d'une Ame (Story of a Soul)* was published. . . ."[2]

Thérèse had entered upon this private retreat in the evening of September 7, 1896, evidently because she would be celebrating the sixth anniversary of her Profession on September 8. There was a certain freedom permitted the nuns, and during the retreat Thérèse received the following note from her sister Marie. We should note once again Marie's reference to Thérèse's approaching end:

> I am writing you not because I have something to tell you but I want to receive something from you . . . from you who are so close to God, from you who are His little privileged spouse, to whom He confides all His secrets. . . . Jesus' secrets to Thérèse are very sweet, and I would like to hear about them once more. Write me a short note. This is perhaps your last retreat, for the *ripe grape* of Jesus must make Him desirous of taking it. . . .[3]

This is only part of the note, perhaps one-third, and the remainder contains many expressions of affection for Thérèse as the youngest in the family. Some of the statements give evidence that Marie really appreciated the "closeness" of her sister to God. Thérèse was very quick to answer the request. Within a few days, in very small writing, on three sheets of folded paper, Thérèse reveals the secrets of her own heart. There are many corrections on this manuscript which are indicative of the fact that it was written in great haste and in a state of

---

²  Ibid., p. 84.
³  See *Correspondance Générale,* 2:887.

extreme fatigue. Be that as it may, it is her "masterpeice," and it has been considered by many as "a jewel of Christian literature." The reader is advised to read it in its entirety in the *Story of a Soul,* pp. 187-200.

I will quote only Thérèse's introductory words, simply because they express her attitude towards her sister Marie:

> O my dear Sister! you ask me to give you a souvenir of my retreat, one which will probably be my last. Since Mother Prioress permits it, it will be a joy for me to come to speak with you who are doubly my Sister, with you who lent me your voice, promising in my name that I wished to serve Jesus only. This child, dear godmother, whom you offered to the Lord and who speaks to you this evening, is the one who loves you as a child loves its mother. . . . O my dear Sister, you wish to hear about the secrets Jesus confides to your little sister; however, I realize He confides these secrets to you too, for you are the one who taught me how to gather the divine instructions. Nevertheless, I am going to stammer some words, even though I feel it is quite impossible for the human tongue to express things which the human heart can hardly understand. . . .[4]

She continues to address Marie in this manuscript, and then she tells her that her words will be better expressed if addressed directly to Jesus, to whom she owes so much:

> When writing these words, I shall address them to Jesus since this makes it easier for me to express my thoughts, but it does not prevent them from being poorly expressed!

Thérèse does express herself perfectly, and her eloquence reaches a very high degree when she speaks about her "vocation" in the Church. She wrote:

> To be Your *Spouse,* to be a *Carmelite,* and by my union with You to be the *Mother* of souls, should not this suffice me? And yet it is not so. No doubt, these three privileges sum up my true *vocation: Carmelite, Spouse, Mother,* and yet I feel within me other *vocations.* I feel the *vocation* of the WARRIOR, THE PRIEST, THE APOSTLE, THE DOCTOR, THE MARTYR. Finally, I feel the need and the desire of carrying out the most heroic deeds for *You, O Jesus.* I feel within my soul the courage of the *Crusader,* the *Papal Guard,* and I would want to die on the field of battle in defense of the Church.[5]

---

[4]  See *Story of a Soul,* p. 187.
[5]  Ibid., 192.

Thérèse beautifully develops her thoughts, or perhaps I should say, she faithfully follows her interior inspirations, ending up with that cry which came from the very depths of her soul:

> ... I understood that LOVE COMPRISED ALL VOCATIONS, THAT LOVE IS EVERYTHING, THAT IT EMBRACED ALL TIMES AND PLACES. ... IN A WORD, THAT IT IS ETERNAL! Then, in the excess of my delirious joy, I cried out: O Jesus, my Love ... my *vocation,* at last I have found it. ... MY VOCATION IS LOVE!
>
> Yes, I have found my place in the Church, and it is You, O my God, who have given me this place; in the heart of the Church, my Mother, I shall be *Love.* Thus I shall be everything, and thus my dream will be realized.[6]

Marie read these pages over, and we have her reaction to them in a letter to Thérèse, dated in *Correspondance Générale* as September 17, 1896. The date is uncertain but is deduced from the content of the note Marie writes:

> Dear little sister, I have read your pages burning with love for Jesus, and your little godmother is very happy to possess this treasure and is very grateful to her little child, who has thus unveiled the secrets of her soul. ... Oh! how I wanted to weep when reading these lines which are not of this earth but from the very heart of God Himself. ...[7]

The note is rather lengthy. Marie brings her thoughts to a conclusion by telling her sister that: ". . . you are possessed by God!"

There is one more writing that Marie is responsible for getting Thérèse to undertake, and this is her poem entitled: *Why I love thee, Mary.* Thérèse had sometimes expressed the desire to be a priest in order to preach about the Blessed Virgin. There are several references to this in the "Yellow Notebook." One very long statement made by Thérèse on August 21, begins this way:

> "How I would have loved to be a priest in order to preach about the Blessed Virgin! One sermon would be sufficient to say everything I think about this subject. ..."

Her thoughts are developed at great length, but the reader is referred to this passage in the "Yellow Notebook." Thérèse's devotion to the Blessed Virgin Mary was always very deep. It had

---

[6]  See *Story of a Soul,* p. 194.
[7]  See *Correspondance Générale,* 2:893.

begun in the early years of her childhood when she was given proper direction in this matter. But it reached its height at the time of her miraculous cure at the age of ten. She tells us in the *Story of a Soul* about this memorable incident of her "childhood."[8] When all hope was lost, Marie, who was attending Thérèse in her illness, and her other sisters, knelt down around Thérèse's bed and prayed fervently to the Blessed Virgin. Speaking of the statue in her room, Thérèse said it suddenly seemed to come to life:

> . . . All of a sudden the Blessed Virgin appeared *beautiful* to me, so *beautiful* that never had I seen anything so attractive; her face was suffused with an ineffable benevolence and tenderness, but what penetrated to the very depths of my soul was the ravishing smile of the Blessed Virgin. . . .

Thérèse was cured. She was never to forget that smile.

We have the following conversation between Thérèse and Marie which explains the origin of Thérèse's poem: *Why I love thee, Mary.* Thérèse said to Marie:

> "When we address ourselves to the saints, they make us wait a little, and we feel that they have to go and present their request; but whenever I ask a favor from the Blessed Virgin, I receive immediate help." *She added:* "Haven't you ever noticed this? Try it yourself, *and you'll see."*
>
> *I then asked her to write for me what she thought about the Blessed Virgin, and she composed, in the month of May, 1897, her last poem in Mary's honor. She said:* "My little Canticle expresses all I think about the Blessed Virgin and all I would preach about her if I were a priest."
>
> She was referring to her poem: *Pourquoi je t'aime, o Marie!* (Why I love thee, Mary.)

This beautiful poem, made up of some twenty-five verses, contains Thérèse's thoughts on Mary's life as it is depicted in the Gospel, a life of simplicity, humility, and total devotedness to Jesus, her Son. Thérèse points out how the Blessed Virgin walked the ordinary way, and therefore she can be followed by "little ones." There were no miracles, no raptures, no ecstasies—only service.

During the closing days of her own life, in the midst of her sufferings, especially in the darkness of her "trial of faith," Thérèse

---

[8] See *Story of a Soul*, p. 64.
[9] See *Derniers Entretiens*, 1:649.

frequently prayed to the Blessed Virgin to help her. And she was sometimes heard repeating the closing lines of her beautiful poem to Mary:

O thou who cam'st to smile on me at dawn of Life's beginning!
Come once again to smile on me . . . Mother! the night is nigh.[10]

[10] See *Saint Thérèse of Lisieux, The Little Flower of Jesus,* p. 384. See also *Poems of St. Thérèse of the Child Jesus,* translated by the Carmelites of Santa Clara, Cal. (London: Burns Oates and Washbourne Ltd.)

July 8.

1.   *With regard to a certain novice who was tiring her out, I said:*
*"It's a mighty big struggle for you. Are you afraid?"*
   "A soldier is not afraid of combat, and I am a soldier."
   *After she had scolded the novice:*
   "Didn't I tell you that I will die with my weapons in my hands?"

\* \* \*

2.   "The 'Thief'[1] is very far away; He has gone off to steal other children!"

\* \* \*

3.   "We are now at July 8, and on June 9, I saw the Thief. If this is the way He acts, He isn't near to stealing me."

\* \* \*

4.   "They have placed me in an 'unlucky bed,' in a bed that makes me miss the train."
   *She was making allusion here to Mother Geneviève, who had received Extreme Unction three times in this same bed.*

\* \* \*

July 9.
   *After the doctor's visit when he found her much better:*
   "The 'Thief' is still absent! Well, as God wills it!"

\* \* \*

July 12.
   *I asked: "If you had to begin your life over again, what would you do?"*
   "I would do exactly what I did."

[1]   See the "Yellow Notebook," June 9.

July 13.

1.   "If you only knew the projects I'll carry out, the things I shall do when I'm in heaven. . . . I will begin my mission."

*"What are your projects?" I asked:*

"Projects such as coming back with my sisters, and going over there to help the missionaries, and then preventing little pagans from dying before being baptized."

\* \* \*

2.   *I was telling her that after her death I would no longer have any more courage, that it seemed to me that I would speak no words to anyone, that I'd remain in a state of prostration.*

"This is not according to the law of the Gospel. We must be all things to all men."[2]

\* \* \*

3.   *"Rejoice, you will soon be freed from the pains of this life!" I said:*

"I who am such a brave soldier!"

\* \* \*

4.   *"And what must little godmother do?"*

"Let her rise above everything the Sisters may say, everything they may do. You must act as though you were not in your monastery, as though you had to spend only two days here. You must take care not to say what displeases you, since you must leave it."

*When I was finishing the writing of these words, the bell for the "Salve Regina" was ringing, and she said:*

"It would have been better, far better, to lose these words and to go and perform a community act. If we only realized what this means!"

---

[2]   1 Corinthians 9:22.

July 16.

"If God were to say to me: 'If you die right now, you will obtain great glory; if you die at the age of eighty, your glory will be far less, but it will please me much more,' I would not hesitate to answer: 'My God, I want to die at eighty, for I am not seeking my own glory, but I only want to please You.'

"The great saints have worked for God's glory, but I, who am only a very little soul, I work only for His pleasure, His whims. And I would be happy to bear the greatest sufferings—even without God's knowing it, if this were possible—not for the purpose of giving Him a passing glory, but if only I knew that in this way a smile would rise to His lips."

\* \* \*

July 25.

"When bending over a little, I saw through the window the setting sun that was casting its rays over nature, and the tops of the trees appeared to be golden. I said to myself: What a difference if one remains in the shadows or, on the contrary, if one exposes oneself to the sun of Love. Then we appear all golden. In reality, I am not this, and I would cease to be this immediately if I were to withdraw myself from Love."

\* \* \*

July 28.
1.   *We were telling her it would cost us much to lose our recreations for anyone else but her; she answered immediately:*

"And I'd be so happy to do it! Since we are on earth to suffer, the more we suffer, the happier we are. . . . We practice charity much better when we are helping a person who is less appealing to us. Oh! how badly we know how to arrange our little affairs on earth!"

\* \* \*

2.   *I was saying to her: "We are happy to die after having spent our life in loving."*

"Yes, but we must also not fail in charity towards the neighbor."

July 29.

*I was telling her that a certain little hymn in honor of St. Martha had been the occasion of merits for her; she said:*

"Not merits! To please God. . . . If I had amassed merits, I would have despaired immediately."

* * *

August 1.

"I don't know what I'll do to die. . . . Ah! I am abandoned. As God wills!"

* * *

August 10.

*I was saying to her: "I asked God not to let you suffer very much, and you are suffering so much!"*

"I begged God not to hear the prayers which would place an obstacle in the accomplishment of His designs for me, and that He remove all the difficulties opposed to these designs."

* * *

August 11.

*I was telling her: "I won't be able to confide in Mother Agnes of Jesus."*

"It wouldn't be necessary except in the event that she needed some consolation. In your case, you would never have to speak to her for your own consolation as long as she'll not be Prioress. I assure you, this is always what I did. Thus, Mother Prioress gave her permission to talk to me, but I didn't talk to her, and I said nothing to her about my soul. I find that it's this that makes the religious life a martyrdom. Without this, it would be an easy life and without any merits."

* * *

August 15.

1. *On August 13,[3] before Communion, she was particularly moved when listening to the whole community recite the* "Confiteor."

---

[3]    It was August 12.

"When I was listening to all the Sisters say for me: 'I confess to God, the Father Almightly, to the Blessed Virgin Mary, and to all the saints,' I was thinking: Oh! yes, they do well to beg pardon from all the saints. I can't tell you how I felt then. This is how God makes me feel that I am little. It makes me so happy!"

* * *

2.   *I was saying: "What grieves me is that you're still going to suffer very much."*
"It doesn't bother me, because God will give me the courage I need."

* * *

3.   *We were saying: "If God were to take her tonight, she would go without our being aware of it; what pain we would experience!"*
"Ah! I find this would be very charming on His part; He would be stealing me!"

* * *

August 20.
"This isn't like persons who suffer from the past or the future; I myself suffer only at each present moment. So it's not any great thing."

* * *

August 22.
"People don't know what it is to suffer this way. No! they would have to feel it."
*After this same day of continual sufferings:*
"See how good God is! Today, I didn't have the strength to cough, and I hardly coughed at all. Now that I'm a little better, the coughing is about to begin."

August 27.

*I said: "Do you want some cold water?"*

"Oh! I'm dying to have some!"

*"Mother Prioress has told you to ask for what you need; do it out of obedience."*

"I do ask for what I need."

*"Not for what gives you pleasure?"*

"No, only what I need. Thus, when I don't have any grapes, I don't ask for any."

*A short time after she had taken a drink of water, she was looking at her glass, and I said: "Drink a little."*

"No, my tongue isn't dry."

*"When I think that sick as you are you still find ways to mortify yourself."*

"What do you expect? If I listened to myself I would be drinking too often."

\* \* \*

September 1.

*With reference to Mother H. of the Heart of Jesus, to whom the in-firmarians had to pay much attention:*

"How happy I would have been to be her infirmarian. This would have cost me much according to my natural inclinations, but it seems to me I would have taken care of her with so much love, because I think of what Our Lord said: 'I was sick and you visited me.' "[4]

\* \* \*

September 8.

"Ah! the Blessed Virgin! She hasn't come to get me!"

\* \* \*

September 17.

*(With regard to the cemetery.)*

"I understand the thought does something to you. But as for me! What do you want it to do to me! . . . They will place something dead

---

4    Matthew 25:36.

into the ground; it's not as though I were in a trance; then it would be cruel."

* * *

September 21.

*I wanted a word from her, such as whether she remembered the past and the devotedness with which I surrounded her in her childhood. Scarcely had the thought come, when she raised eyes filled with tears to Mother Agnes of Jesus and myself, and said:*

"Little sisters . . . it's you who raised me! . . ."

* * *

September 25.

*I looked at her tenderly:*

"Godmother, how beautiful you are when your face is lit up with a ray of love. . . . It's so pure!"

* * *

September 30.

"Oh! it's pure suffering because there are no consolations! No, not one!"

"O my God! Nevertheless, I love God. . . . O good Blessed Virgin, come to my aid!"

"If this is the agony, what is death?"

"O my poor little Mother, I assure you, the cup is filled to the brim!"

"Yes, my God, everything that You will! . . . But have pity on me!"

"Little sisters! . . . Little sisters! . . . My God! . . . My God, have pity on me! I can't take anymore! . . . I can't take anymore! . . . And yet I must endure. . . . I am . . . I am reduced. . . . No, I would never have believed one could suffer so much . . . never! never!"

"O Mother, I no longer believe in death for me. . . . I believe in suffering!"

"Tomorrow, it will be worse! Well, so much the better!"

*Last words, looking at the Crucifix:*

"Oh! I love Him. . . ."

"My God, I love You! . . ."

# LAST CONVERSATIONS WITH COUSIN M. GUÉRIN

## INTRODUCTORY REMARKS

We read in the "Yellow Notebook," August 15, the following conversation between Mother Agnes and Sister Thérèse:

> *I was recalling for her what St. John of the Cross said on the death of those who were consumed by love. She sighed and said:*
>
> "I shall have to say that 'joy and transports' are at the bottom of my heart. . . . But it would not encourage souls if they didn't believe I suffered very much."
>
> *I said: "How I sense your agony! And yet it's a month ago that you were saying such beautiful things about the death of love."*
>
> "What I was saying then, I would say right now."

Perhaps it would help the reader to have St. John of the Cross' words before him, the ones to which Mother Agnes was making reference. In his book *The Living Flame of Love,* St. John wrote:

> It should be known that the death of persons who have reached this state is far different in its cause and mode than the death of others, even though it is similar in its natural circumstances. If the death of other people is caused by sickness or old age, the death of these persons is not so induced, in spite of their being sick or old; their soul is not wrested from them unless by some impetus and encounter of love, far more sublime than previous ones, of greater power, and more valiant, since it tears through this veil and carries off the jewel, which is the soul.[1]

St. John of the Cross goes on to say in his commentary that the death of such persons is very "gentle and sweet," and that it takes place in the midst of the "most sublime impulses" and "delightful encounters of love." The comparison he used to make his point is that of the death of a swan "whose song is much sweeter at the moment of death." Thérèse had frequently read these passages of St. John's

---

[1]  John of the Cross, St., *The Living Flame of Love,* st. 1, no. 30. See *The Collected Works of St. John of the Cross,* trans. Kieran Kavanaugh, O.C.D. and Otilio Rodriguez, O.C.D. (Washington, D.C.: ICS Publications, Institute of Carmelite Studies, 1973), p. 591. (See also nos. 33 and 34 which were much read by St. Thérèse and were marked off in pencil by her.)

teachings,* and she had spoken of her own intense desire to die in this way, that is, to die of love. She was certain that God, as He had done in all her other desires for certain things, would really allow her to realize this one. This certitude persisted even through all her sufferings. However, when these became so intense, Mother Agnes seemed to think there was some kind of contradiction between what was said in St. John's writings and what she saw in Thérèse's sufferings. Thérèse had to remind her of something which all of us should know. On July 4, 1897, she said:

> "Our Lord died on the Cross in agony, and yet this is the most beautiful death of love. This is the only one that was seen; no one saw that of the Blessed Virgin. To die of love is not to die in transports. I tell you frankly, it seems to me that this is what I am experiencing."

Just as she has done in so many other matters of a deep spiritual nature, St. Thérèse has succeeded here in shedding light on this one—dying of love—by her simple words and perfect comparisons. When we read St. John of the Cross' teachings on the "death of love," and then compare how Thérèse actually died, we find that here again God had carried out her desires, she died the "death of love."

The "Yellow Notebook" contains a vivid description of St. Thérèse's death, September 30, 1897:

> *And looking at her Crucifix:*
> "Oh! I love Him! . . . "
> "My God! . . . I love You! . . . "
> *Suddenly, after having pronounced these words, she fell back, her head leaning to the right. Mother Prioress had the infirmary bell rung very quickly to call back the community.*
> *"Open all the doors," she said at the same time. These words had something solemn about them, and made me think that in heaven God was saying them also to His angels. The Sisters had time to kneel down around her bed, and they were witnesses to the ecstasy of the little, dying saint. Her face had regained the lily-white complexion it always had in full health; her eyes were fixed above, brilliant with peace and joy. She made certain beautiful movements with her head, as though Someone had divinely wounded her with an arrow of love, then had withdrawn the arrow to wound again.*

---

(*) Therese had a book containing St. John's *Spiritual Canticle* and The *Living Flame of Love* at her bedside in the infirmary. She marked off certain passages pertaining to the death of love. This book is still at the Lisieux Carmel.

*Sister Marie of the Eucharist approached with a candle to get a closer view of that sublime look. In the light of the candle, there didn't appear any movement in the eyelids. This ecstasy lasted almost the space of a "Credo" and then she gave up her last breath.*

Mother Agnes' description of her sister's death—so perfectly fulfilling St. John of the Cross' teaching—was not something made up by her. It was witnessed by over twenty other nuns, some of whom were to give the same description when they testified at the beatification process. Each one, of course, was affected in a different way. For instance, when Mother Agnes of Jesus was recalling this event, she described Thérèse as being wounded with an arrow several times. This naturally recalls to our mind St. Teresa of Avila's description, in the twenty-ninth chapter of her "Life," of certain raptures of love, and even of her own mystical experience in this regard. However, Thérèse's sister Céline (Sister Geneviève) was affected in a different way. she felt she was present at her young sister's "judgment." Perhaps the reason why this event was witnessed by so many was to teach us all the lesson that the death of the ordinary Christian can really be a "death of love."

What we must keep in mind, however, when reading about St. Thérèse's holy death is this: her ecstasy had been preceded by months of sufferings, both physical and spiritual sufferings, for example, the "trial of faith" lasting eighteen long months. And it is these "sufferings" that Thérèse begged her sisters to make known to others. She was convinced that her "mission" would never be understood except in the light of her "sufferings." Then only could she be a source of inspiration and strength.

Perhaps we could say that Marie Guérin (Sister Marie of the Eucharist) was the member of her family—she was a cousin—chosen to emphasize these sufferings. She didn't do it consciously, but she did it nevertheless. I am referring here, not to the content of her "conversations" with Thérèse but to the section entitled: Letters concerning the *sickness* of Sister Thérèse of the Child Jesus. True, Marie did not write all of them, but she did write the greater part (with an additional thirty conversations of St. Thérèse). Fortunately for us, Marie was permitted by Mother Marie de Gonzague free access to Thérèse's bedside during those final months. There she observed closely the sufferings of Thérèse and listened to her "last conversations." M. and

Mme. Guérin, very much attached to Thérèse, were kept perfectly informed about her condition by their daughter Marie. She seemed to be especially prepared for this task, for she was the daughter of a pharmicist, the sister-in-law of a doctor, Dr. La Néele, and she had lived for some years with her mother and her sister Jeanne, both of whom were frequently ill. This accounts, no doubt, for the excellent medical reports that her letters turn out to be.

There is very much that is interesting in St. Thérèse's relationship with this young cousin of hers. We meet Marie Guérin very early in the pages of the *Story of a Soul,* for she was a childhood companion of the saint—she was only two years and four months older than Thérèse—and she plays a part in the "childhood memories." In fact, Thérèse's memories of little Marie are somewhat pleasant as the following account will prove:

> What pleased me was when by chance I was alone with little Marie, not having Céline Maudelonde dragging her into *ordinary games,* she left me free to choose, and I chose a game that was entirely new. Marie and Thérèse became *two hermits,* having nothing but a poor hut, a little garden where they grew corn and other vegetables. Their life was spent in continual contemplation; in other words, one *hermit* replaced the other at prayer when she was occupied in the active life. Everything was done with such understanding, silence, and so religiously that it was just perfect. . . .[2]

Both these children were to undertake this form of life in later years. Thérèse was to leave home very early and enter the Lisieux Carmel on April 9, 1888. She was followed some seven years afterwards by Marie Guérin, who entered the same Carmel on August 15, 1895. Marie was placed under the guidance of her younger cousin Thérèse, who, as we have seen, was given charge of the novices in the month of February, 1893. Father Guy Gaucher,O.C.D. has the following remarks to make about this:

> Family ties did not facilitate Thérèse's task. We have seen this already in the case of Sister Geneviève. It is true, too, for her cousin Marie, who has now become Sister Marie of the Eucharist. Being introduced to the contemplative religious life by one's companion in games, when one is both compulsive and scrupulous, can give rise to many difficulties. It was not without some difficulty, then, that Thérèse won the confidence

---

[2]  See *Story of a Soul,* p. 54.

of her cousin. The health reports which Marie was very soon to be writing to her family give proof of the admiration and attachment she had for her Mistress.[3]

Father Gaucher's observation reminds us of what he said about Thérèse and her sister Céline (Sister Geneviève). The situation was practically the same: Marie Guérin, like Céline, was twenty-five years old when she entered. She, too, had grown accustomed to an independent way of life. She had lived with Céline through those years, and especially through the six years of M. Martin's illness, for he was taken into M. Isidore Guérin's home during those years. We can understand, then, how Marie would react to Thérèse's direction. What made it even more difficult for her was the fact that she had, in the years preceding her entrance into the monastery, confided much of her spiritual trouble to Mother Marie de Gonzague, who was officially Novice Mistress when Marie Guérin entered. Hence Thérèse's spiritual direction must have appeared superfluous.

Father Gaucher states that Marie Guérin suffered from scruples. This was very true and even in the month of June, 1897, when Thérèse was no longer able to function as "head" of the novitiate, we find that Marie was still plagued by "scruples." What is very interesting in this matter is that there is a letter extant written by Thérèse—only a novice—advising Marie about these scruples. It is worthwhile quoting because of its historical importance. Marie Guérin had written Thérèse on May 29, 1889, concerning her reluctance to receive Holy Communion because of certain scruples she was experiencing. Thérèse—age sixteen—gives her the following answer on May 30, 1889:

> You did well to write me, and I understand everything, everything, everything!
>
> You haven't committed the slightest sin; I can assure you of this without any fear, for I know so well these kinds of temptations, and besides Jesus tells me so at the bottom of my heart. . . . One must despise all these temptations, paying them not the slightest bit of attention.
>
> Must I tell you something which has caused me very much pain?
>
> It is that my little Marie has not received Communion . . . on the feast of the Ascension and on the last day of Mary's month! . . . Oh, how this has pained Jesus! . . .

---

[3] See *La Passion de Thérèse de Lisieux,* pp. 31-32.

The devil has to be very clever to so deceive a soul! But don't you know, my dear, that this is the only thing he wants. He knows, this perfidious one, that he can't make a soul sin when that soul wants to belong entirely to Jesus, and so he tries to make it believe it has sinned. . . .[4]

I said that this letter is worthwhile because of its historical importance. When Sister Thérèse of the Child Jesus was attracting world-wide attention after her death, the possibility of her future "canonization" was considered. Her writings came under close scrutiny. This particular letter to Marie Guérin came into the hands of Monsignor de Teil, the vice-postulator for Thérèse's cause. He brought it to Pope Pius X, October 28, 1910, making this comment: "Holy father, this little saint has made the following 'anticipated' commentary on your Holiness' decree on 'frequent communion.' " After the Holy Father read the letter he said: "This is most opportune! It gives me great joy. This process must be advanced quickly."[5]

There are two more things I would like to point out regarding Marie Guérin's relationship with St. Thérèse. The first has reference to the saint's attitude in the monastery towards her cousin. In spite of the differences between them—Sister Marie of the Eucharist's lack of confidence in her—Thérèse nevertheless looked upon her cousin as a kindred spirit. In a letter dated July 12, 1897, Marie wrote:

. . . There is something, dear Father, which has afforded me much happiness; it's something Thérèse said to me a few days before I received the veil. I regard it as her "will and testament" to me. . . . There was, at this time, no question of her death, her condition was not yet known; she said to me all of a sudden, looking at me with such a profound gaze that I'll never forget it: *"Oh, little Sister, promise me you'll become a saint, a great saint."*

When I looked at her in amazement, she continued: *"Yes, and if I say this to you, it's because I find in you all that is necessary for this; and if you don't become one, believe me, you'll be unfaithful to grace. Oh! I beg you, become a saint. God is begging this from you. When I'm no longer on earth, you'll have to be a saint for two, in order that God lose nothing; I feel that your soul is being called to the same type of perfection as my own, and you must replace me when I'm gone."*

---

[4]   See *Correspondance Générale*, 1:486.

[5]   Ibid., p. 488, note -d-.

We have, too, the following letter from Marie Guérin, dated July 20, 1897, and addressed to Mme. Gaston Pottier, who happens to be the same person mentioned in the childhood games *(Story of a Soul,* p. 54), Céline Maudelonde (Marie's first cousin):

> I thank God for permitting me to know this little saint, for here in the community she is loved and appreciated as such. . . . Hers is not an extraordinary sanctity; there is no love of extraordinary penances, no, only love for God. People in the world can imitate her sanctity, for she has tried only to do everything through love and to accept all little contradictions, all little sacrifices that come at each moment as coming from God's hands. She saw God in everything, and she carried out all her actions as perfectly as possible. Daily duty came before everything else; as for pleasure, she knew how to sanctify it even while enjoying it, offering it up to God. . . . I asked her the other day: "Did you sometimes refuse God anything?" She said: *"No, I don't remember refusing Him anything. Even when I was very little, at the age of three, I began to refuse God nothing He was asking from me."* This is saying everything, isn't it, to be able to make such an answer, and it's rare to hear it even in our Carmels. Never to have refused God anything! . . .

What a perfect testimony we possess of Marie Guérin's attitude towards Sister Thérèse of the Child Jesus. It was written on July 20, 1897, thus anticipating, by quite a number of years, what was to be the official teaching of the Church, namely, that Thérèse's sanctity was imitable by all. Unfortunately, we don't have any further testimony of this nun regarding Thérèse's life in the monastery and her practice of virtue, but this one is sufficient. Marie Guérin (Sister Marie of the Eucharist) died on April 14, 1905, from the same disease as did Thérèse.

July 11.

"I advise you, when you have struggles against charity, to read this chapter of the Imitation: 'We must bear with the faults of others.' You will find that your struggles will disappear; it always did me a lot of good. It's very good and very true."[1]

\* \* \*

July 18.

*I asked her to obtain great graces for me when she was in heaven:*

"Oh! when I am in heaven, I will do very many things, great things. . . . It is impossible that it is not God, who has given me this desire; I am sure He will answer me! And also, when I am up there, I will follow you very closely!"

*And when I told her that this would frighten me:*

"Does your guardian angel frighten you? He follows you nevertheless, all the time; well, I will follow you in the same way, and even closer! I won't let anything pass you."

\* \* \*

July

"It always gives God a very little pain when we rationalize a very little about what Mother Prioress has said; and it gives Him much pain when we rationalize much, even in our heart."

\* \* \*

August 2.

"I don't find any natural pleasure in being loved, coddled, but I find great pleasure in being humiliated. When I make a bad blunder which humiliates me and makes me see what I am, oh! then, I experience a natural pleasure; I experience a real joy such as you experience at being loved."

[1] DE 1:777.

September 11.

"You must become gentle; never any harsh words, never a harsh tone; never take on a harsh look, always be gentle.

"For example, you gave Sister X some trouble yesterday; a few moments afterwards, another Sister did the same. What happened? She cried! Well, if you hadn't treated her harshly, she would have been able to accept the second rebuff better, it would have passed unobserved. But two rebuffs coming close together put her in a state of great sadness; had you been gentle, nothing would have happened."

*One day, she made me promise that I would be a saint; she was asking me if I were making any progress, and I answered: "I promise you that I'll be a saint when you have left for heaven; at that moment, I'll put my whole heart into it."*

"Oh! don't wait for that. Begin now. The month which preceded my entrance into Carmel has remained for me a very sweet memory. At first, I said to myself: I'll be a saint when I'm in Carmel; while waiting, I won't put myself out. But God showed me the value of time; I did just the opposite of what I was thinking. I wanted to prepare myself for my entrance by being very faithful, and it's one of the most beautiful months of my life.

"Believe me, don't wait until tomorrow to begin becoming a saint."

\* \* \*

# ADDITIONAL CONVERSATIONS*

## MOTHER AGNES OF JESUS

May

*One day, when she attended Mass and received Communion, although shortly before she had received a vesicatory (blistering), I began to cry and was unable to attend the Divine Office. I followed her into her cell, and I shall always see her seated on her little bench, her back supported by a partition of rough boards. She was quite exhausted and was gazing at me with a sad but very gentle look! My tears redoubled, and, guessing how much I was causing her to suffer, I begged pardon on my knees. She said simply:*

"This is not suffering too much to gain one Communion!"

*To repeat the phrase is nothing; one had to hear her state it.* [1]

\* \* \*

*She was coughing very much at this period, especially at night. She was obliged to sit up on her "paillasse" (straw mattress) to lessen the suffocation and to enable herself to breathe. I would have preferred to see her taken down to the infirmary where she would have had a better mattress, but she said that as long as she was happy in her cell she should be left there till the last extremity:*

"Here they don't hear my coughing, so I don't disturb anyone. Besides, when I'm too well cared for, I'm not happy."

(*) Most of the following references are to the testimonies given at the "beatification and canonization process" of Sister Thérèse of the Child Jesus. Two ecclesiastical tribunals were set up to examine into her life, virtues, writings, etc.; the first, August 3, 1910, was set up by the bishop, with the Holy See's approval, and is referred to in these notes as "the diocesan process" (DP); the second, March 17, 1915, was set up by the Holy See, and is referred to as the "apostolic process"(AP). Mother Agnes prepared notes for each process, and these are referred to as "preparatory notes to diocesan process" (PNDP), and "preparatory notes to the apostolic process" (PNAP).

[1]   This text and the two following appear in the "Green Copybooks *(Cahiers verts),* May 21/26.**

(**)   See Thérèse de l'enfant-Jésus et de la Sainte-Face, Ste., *Derniers Entretiens avec ses soeurs,* 2 vols. (Paris: Cerf-Desclée de Brouwer, 1971), 2:38,40. (These will be hereafter referred to as DE 1 and DE 2).

*For another vesicatory, her infirmarian, an old venerable nun, very good and well-intentioned, had placed her in the armchair of the infirmary. In order to make the seat more comfortable, the infirmarian had placed pillows, one before the other, against the back of the chair; the poor patient found herself sitting on the edge of the chair, running the risk of falling off at any moment. Rather than complain, she thanked the Sister, and then had to listen to the remarks of the other Sisters who paid her visits during the day: "Well, I hope you're comfortably installed! How many pillows you have! We can see you're taken care of by a real Mamma, etc."*

*I was rather surprised when I saw her, but she gave me a knowing smile and then I understood what happened. It was too late, however, to remedy the matter.*

June

*On June 9, 1897, Sister Marie of the Sacred Heart told her we would be very sorry after she died. She answered:*

"Oh! no, you will see . . . it will be like a shower of roses."

*She added:*

"After my death, you will go to the mail box, and you will find many consolations."[2]

\* \* \*

*Mother Agnes of Jesus had retained this souvenir, dating from June, 1897, relative to the bottles of milk.*

*This cartoon, cut out of a newspaper found accidentally, was brought to me by Sister Thérèse of the Child Jesus, who had a mischievous smile on her face. She gave it to me at a time when I was quite desolate because she, being too sick, was able to take nothing but milk. She did it to cheer me up:*

"My bottle of milk follows me as faithfully as this drunkard's bottle. Look, you can see nothing but the end of his cane!"

*The cartoon in question depicted a dog, urged on by his invisible master's stick and coming at a gallop, carrying a bottle in his mouth.*

[2]   AP, 2337 (DE 1:438).

July

*Heaven, in Thérèse's mind, was God seen and possessed fully. Following the example of other saints, St. Thomas Aquinas in particular, she longed for no other reward than that of God Himself. She remembered the words of Our Lord: "And this is eternal life, that they know you . . . . " and, for her, to know God was to love Him, and so she could say:*

"One sole desire makes my heart beat, and it is the love I shall receive and the love I shall be able to give."[3]

\* \* \*

*I was asking her about the "way" she wanted to teach to souls after her death:*

"Mother, it's the way of spiritual childhood, it's the way of confidence and total abandon. I want to teach them the little means that have so perfectly succeeded with me, to tell them there is only one thing to do here on earth: to cast at Jesus the flowers of little sacrifices, to take Him by caresses; this is the way I've taken Him, and it's for this that I shall be so well received."[4]

\* \* \*

August

*One evening, in the infirmary, she was drawn to confide her troubles to me more than she usually did. She had not yet opened up in this way on this subject. Up until then, I had known her trial of faith only vaguely:*

"If you only knew what frightful thoughts obsess me! Pray very much for me in order that I do not listen to the devil who wants to persuade me about so many lies. It's the reasoning of the worst materialists which is imposed upon my mind: Later, unceasingly making new advances, science will explain everything naturally; we shall have the absolute reason for everything that exists and that still remains a problem, because there remain very many things to be discovered, etc., etc.

"I want to do good after my death, but I will not be able to do so! It

[3]    PNAP, Hope of heaven (DE 2:448).
[4]    *Novissima Verba,* July 17 (DE 2:169).

will be as it was for Mother Geneviève: We expected to see her work miracles, and complete silence fell over her tomb. . . .

"O little Mother, must one have thoughts like this when one loves God so much!

"Finally, I offer up these very great pains to obtain the light of faith for poor unbelievers, for all those who separate themselves from the Church's beliefs."

*She added that she never reasoned with these thoughts:*

"I undergo them under duress, but while undergoing them I never cease making acts of faith."[5]

\* \* \*

"I've suffered from the cold in Carmel even to the point of dying from it."

*I was astonished to hear her speak in this way, because in the winter time her conduct revealed nothing of her suffering. Not even in the coldest weather did I see her rub her hands together or walk more rapidly or bend over more than was her usual habit, as all of us do naturally when we are cold.*[6]

\* \* \*

*During this phase of her sickness, how many times must her patience have caused God to smile! What sufferings she had to endure! She sighed many times like a poor little lamb about to be immolated. She told me:*

"Watch carefully, Mother, when you will have patients a prey to violent pains; don't leave near them any medicines that are poisonous. I assure you, it needs only a second when one suffers intensely to lose one's reason. Then one would easily poison oneself."[7]

\* \* \*

September

*One day, in her presence, Mother Prioress was speaking to the doctor about the purchase just made of a lot in the city cemetery because*

---

5    PNAP, her "trial of faith" (DE 1:525).

6    PNAP, Temperance (DE 1:537).

7    "Green Copybooks," August 30 (DE 2:348).

*there was no longer any room in the old one. She added that they would henceforth dig the graves deep enough so that it would be possible to superimpose three coffins. Sister Thérèse of the Child Jesus said, laughing:*

"Then it's I who will do first honors to this new cemetery?"

*The doctor was surprised and told her not to be thinking of her burial. She replied:*

"However, it's a happy thought. But if the hole is so deep, it will disturb me, because some accident could happen to those who were lowering me into it."

*And continuing in this same vein:*

"I already hear one undertaker crying out: 'Don't pull the cord there!' Another who answers: 'Pull it that way! Hey, be careful! So that's that!' They will throw some earth on my coffin and then everybody will leave."

*When Doctor de Cornière left, I asked her if she really felt nothing at the thought of being placed so deeply in the earth. She answered with surprise:*

"I don't understand you! What does it matter to me! I would not even experience the least repulsion at knowing that I will be thrown into a common grave."[8]

## CÉLINE(SISTER GENEVIÈVE)

June

*During her illness, she had painfully accompanied the community to the hermitage of the Sacred Heart, and she was seated during the singing of a hymn. A Sister made a sign for her to join the choir; she was exhausted and could not stand up, but she stood up nevertheless. When I reproached her for it after the reunion, she answered simply:*

"I formed the habit of obeying each one as though it were God who was manifesting His will to me."[9]

---

[8]   PNAP, Humility (DE 1:661).
[9]   DP, 1029. **\*\*\***

(\*\*\*)   See *St. Thérèse of Lisieux by those who knew her*, p. 147.

*During the course of the year 1897, Sister Thérèse of the Child Jesus told me, even before she became sick, that she expected to die during the year, and this is the reason she gave me in the month of June when she was seized with pulmonary tuberculosis:*

"Don't you see that God is going to take me at an age when I would not have had the time to become a priest. If I had been able to become a priest, it would have been in this month of June, at this ordination that I would have received holy orders. So in order that I may regret nothing, God is allowing me to be sick; I wouldn't have been able to present myself for ordination, and I would have died before having exercised my ministry."[10]

\* \* \*

July

*A Sister had told her that she could experience an hour of fear before her death in order to expiate her sins:*

"The fear of death to expiate my sins? This would have no more strength than some muddy water! Also, if I have these fears, I shall offer them to God for sinners, and since this will be an act of charity, this suffering will become for others much stronger than water. As for me, the only thing that purifies me is the fire of Divine love."[11]

\* \* \*

*One day after Communion.*

"It was as though one had placed two little children together, and the little children said nothing to each other; however, I did say some little things to Him, but He didn't answer me; undoubtedly He was sleeping."

\* \* \*

"When I am dead, I shall say nothing, I'll give no advice. If they place me on the right or the left, I'll not help them. One will say: She is better on this side; they will be able to place fire at my side, I'll say nothing."

[10] DP, 2740 (DE 1:619, note 4).
[11] For the source of this text and the ten following (DE 1:588).

*One day when she was standing in front of a library:*
"Oh! I would have been sorry to have read all those books!"
*I asked: "Why? This would have been quite an acquisition. I would understand your regretting to read them, but not to have already read them."*
"If I had read them, I would have broken my head, and I would have wasted precious time that I could have employed very simply in loving God."

\* \* \*

*"I am in a disposition of mind where it seems to me I am no longer thinking."*
"This doesn't matter, God knows your intentions. As long as you're humble you will be happy."

\* \* \*

*Once when the community bell sounded for something, and I did not move fast enough, she said:*
"Go to your little *duty.*"
*Then, correcting herself:*
"No, to your *little love!*"
*Another time, I said to her: "I must work because Jesus will be sad," she replied:*
"No, it's you who would be sad; He cannot be sad with our arrangements, *but what sadness for us not to give Him as much as we can!*"

\* \* \*

*When some hemorrhages occurred, she was rejoicing, thinking she was shedding her blood for God:*
"It could not be otherwise, and I knew I would have this consolation of seeing my blood poured out since I am dying a martyrdom of love."

*Another time, I said to her: Since you want to go to Saigon, perhaps
when you are in heaven, I shall go in your place to complete your
work, and the two of us will do a perfect work:*

"Ah! if you ever go over there, don't think it's to complete
something. There is no need of this. Everything is good, everything is
perfect, accomplished, it is love alone that counts. If you go there, this
will be a whim of Jesus, nothing else. Don't think this would be a
useful work, it would be a whim of Jesus."[12]

\* \* \*

### SISTER MARIE OF THE SACRED HEART (MARIE)

May

*The infirmarian had told her to take a little walk for a quarter of an
hour each day in the garden. I met her walking painfully and
seemingly at the end of her strength. I said: "You would do better to
rest; this walking can do you no good under such conditions. You're
exhausting yourself."*

"It's true, but do you know what gives me strength? Well, I am
walking for a missionary. I think that over there, far away, one of
them is perhaps exhausted in his apostolic endeavours, and, to lessen
his fatigue, I offer mine to God."

\* \* \*

July

*At Carmel, her great suffering had been not being able to receive
Communion each day. She said, a short time before her death, to
Mother Marie de Gonzague, who was afraid of daily Communion:*

"Mother, when I'm in heaven, I'll make you change your opinion."

*This is what happened. After the death of the Servant of God, the
chaplain gave us Communion every day, and Mother Marie de Gonzague, instead of being repelled by it, was very happy about it.*[14]

---

[12] From Sister Geneviève's notebooks (DE 2:482).
[13] DE 1:635.
[14] DP, 1647 (DE 1:659).

*One day I said to her: "Ah! if I were alone in suffering from your death, it would not be so hard; but how will I be able to console Mother Agnes of Jesus, who loves you so much?"*

"Don't worry, she will not have time to think of her pain, for until the end of her life she will be busied about me, she won't even have time to do everything."[15]

\* \* \*

*During the month of August, 1897, about six weeks before her death, I was at her bedside with Mother Agnes of Jesus and Sister Geneviève. Suddenly, without any provocation, she looked at us with a heavenly air and said very distinctly:*

"You know well you are taking care of a little saint."

*When she was asked in the process of beatification, whether the Servant of God had given any explanation or correction to this statement, Sister Marie of the Sacred Heart answered:*

*"I was very much moved by these words as though I had heard a saint predict what would happen after her death. Under the influence of this emotion, I withdrew a short distance from the infirmary, and I don't remember having heard anything else."[16]*

\* \* \*

## SISTER MARIE OF THE TRINITY, ONE OF THE NOVICES OF ST. THÉRÈSE

April

*She told me about the following incident which took place five months before her death:*

"One evening, the infirmarian placed a hot-water bottle on my feet and some tincture of iodine on my chest. I was consumed with a fever, a burning thirst was devouring me. When submitting to these remedies, I couldn't resist complaining to Our Lord: 'My Jesus, You are my witness, I am burning, and they bring me still more heat and

---

[15] NPDP, 1908, (DE 1:659).
[16] AP. 2339 (DE 2:651).

fire! Ah! if only I had in place of all this a glass of water! . . . My
Jesus, your little girl is very thirsty! However, she's happy to find the
opportunity of lacking what is necessary in order to resemble You better and to save souls.' Soon the infirmarian left me, and I didn't expect to see her again except the next morning, when to my great surprise she returned a few moments afterwards, bringing me a refreshing
drink. . . . Oh! how good our Jesus is! How sweet it is to confide in
Him!''[17]

\* \* \*

May
*Yesterday, the singing of the "Unpetalled Rose" brought back to
my mind a cherished memory. Mother Marie-Henriette of the Paris
Carmel, on Messine Avenue, had asked me to beg Sister Thérèse to
compose a poem on this subject. As this corresponded with the sentiments of our dear Saint, she put her whole heart into the com-
position. Mother Henriette was very happy to receive it, only she
wrote to tell me that a last stanza was missing; it should explain that
God, at death, would gather together these plucked petals to form
them into a beautiful rose which would shine for all eternity. Then
Sister Thérèse said to me:*
"Let the good Mother make the stanza herself as she understands it;
as for me, I'm not in the least bit inspired to do so. My desire is to be
unpetalled forever in order to give joy to God. Period. That's all!''[18]

\* \* \*

June
*I have always felt the three long months of our Angel's agony. I'd
been forbidden to speak to her under the pretext that as I was young I
might contract her sickness! (I was certain of the opposite, for Sister
Thérèse had told me nobody would catch her disease, that she had
asked God for this.) Each day, news of her health was sadder and sadder, and I was smothered with pain. One day, I went to take a walk in
the garden, and I saw her in her wheelchair under the chestnut trees.*

[17]  NPAP, (DE 1:785).
[18]  A note from Sister Marie of the Trinity to Mother Agnes, January 17, 1935.

*She was all alone and she made a sign for me to approach. "Oh! no, they would see us, and I have no permission." I entered the grotto of the Holy Face where I began to cry; lifting up my head, I saw with surprise little Sister Thérèse seated on a trunk of a tree at my side. She said:*

"I haven't been forbidden to come to you, and even though I should die of it, I want to console you."

*She dried my tears and placed my head on her heart. I begged her to return to her wheelchair, for she was trembling with fever:*

"Yes, but not before you have laughed for me!"

*This I did immediately for fear she would get worse, and I helped her regain her wheelchair.* [19]

\* \* \*

*I had very much pain at seeing her sick, and I often repeated to her: "Oh! life is sad!" But she took me up immediately, saying:*

"Life is not sad! On the contrary, it is very happy. If you were to say: 'The exile is sad,' I would understand you. We make a mistake in giving the name of life to what must come to an end. It is only to the things of heaven, to what must never die that we must give this real name; and, under this title, life is not sad, but happy, very happy!" [20]

\* \* \*

July-August

*One feast day, in the refectory, they had forgotten to give me my dessert. After dinner, I went to see Sister Thérèse in the infirmary, and, finding my neighbor at table there, I made her understand in no uncertain terms that I had been forgotten. Sister Thérèse, having heard this, made me go tell the Sister in charge of the food, and when I begged her not to impose this on me, she said:*

"No, this is your penance; you're not worthy of the sacrifices God is asking of you. He was asking the deprivation of your dessert, for He was the one who permitted them to forget. He believed you were

[19] Letter to Mother Agnes, November 27, 1934. (DE 1:780).
[20] *Histoire d'une Ame,* 1907, p. 296 (DE 1:781).

generous enough to make this sacrifice, and you aren't measuring up to His expectation when going to claim it.''

*I can say that her lesson bore fruit and cured me forever of any desire to do it again.*[21]

\* \* \*

August

*This recalls to my mind an intimate memory with Sister Thérèse of the Child Jesus. It was about a month before her death: the whole community was very sad, and I was second to none in my own sorrow. When going to see her in the infirmary, I noticed a large red balloon at the foot of her bed; it had been given her as a distraction. This balloon excited my interest, and I couldn't help telling her: "How I would love to play with it!" She smiled, but since her weakness was so great that she couldn't bear any noise whatsoever, she said:*

"Get behind me while there is no one here, and play with it; I'm going to close my eyes so that I won't get dizzy."

*Delighted, I took the balloon and I was enjoying my game so much that little Thérèse partly opened her eyes to look at me without seeming to do so, and she couldn't help laughing. Then I said to her: "It's too long a time for me to be sad! I can't stand it any longer! I have temptations to distract myself, desires to play with the top you gave me at Christmas, but if they see me, they might be scandalized and say that I haven't any heart.''*

"No, no, I oblige you to take your top and go and play for one hour in the attic of the novitiate; no one will hear you there, and if anyone sees you, tell them that I was the one who told you to do it. Go quickly, it will give me much pleasure to think you are going to enjoy yourself.''[22]

"When I am in heaven, you will have to fill my little hands with prayers and sacrifices to give me the pleasure of casting these as a shower of graces upon souls.''[23]

[21] NPAP, (DE 1:781).
[22] Letter to Mother Agnes of Jesus. Good Friday, 1906 (DE 1:780).
[23] NPAP, (DE 1:582).

September

*Eight days before her death, I had cried all evening when thinking of her approaching death. She noticed it and said:*

"You have cried. Was it into the shell?"[24]

*I couldn't lie, and my admission that I didn't do this saddened her. She answered:*

"I'm going to die, and I won't be at ease regarding you unless you promise to follow my recommendation faithfully. I attach great importance to this for the good of your soul."

*I had only to give in and I gave her my word, asking however, as a favor, permission to cry freely over her death.*[25]

* * *

*The day of her death, after Vespers, I went to the infirmary where I found the Servant of God sustaining with invincible courage the last struggles of the most terrible agony. Her hands were blue; she joined them with anguish and cried out in a voice which the over-stimulation of a violent suffering made clear and strong:*

"O my God! . . . have pity on me! . . . O Mary, come to my aid! . . . My God, how I am suffering! . . . The chalice is full. . . . Full to the brim! . . . never will I know how to die!"

*Mother Prioress was saying: "Courage, you're coming to the end, a little while and everything will be finished."*

"No, Mother, it's still not finished! . . . I feel that I'm going to suffer in this way for months."

*"And if this were the will of God to leave you for a long time on the cross, would you accept it?" With an accent of extraordinary heroism, she said:*

"I would."

*And her head fell back upon the pillow with so calm, so resigned an air that we couldn't hold back our tears. She was absolutely like a martyr awaiting new tortures. I left the infirmary, not having the courage to bear with the very sad spectacle any longer. I didn't return*

---

[24] A shell Thérèse used in her painting; she had told one novice, Sister Marie of the Trinity, to collect her tears in it each time she wanted to cry, to get her out of the habit of crying.

[25] *"Conseils et Souvenirs"* from *Histoire d'une ame,* 1899, pp. 280-281 (DE 1:783).

*except with the community for the last moments, and I was witness to
her beautiful and long ecstatic gaze at the moment when she died,
Thursday, September 30, 1897, at seven o'clock in the evening.*[26]

* * *

### SISTER THÉRÈSE OF ST. AUGUSTINE

July
  *"Tell me, have you had any struggles?"*
  "Oh! yes, I have had some. I've had a nature that wasn't easy-
going; this wasn't apparent exteriorly, but I know it well, and I can
assure you that I wasn't a day without suffering, not a single day."
  *"But some think you had none."*
  "Ah! the judgments of creatures! Because they don't see, they
don't believe!"[27]

* * *

  *"There are some Sisters who believe you will experience the fears of
the dying."*
  "These haven't come to me as yet. If they should come, I'll bear
them; but if I should have them, they would not be sufficient to purify
me, they would be no more than Javel water. What I need is the fire of
love."[28]

* * *

### SISTER MARIE OF THE ANGELS

  *Mother Agnes of Jesus said to her one day when the community was
standing around her bed: "Will you cast some flowers at the community?"*
  "Oh, no, little Mother, don't ask me to do this, I beg you; I don't

---

[26] DP, 2793-2794 (DE 2:486).
[27] *Souvenirs d'une sainte amitié*, p. 12; (DE 1:788).
[28] Ibid., (DE 1:421).

want to cast flowers at creatures. I would do it for the Blessed Virgin or St. Joseph but not at any other creatures."[29]

\* \* \*

*A few days before her death, we had rolled her bed out under the cloister walk. Sister Marie of the Sacred Heart, in charge of the cloister courtyard, said to her: "Here's a rhododendron shoot that's dying, I'll pull it out."*

"Oh, Sister Marie of the Sacred Heart," *she answered in a little supplicating tone of voice,* "I don't understand you. . . . I beg you, leave life to this poor rhododendron, for me who am about to die."

*She had to insist further, but her desire was respected.*[30]

\* \* \*

### SISTER AIMÉE OF JESUS

*In the last days of September, 1897, when the weakness of our dear Saint prevented her from being moved, it became necessary to place her for a few moments on a temporary bed in order to make up her own bed. Seeing the embarrassment of the infirmarians who were afraid to hurt her, she said:*

"I believe that Sister Aimée of Jesus would easily take me into her arms; she's big and strong and very gentle around the sick."

*They called, then, our good Sister, who lifted the holy little patient as though she were a light burden, without giving her the least jolt. At this moment, with her arms around Sister's neck, this Angel thanked her with such a smile of affectionate gratitude that she will never forget that beautiful smile. It even became for her a compensation for her regrets at having been the only one not to hear the infirmary bell which convoked the Sisters at the last moment of the most beautiful death which was ever seen at the Carmel of Lisieux.*[31]

---

[29] DP, 2016 (DE 1:791).

[30] Slips of paper attached to NPAP (DE 1:545).

[31] Obituary notice of Sister Aimée de Jésus, January 17, 1930; see DP, 2222 and AP, 2455 (DE 1:561).

### ANONYMOUS

*We asked her what name we should call her when we prayed to her in heaven:*

"You will call me little Thérèse," *she answered humbly.* [32]

* * *

[32] *"Conseils et Souvenirs"* from *Histoire d'une Ame,* 1953, p. 248.

Infirmary where Thérèse died.

The sick Thérèse, August 30, 1897.

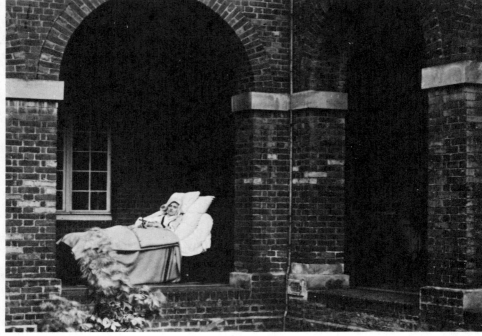

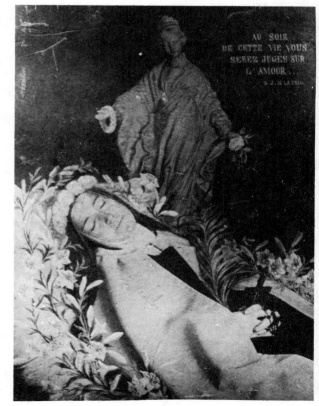

AU SOIR
DE CETTE VIE VOUS
SEREZ JUGÉS SUR
L'AMOUR...
S. J. DE LA CROIX

The four Martin sisters and their cousin, Marie Guérin. (l.r.) Marie, Pauline, Céline, Marie Guérin, Thérèse.

Thérèse in death.

## LETTERS CONCERNING THE SICKNESS
## OF SISTER THÉRÈSE OF THE CHILD JESUS

From Sister Marie of the Eucharist to M. Guérin,
June 5, 1897.

My dear little Father,

Our little Sister Thérèse of the Child Jesus is really very sick and we are deeply disturbed. Dr. de Cornière has to come to see her this morning. She's up and around, but she's experiencing a general state of weakness. She herself now realizes that she's very ill. She feels sharp pains in her side and can eat hardly anything. Yesterday, she threw up her dinner, and, frequently, in her coughing spells, she vomits. We are really upset.

Mother Prioress takes good care of her, none could do better. Since Sister Thérèse is changing very much and won't be able to stay up, we would like to take a picture of her for Mother Prioress' feast day. Should her condition continue, by the end of the week, her appearance would be so bad, it would be impossible to dream of doing this; especially if Dr. de Cornière prescribes vesicatories. With reference to these, in her weakened state, she'll have trouble recovering from them.

I fear I'm disturbing you, dear Father, but we are very much upset. If you could only see the progress her illness has made in one week, and even since I received the Veil.[1] She's in a state of great exhaustion; she feels at times, as she tell us, agonies as though she were going to die; she feels that life is leaving her.

Would Mamma please send us some little dishes for her? She'll be able to choose nice little things which will do our little Angel some good. I believe she is going to fly away to heaven very soon.

She said last night: *"I will be content to die or to live, for I will only what God wills; everything is for His love."* We are making a novena to Our Lady of Victories, and Mother Prioress is having Masses offered up there. Besides, during this novena, Mother is putting Lourdes water in everything Sister Thérèse takes. She told us last night:

[1]   June 2, 1897.

*"Either the Blessed Virgin will cure me or take me off with her; this can't last a long time."* We have great confidence in Our Lady of Victories.

From Mother Agnes of Jesus to M. and Mme. Guérin,
June 7, 1897.

Dear Aunt and Uncle,
Our little Angel is doing much better. She's coughing less and our hearts are consoled. Her appetite, however, is gone completely, but, with the good things Mamma[2] is sending her, we will break this terrible weakness, I trust.

Yesterday evening, we took her for a ride in the garden in Papa's old wheelchair, and, I assure you, Sister Marie of the Eucharist was repaid for the trouble we've brought upon her, so greatly did she enjoy herself.

Thanks for all you've sent us, and for the trouble you are going to in order to carry out our smallest wishes.

Our good Mother Prioress is very grateful to you, and she begs that you join us in our novena to Our Lady of Victories. Last Saturday, poor Mother shed warm tears when she began the chanting of the "Salve Regina." It's true, on that day, our little Angel was very sick.

From Sister Marie of the Eucharist to M. Guérin,
July 8, 1897.

Dear little Father,
I come to give you news of your little Queen's health. The news is more and more disturbing. Yesterday, Dr. de Cornière came twice during the day. He's terribly worried. It's not tuberculosis,[3] but an accident which happened to the lungs, a real lung congestion.

Yesterday, she coughed up blood twice. These are particles of blood that look as if she's vomiting some liver, and all through the remainder of the day, she was coughing up blood. Dr de Cornière, yesterday morning, forbade her to make any movements; he won't even

[2]  Mme. Guérin.
[3]  Concerning Dr. de Cornière's diagnosis, see *La Passion de Thérèse de Lisieux,* pp. 218ff.

allow her to be taken down to the infirmary until the wound in her right lung is healed. She is constantly taking ice, a drink which is to stop the blood. I think, too, she's being given mustard poltices and mustard under other forms. The doctor is caring for her admirably. He applied two dry-cups. She had a very bad night, and this morning she was telling us that the souls in purgatory couldn't burn any more than she did, her fever was so strong, and, in addition, she was seized with fits of suffocation.

Today, she is perhaps a little better. The fever has dropped, but she feels very weak and isn't able to raise her hand to her mouth, it just falls by her side. Dr. de Cornière came this morning, and he discovered she was able to breathe a little more but that her right side is still congested. He said there wasn't great damage to the chest but there was pain in the lung. Her great weakness disturbed him very much, and he told Mother Prioress this morning that, in her present state, only two percent recover. If she were able to receive food, he said, we could prolong her life, but a cure is impossible. And if she can't digest milk, he gives her only a few days to live.

When we visit her, we find her very much changed, very emaciated, but she's always calm, always ready to joke. She sees death coming and she's happy; she hasn't the least fear of it. This will sadden you, dear little Father, and it's quite understandable. All of us will be losing the greatest of treasures, but she's not to be pitied: loving God the way she does, how well received she'll be up there in heaven. She'll go straight to heaven, that is certain. When we spoke to her about purgatory for ourselves, she said: *"Oh! how you grieve me! You do a great injury to God in believing you're going to go to purgatory. When we love, we can't go there."*

To mention the state the community is in, there are tears, sobs, and grief on all sides. Mother Agnes of Jesus is to be admired for her courage and resignation; our Mother Prioress has a real motherly tenderness towards all of us in the midst of the greatest of pains, for Sister Thérèse of the Child Jesus was her greatest treasure.

From Sister Marie of the Eucharist to M. Guérin, July 9, 1897.

The news today is a little more encouraging. It's now two days since she hasn't vomited blood or even spit it. Dr. de Cornière is much happier this morning. He was asked about her receiving Extreme Unction, and he answered: "Oh! fortunately she isn't that bad; she could even have a few accidents of coughing up blood without her being entirely lost." If she eats, then, if she digests some milk, she'll be able to recover a little; her weakness is the most disturbing. In a word, after yesterday's day of trial, we've regained a little bit of hope. Yesterday, she was able to keep down seven cups of milk, but, except for the ice they gave her afterwards, I think she would have thrown up everything.

I really disturbed you yesterday, dear little Father; we too were disturbed, however, and so was Dr. de Cornière.

If you were to see our little patient, you wouldn't be able to stop laughing. She has to be always saying something funny. Ever since she has become convinced she is going to die, she has been as gay as a little finch. There are times when one would pay to be near her. All of a sudden this morning she began to say: *"But if I am going to be one of the two, alas! . . ."* We looked at one another, wondering what she meant, and she went on: *"Yes, one of the two percent; that would be unfortunate!"* Very simply stated, because Mother Prioress told her that Dr. de Cornière said that only two percent of those in her present condition recover, she is afraid she might be one of those who will recover.

It's somewhat amusing to see her laugh and to see her mischievous look when she is telling us all this. When I told her I was going to write you, giving you a little bit of assurance, she said: *"Tell them that I love them very much, and that I'm a child of contradiction: They think I'm dying, and I don't turn up my eyes; then they think I'm alive, and I'm on the threshold of death. I'm a real contradiction. Tell them, however, that I love them all very, very much."*

Our Father[4] came to see her this morning and he exclaimed: "Oh! you're only trying to mislead us; you're not about to die, and very soon you'll be running in the garden. You don't look like one who is dying. Give you Extreme Unction? But the sacrament wouldn't be valid; you're just not sick enough!" Father was a little rough, but, I believe, he did this purposely, for when he came out of the room, he was vey much edified to see a child so young with such a desire to die and to see, with so much joy, death coming.

---

[4]   Canon Charles Maupas.

When he left, our little patient was aggravated at him for not being willing to give her the last sacraments, and she said: *"The next time I'll not go to so much trouble. I sat up in bed out of politeness, I was very pleasant with him, I paid him special respect, and he refused what I was asking of him! Another time, I'll use a little pretence; I'll take a cup of milk before his arrival because then I always have a very bad face; I'll hardly answer him, telling him I'm in real agony."* (Then she put on a real comedy for us.) *"Yes, I really see I don't know my business; I don't know how to go about things!"*

She's a charming little patient, extremely amusing; she knows only how to make us laugh; however, she's forbidden to talk lest she tire herself too much.

From Sister Marie of the Eucharist to M. Guérin, July 10, 1897.

Our little patient is always in the same condition. There is constant anxiety about her state, and I believe that, without some accident, she can go on for another few weeks. Last night, she was seized with a coughing spell, coughing blood, and this was stopped by giving her a lot of ice. Dr. de Cornière said he was surprised at this; that she'll still have more than one of these spells. But her weakness continues day by day, and she is becoming perceptibly emaciated. As for food, it's always the same thing: she throws up the two or three cups of milk she takes in a day. Dr. de Cornière, today, tried to give her an eggnog. She didn't throw it up, but she suffered very much in her stomach and head. She had great abdominal pains, and her digestion was very bad.

She's so weak, she can't wash her hands any longer by herself; it's a real task for her, and it causes her suffering in all her limbs. Last night, before her vomiting spell, she underwent such a session of perspiring that her pillows were soaked through, and we had to change her. With regard to her morale, it's always the same: she is gaiety itself, making all those who come near her laugh, talking joyfully about the thief (God) who is coming to get her very soon. Oh! she's not to be pitied, this little sister of ours! She'll be so happy, and she's so well prepared. She will be such a great protection to us in heaven. She said: *"I'll still be even more with you than I was before; I'll not leave you. I will watch over Uncle and Aunt, over my little Léonie, over all of you.*

*When they are ready to enter heaven, I'll go very quickly to meet them. And for my little Jeanne, the first thing I'll do upon entering heaven will be to go into the little angels' big store and there I'll choose the most charming one and I'll tell him: 'You must go very quickly to Mme. La Néele to give her happiness and joy.'"*

Our Father said to her yesterday: "You're . . . going to heaven soon! But your crown isn't made yet, you've only just begun making it!" Very angelically she replied: *"Oh! Father, it's true, I haven't made my crown, but it's God who made it!"*

Ah! yes, her crown is really made up!

From Sister Marie of the Eucharist to M. Guérin, July 12, 1897.

My dear little Father,

It seems that little Queen's sickness had made you sad, and this grieves her; she'd like you to rejoice with her over her entrance into heaven which is being delayed from day to day.

The news is better. Dr. de Cornière said yesterday evening: "I'm really content. There is an improvement." This is true, she is better; she's taking some pancreatin to help her digest the milk, and for two days now she hasn't thrown up, nor has she had diarrhea. As for the fever, she doesn't have a fever high enough to measure by degrees;[5] on the first two days of last week, she had a very high fever, but since then it's an ordinary one which she gets at times for half an hour, an hour, but it doesn't last all day long. It's very benign.

She has not had any new accident since Saturday. And so, yesterday and today, we revived our hopes, not for a cure because that would be a miracle, but in keeping her with us for a little while. It's true, as Dr. de Cornière has said, that she can still have more than one accident; she's certainly not dying at the moment, and provided there is no hemorrhage, she can still go on for some weeks, perhaps even a few months, especially if she gets nourishment. In fact, I believe, dear little Father, from what I see, that she will be left with us for some time, unless the accidents become more serious and frequent; but in her present state there is a little hope.

---

[5]    The "Green copybooks" state: "We never took her temperature, but we judged it must have been very high during April, 1897, because her color was high and she was usually pale. She could barely stand, because she was burning with fever and was exhausted."

Don't think she is suffering much; she suffers only from weakness, exhaustion, several bearable pains in the side, some heart aches, but all that doesn't make her suffer as much as you think. Last night, she slept a good sleep of six hours.

You see, my dear little Father, that she's much improved; that, it's true, can change from day to day.

Little Queen is always very happy; they brought her down and placed her in Mother Geneviève's bed in the infirmary, and since Mother Geneviève (she was foundress of the Lisieux Carmel, and she died December 5, 1891) more than once waited for death and desired it very much, and since she was more than once frustrated in her hopes, little Queen often says: *"What an unfortunate bed! When one is in it, one always misses the train!"* And: *"The Thief has gone off far away; He has left me to go and steal other children. . . . When my own turn will come, I know nothing about it now. . . . Tell dear little Uncle, Aunt, Léonie, everybody, that when I'm in heaven, my greatest happiness will be the power to express all the love I have for them. I can't do this here on earth, my love is too strong; but in heaven when I am up there, I'll be able to make them understand . . . this is what gives me joy!"* And this morning when I was wondering what she would do, and what she would say when seeing God for the first time, she answered: *"Don't talk to me about that; I can't think of it, so much happiness does it give me! What I'll do . . . I will cry with joy!"*

Ah! what a beautiful little soul she is, and how, in fact, I have thanked God for making me know her; she can no longer give us her counsel, but what remains with us, and will always remain with us, is her example.

There is something, dear Father, which has afforded me much happiness; it's something she said to me a few days before I had received the Veil. I regard it as her "will and testament" to me. It was the last time I had seen her and was able to speak to her about my spiritual life. There was, at this time, no question of her death, her condition was not yet known; she said to me all of a sudden, looking at me with such a profound gaze that I'll never forget it: *"Oh! little sister, promise me you'll become a saint, a great saint."*

When I looked at her in amazement, she continued: *"Yes, and if I say this to you, it's because I find in you all that is necessary for this; and if you don't become one, believe me, you'll be unfaithful to grace.*

*Oh! I beg you, become a saint, God is begging this from you. When I'm no longer on earth, you'll have to be a saint for two, in order that God lose nothing; I feel that your soul is being called to the same type of perfection as my own, and you must replace me when I'm gone."*

I cannot express, dear little Father, what these words engraved on my heart; yes, it was really her "last will and testament" to me, and from that day onward I never doubted she was near her entrance into heaven.

From Sister Geneviève to Mme. La Néele,
July 12, 1897.

Dear little Jeanne,
    Your letter touched me very much. You can understand all I have to suffer. It's true that the older ones (her sisters Marie and Pauline) could call themselves our mothers, but we two, the two little ones, we formed one, we had never left each other, our souls, our hearts were beating in unison. Now God is about to take her from this exile, and am I to argue with Him over her? Oh! no, our dear little Angel has often repeated to us the words of Our Lord: "Nevertheless I tell you the truth: it is to your advantage that I go away, for if I do not go away, the Counsellor will not come to you; but if I go, I will send him to you."[6] She told me too: *"You recall the two little bluebirds I bought you at Le Havre,[7] how they never sang; then when the first one died, the second began to warble, and it sang its most beautiful song and afterwards died."* When my dear Thérèse has died, I shall try to offer to the Lord a song which I haven't sung as yet; the bitterness of this suffering will provide me with a new voice.
    But I'll stop here; I can say no more because my grief is too great. My little companion, my dear sister, my friend, my little better half, this is the one who is leaving. I can't understand what will happen; it will make a void in my spirit. It's the keenest blow that could touch me, and perhaps it will be the last.
    The news is always the same, not worse. Dr. de Cornière says the situation is always serious and tense, but there's no danger of death,

---

6    John 16:7.
7    See *Correspondence Générale*, 1:235.

except in the event of an accident; otherwise, she can go on for some weeks.

She's an angel and there hasn't been a soul like her. How much I could say!

From Sister Marie of the Sacred Heart to Mme. Guérin,
July 14, 1897.

Her condition isn't any worse, but it isn't better either. Yesterday, Dr. de Cornière said: "I'm always without any hope, for instead of being on the decline the disorder increases." Our dear one was aware of this; if you only could see her radiant face. When I wanted to write you yesterday, she told us: *"No, it's better that they don't receive any news; after all, it's always the same thing; leave them alone, they will think that I'm better; we must give them little joys."*

We received the large basket of flowers from Beuvillers,[8] and I brought them to our little Thérèse's bed. She was delighted with all the trimmings for her King.[9] How much your little Queen loves you; we see she'd like to try in every way to spare you from grieving over her. Recently, she said: *"Oh! if Mother Prioress permits me, I'll write them at La Musse and make them laugh at me!"*[10] She isn't suffering much at the present, or, I should say, when she is suffering very much, she has so much strength and virtue that she doesn't complain about it. She is like a little lamb that allows Jesus to pluck her fleece, one piece at a time.

Dr. de Cornière came today; he thinks her condition will go on a little longer. This gives us a little bit of a respite, without, however, removing our anxieties.

You cannot imagine how kind Mother Prioress is to us, expecially to our little Thérèse. This dear little one said to her this morning, in her delightful, smiling way: *"Mother, I want to die in your arms . . . not on the pillow, but on your heart."*

Oh! dear little Angel, her life will have been nothing but a heavenly melody!

---

[8]  A commune on the edge of Lisieux, where the Guérin family owned a property.

[9]  In view of her reception of Holy Communion, July 16.

[10]  See *Correspondance Générale*, 2:1033.

From Mother Agnes of Jesus to M. and Mme. Guérin,
July 16, 1897.

The condition of our dear little patient is always the same. I don't believe the end is as close as we had at first thought. This Angel is going to remain with us in order to edify and prepare us for her departure.

She said to me just now, with almost a tone of anxiety in her voice: *"Alas, if I were to be cured!"* I quickly reassured her because I had no hope of this whatsoever.

Distract yourselves as much as possible at La Musse, this is what your little girl desires very much, and, in fact, why be sad about a departure which causes her so much joy? It's even curious and amusing to listen to her; she sees herself become emaciated and is happy about it: *"How happy I am,"* she said, when looking at her hands. *"How pleasant it is to see my destruction."* And again: *"This poor M. Clodion* (she calls Dr. de Cornière this because of his long hair), *you'll have to see him when he withdraws his head from my shoulder; he'll no longer know what to do, and he'll be so nettled, he'll jump around. And he will find nothing but rags, bones, and old habits!"*

A Sister said to her recently: "You haven't the least bit of fear for death, and still death is a terrifying thing." She answered: *"Yes, it frightens me very much when I see it represented in pictures as some huge spectre, but death isn't this. This idea is foolish, it's not true, and all I have to do to chase it away is recall the answer in my catechism: death is the separation of the soul from the body. That's what it is! Well, I haven't any fear of a separation which will reunite me forever with God."*

Only a few days ago, I was saying to her, her happiness was going to be great when she would finally leave this world of miseries to go and enjoy the delights of eternity. This was her answer: *"Ah! little Mother, this evening, I was listening to some beautiful music in the distance, near the train station, and I was thinking that very soon I was going to hear much more beautiful harmonies. But this feeling of joy passed off quickly; for a long time now I no longer know what a living joy is, and it's impossible for me to make a feast of rejoicing. That isn't what attracts me. I can't think very much about my joy. I think only of the Love I'll receive and the love I'll be able to give."*

From Sister Marie of the Eucharist to M. Guérin,
July 20, 1897.

First, I'll give you some news about your little Queen. She coughed
up blood again this morning. It has become a regular affair, happening every third day in the morning. She'll cough up a generous
glassful in a quarter of an hour. Today, she's more tired because she
coughed up so much. Dr. de Cornière has just left; he's not at all content to see her condition continue in this manner. He discovers more
and more damage to the lung, and this damage is climbing to the top
of the lung and extending into the shoulder. He also is finding several
cavities. He says she's lost unless a great miracle takes place, which, of
course, makes our little patient jubilant. As for the rest, fever and
such things, her condition remains the same, the same details. She's
digesting milk a little better, but it's hardly helping her as her
emaciated condition continues each day. Ah! now we're resigned and
prepared for sacrifice, for God has given us enough warnings of this
nature. It's a consolation for us to see that she's not suffering more
and to see the joy with which she's leaving for heaven.

From Sister Marie of the Eucharist to Mme. Gaston Pottier (Céline
Maudelonde), July 20, 1897.

I thank God for permitting me to know this little saint, for here in
the community she is loved and appreciated as such. . . . Hers is not
an extraordinary sanctity; there is no love of extraordinary penances,
no, only love for God. People in the world can imitate her sanctity,
for she has tried to do everything through love and to accept all little
contradictions, all little sacrifices that come at each moment as
coming from God's hands. She saw God in everything, and she carried
out all her actions as perfectly as possible. Daily duty came before
everything else; as for pleasure, she knew how to sanctify it even while
enjoying it, offering it up to God. . . . I asked her the other day:
"Did you sometimes refuse God anything?" She said: *"No, I don't
remember refusing Him anything. Even when I was very little, at the
age of three, I began to refuse God nothing He was asking from me."*
This is saying everything, isn't it, to be able to make such an answer,
and it's rare to hear it even in our Carmels. Never to have refused God

anything! . . . And if you could only see her joy at the thought of death. To die to go and live God's life, to die and go to heaven, that's her only wish. And her face lights up when we tell her that her desire is going to be realized. It's very beautiful to view death in this way, and it's a consolation for those left behind. This prevents you from fearing it, and you view it yourself with more joy.

I thought, little Céline, that in giving you our little patient as an example, I couldn't give you better counsel. Oh! if she were in your place, if she had like you a little family trial, how she would be able to profit from it. She'd see God in all the circumstances, and she'd offer to Him each little thorn wounding her heart as an act of perfect love. This is what she would do and she would experience a great peace. But she often said to me: *"This doesn't mean that we must not feel the pain, the suffering; where would the merit be if one didn't feel it? One can feel suffering very intensely even, but can offer it to God and find in this offering, in the midst of the greatest sufferings, a great peace."*

I read your little letter to her and she told me to give you this answer: *"Tell Céline that I shall never forget my little childhood friend, and when I am in heaven, I shall watch over her in a very special way. Tell her that God is calling her to be a saint in the world, and that He has special plans for her and a special love."* I transmit her words just as she has spoken them.

From Sister Geneviève to Mme. Guérin,
July 22, 1897.

My little patient isn't worse, but she isn't better. The sickness pursues its course, says Dr. de Cornière, and he adds that cavities are forming in the lung; this makes him fear the formation of sores, etc. He was telling us the other day: "She's going to win her canonization process!" Our dear little angel is always the same, a model of patience, gentleness; she's grace personified. The other day, I was reading a passage to her on the happiness of heaven, and she interrupted me by saying: *"Oh! that's not what attracts me!"* I asked: "What then?" *"Oh! it's love, to love, to be loved, and to return to earth . . . ."*[11]

My dear Aunt, guess for yourself what is taking place within my heart. The trial which faces me makes me shudder. I'm in the Garden

---

[11]  See note "5" of *Last Conversations with Céline.*

of the Agony, and the prayer of Our Lord bursts from my heart at each instant.

From Sister Marie of the Eucharist to Mme. Guérin,
July 30, 1897.

My dear little Mother,
   The news is not good ever since yesterday, July 29. Dr. de Cornière finds that her sickness has become worse. She's coughing blood every day now, even two and three times a day. It was continuous this morning. She is having chest pains and difficulty in breathing; for minutes she's positively choking. She has to breathe in ether continually, and, at times, her breathing is so bad that the ether has no effect. Mother Prioress spoke this morning to Dr. de Cornière about her receiving Extreme Unction. He answered that this would be perhaps prudent since we don't know what will happen. He finds a great change in her since yesterday.
   We are under no illusions, and we see that this cannot last very long. Last night, for example, she had such an intense fever that her back was burning like fire, and she said that she felt she was in prugatory so much was the fever burning. I believe our Father will administer the last sacraments today or tomorrow.

From Sister Marie of the Eucharist to M. Guérin,
July 31, 1897.

My dear little Father,
   I'm writing you a few words to give you news about little Queen. The news is always very bad; however, today she has coughed up less blood, but yesterday we believed she wouldn't last through the night. Dr. de Cornière feared this, too, for when he saw her at four o'clock, he saw that the blood hadn't stopped since the evening before, and he told Mother Prioress not to wait until tomorrow to give her Extreme Unction.
   Father came at six o'clock. He administered Extreme Unction and afterwards gave her Holy communion. It was very touching, I assure you, to see our little patient with such a calm and pure aspect; when she begged forgiveness from the whole community, more than one

broke down in tears. Last night, she coughed up blood again; tonight, too, hasn't been good, but not as bad as we would have supposed after such a day. This morning was passable; she didn't cough blood until three o'clock this afternoon when she had one spell of coughing. She is always burning with fever, suffers from chest pains, and a pain in her side. In a word, she's very ill, and I believe it is preferable to delay your trip to Vichy, for she can't go many days like this, especially if she has some days similar to yesterday.

It's quite impossible to understand her joy at dying. She is like a little child who wants to go with all her heart to see her Father again. Never was anyone seen to die with such calmness. She says: *"What do you expect? Why should death frighten me? I've never acted except for God."* And when we say: "Perhaps you'll die on this feast day or that," she answers: *"I don't have to choose a feast day on which to die, because the day of my death will be the greatest of all feasts for me."*

Today, because she had coughed up a little less blood and in the container there was only a little since this morning, she looked at it dejectedly: *"So little for so much suffering."* Again: *"So little, ah! I won't be dying today, then . . . I can't die. . . . I think I'll have to be very good now and wait for the Thief very nicely."*

We feared very much yesterday that she wouldn't last through the night, and someone had placed a blessed candle and some holy water in readiness in the room next to hers. She was looking at these with complacence out of the corner of her eye; she said to us: *"See that candle? When the Thief comes to take me away, place it in my hand, but not the candlestick; it's too ugly."*

Then she began amusing herself by talking about everything that would happen at her death. Because of the way she did this, whereas we should have been crying, she had us bursting out with peals of laughter, so amusing was she. She reviews everything; this is her joy, and she shares it with us in words which make us laugh. I believe she'll die laughing because she is so happy.

I interrupted my letter when I heard Dr. de Cornière's ring. After this day's experience, the doctor is rather puzzled, seeing that these coughings of blood are not weakening her in such a way as to reduce her to a state of great feebleness. He says that at her age there's so much life that one is unable to say if this sickness can last a few days or a long time.

From Mother Agnes of Jesus to M. and Mme. Guérin,
August 5, 1897.

Our dear little Angel is not doing too badly; however, she isn't
doing well. Her condition has stablized, although it is very difficult
and more painful than before July 28. But she is suffering with admirable patience and gentleness. She's always very much herself. Oh!
how very true it is to say that death is an echo of one's life! Our little
saint awaits death with patience, she's no longer tormented with ardent desires for it. Each day, she finds her peace in these words of the
psalm which delight her: "You have given me delight, O Lord, in all
your doings."[12] The other day, I really felt sorry for her. She was
gazing at me with such suffering, I said to her: "Ah! you are in pain,
little one, seeing that heaven is not for tomorrow, isn't that so?" She
said: *"Little Mother, you still don't understand me? See, all my sentiments are expressed in this stanza of one of my little hymns:*

> For long on earth would I remain
> If Thou, O Lord, didst will,
> Or join at once Thy heavenly train
> Thy pleasure to fulfill;
> Jesu, thy love, that heavenly fire,
> Consuming joyfully,
> Joins life and death as if the same—
> Thy love is all I see.*

Your letter, dear Uncle, and yours, dear Aunt, gave her such joy
that she wanted to answer them herself. Immediately she wanted
someone to give her a pencil, but she was too fatigued! This would not
be prudent. In the evening, she was suffering so much with chest pains
that I pitied her. Her side, too, causes her violent pain. During the

> (*)   *Longtemps encore je veux bien vivre*
>       *Seigneur, si c'est là ton désir.*
>       *Dans le Ciel je voudrais te suivre*
>       *Si cela te faisait plaisir.*
>       *L'Amour ce feu de la patrie*
>       *Ne cesse de me consumer.*
>       *Que me fait la mort ou la vie,*
>       *Jésus, ma joie c'est de t'aimer.*[13]

[12] Ps. 91:5.
[13] Poem: *"Ma Joie."*

night, she perspires so profusely that her mattress is soaked right through. Poor little thing, how happy she'll be in heaven, how well she'll be received! Yesterday, someone placed an ear of corn laden with kernels in her hands, and she said humbly to me, in a way I cannot express: *"This is how God has laden me with graces."* She is truly laden with His graces!

From Sister Geneviève to Mme. La Néele,
August 8, 1897.

Our little patient is not worse; she hasn't coughed up blood for the past four days. But what is frightening is her extreme weakness which gains each day and her emaciation which is making great progress. Her breathing difficulties also cause her the greatest fatigue; we see very clearly that her poor little life is ebbing away. Ah! life is not gay, what hours of sadness and anguish come to lodge themselves in our hearts! If I were as perfect as she is, I wouldn't become so afflicted. She was saying to me the other day: *"Why are you so grieved over my going? As for myself, I would be very much grieved over leaving you; if I thought I was leaving you, I would be grieved, but since I tell you I will be closer to you without my body than with it, then why are you sad?"*

From Sister Marie of the Eucharist to M. Guérin,
August 17, 1897.

My letter had just been sent when Francis, who came to Lisieux to see grandmother[14] because of her heart, came and asked to see me. Then Mother Prioress allowed him to come in, and he saw our little patient; this visit moved him greatly. He found her very sick, and he doesn't give her any more than two weeks before she leaves for heaven. Since Sunday, the Blessed Virgin seems to have precipitated the advance of the sickness, for on the evening of the feast, she suffered a very violent pain in the other lung. It began to take hold before Dr. de Cornière's departure, and Francis claimed that for the past week the sickness has made progress in this second lung. He told us that the tuberculosis has reached its last stage, that perhaps you would

---

[14] Mme. Fournet, mother of Mme. Guérin.

have time to complete your cure at Vichy, but that it would be cutting it close. He says this could be even much shorter, that one can't really know. He found our little patient admirably cared for, and he said that with all the care Dr. de Cornière has given her, if she was not restored to health, it was because God willed to take her for Himself in spite of everything.

Oh! if you only knew, dear little Father, how charming your little Queen is, and how much she loves both of you; when she speaks to me about you, I feel she has a very great affection for you, and when she is in heaven, she will watch over you as a real daughter. You mustn't think her desire to go to heaven is filled with enthusiasm, oh! no, it's very peaceful. She was telling me this morning: *"If I were told I was going to be cured, don't believe I'd be dejected; I would be happy, just as much as I would be to die. I have a great desire for heaven, but it's especially because I am in great peace that I am happy; as for feeling an immense joy as we sometimes do when our heart beats with happiness, oh! no. . . . I'm in peace, that's why I'm happy."* Francis found her very charming and very angelic.

Sister Thérèse cannot raise herself up, she's altogether too weak and can no longer move by herself. Ever since yesterday, her limbs are beginning to swell, and I believe that's a bad sign. But the coughing of blood hasn't returned. Today, she seems perhaps a little bit better, she's less down, less feverish, but this evening the respiratory difficulties began again.

From Sister Marie of the Eucharist to Mme. Guérin,
August 22, 1897.

The little Queen's sickness pursues its course. She has reached an excessive state of weakness, and you couldn't imagine how bad she is. She can no longer do anything by herself. She suffers very much in the joints, and she has continual pain in both her sides. To prove her illness is becoming worse, I will tell you that she's obliged to deprive herself of Communion. She was receiving every two or three days, but, at present, if she is able, it will be once a week. When Father brings her Communion the whole community enters chanting the "Miserere" and the last time, she was so weak that just hearing us got on her nerves. She is suffering martyrdom.

This morning, for my anniversary, she gave me a picture which she wanted to sign. She had all she could do to sign it and she thought she wouldn't be able to complete it. Also, she wasn't able to answer Papa's letter. This grieved her very much. She said: *"You won't be able to express my feelings. You'll not tell them sufficiently how much I love them, how much I'm touched by their affection."* She did not grow tired of listening to this letter, and you should have seen her beautiful little pensive face while I read it. I had to begin it several times as she couldn't get enough of it. She said: *"Oh! how good Uncle is, he's a great soul!"* But just to say these few words, she had to pause a minute between each word because of her breathing difficulties.

P.S. Our little Thérèse is suffering very much this afternoon. She has intestinal pains, and she can't bear to hear anyone talk or make a move around her. As for her breathing and the fever, they are always the same. She isn't coughing blood, however.

From Mother Agnes of Jesus to Mme. Guérin,
August 24, 1897.

Our poor little patient is very weak and suffering very much. The nights are especially painful and could not be worse. To give her some relief we've stopped giving her the famous milk diet. It's impossible to push this any further. This poor little thing believes she is poisoned, and it required a courage like hers not to have said this before. We were only noticing her very great repugnance when taking the cups. I wonder how one can live in her condition. I assure you, having seen her suffer so much, I'll be consoled more easily by her death. She'll be so happy! When she was seized with those violent intestinal pains, she said this pain was bad enough to make her cry out. *"However, I can control myself. It's not as it is for the choking, for then I cannot stop from crying out."* Do you know, dear Aunt, the agreement she made with Sister Geneviève? These are our Angel's words: *"Sister Geneviève, when I cry out: 'I'm suffering!' and I don't have the strength to say anything else, you answer for me by saying: 'So much the better!'"* This is what takes place; Sister Geneviève is obliged to obey her. She would be afraid to cause her any grief.

From Dr. Francis La Néele to M. Guérin,
August 26, 1897.

I took advantage of my trip to Lisieux to go to the Carmel. I saw, rather I heard Marie,[15] who was very happy to see her big brother. I told her to ask Mother Prioress if I could examine Thérèse in order to know whether our trip to Lourdes was possible. I was brought in immediately, and what a favor this was! I kissed our little saint on the forehead for you, Mamma, and the whole family. I had asked permission, as a matter of form, from Mother Prioress, and without waiting for the answer that perhaps the Rule forbade it, I took what was your right. What a heavenly face! What a radiantly smiling Angel! I was moved to tears when I was speaking to her, holding her transparent hands burning with fever. After I examined her, I had her sit up on her pillows. She asked: *"Am I going to heaven soon?"* "Not yet, dear little sister. God wants you to wait for a few more weeks so that your crown will be more beautiful in heaven." *"Oh! no, I'm not thinking of that! It's only to save souls that I want to suffer more."* I answered: "That's very true, but when you save souls, you climb up higher in heaven, you are closer to God." She answered with a radiant smile which lighted up her face as though heaven had opened before her eyes, flooding her with its divine brightness. "You'll really remember us up there?" I asked: *"Oh! yes, and I'll ask God to send you a little cherub. Yes, that's quite settled! I'll ask for one that is like you."* I said: "No, not like me, but like his mother who is much better than I." *"May he be like both of you. How many days do I have before going to heaven?"* I said: "In your sickness, little sister, it's very hard to say. In a few weeks, a month, perhaps more, unless you have an accident or you're in a hurry to go to see God." She said: *"I'll wait as long as God wills. Besides, I don't want to cause you any inconvenience, you nor Uncle. I'll wait till you return. You will pray for me at Lourdes. Tell Uncle and Aunt how much I love them; kiss them for me, as well as Léonie and Jeanne. In heaven I'll be always with you."* I remained a good half hour with her, along with Céline and Mother Prioress. I kissed her again before I left and she accompanied me to the door with her smile which I'll never forget.

[15] Sister Marie of the Eucharist.

The right lung is totally lost, filled with tubercles in the process of softening. The left lung is affected in its lower part. She is very emaciated, but her face still does her honor. She was suffering very much from intercostal neuralgia, and it was because of this that I had the happiness of seeing her. I returned there the following Wednesday,[16] hoping to enter once more, but Marie and the little Prioress[17] didn't dare ask Mother Marie de Gonzague's permission for me to do so. I gave her a prescription to calm her pains, for she was suffering very much that day, and I made Céline get permission to see me so as to give her some advice.

From Sister Marie of the Eucharist to M. Guérin, August 27, 1897.

Now, dear little Father, you're impatiently awaiting news of your little Queen. It's always the same. She is weaker and weaker, no longer able to bear the least noise around her, not even the crumpling of paper or a few words spoken in a whisper. There is much change in her condition since the feast of the Assumption. And we have even come to the desire of her deliverance, for she's suffering a martyrdom. She was saying yesterday: *"Fortunately, I didn't ask for suffering. If I had asked for it, I fear I wouldn't have the patience to bear it. Whereas, if it is coming directly from God's will, He cannot refuse to give me the patience and the grace necessary to bear it."*
The breathing difficulties always make her suffer much, but what is most painful for her is the difficulty in returning the enemas. She can't do so because of the great suffering she experiences. I believe it is the intestines themselves that are coming out. She retains all these and this causes her stomach to be distended and hard. That is her greatest suffering at the moment. She was saying yesterday: *"I was saying to God that all the prayers offered for me were not to serve to assuage my sufferings but to help sinners."*

---

[16] August 18, 1897.
[17] Mother Agnes of Jesus.

From Sister Geneviève to Mme. Guérin, beginning of September, 1897.

Here's what my little patient said just now: *"I'd love to have something, but only Aunt or Léonie could be able to get it for me. Since I'm eating now, I'd really love to have a little chocolate cake, soft inside."* I mentioned a chocolate patty to her. *"Oh! no, it's much better; it's long, narrow, I believe it's called an éclair."* I understood she thought it was made out of chocolate in the middle. In any case, it has a lot of chocolate on the top, this would amount to the same thing. She said: *"Only one, however!"* Thank you. Thank you.

From Sister Marie of the Eucharist to M. Guérin, September 17, 1897.

The little patient is always very sick. Her feet are constantly swelling. Dr. de Cornière says this is a bad sign. The little patient thanks you for the artichokes. She almost cried when she learned that her Uncle came to bring them. She said to me yesterday: *"Oh! I knew I was loved; I would never have believed they loved me so much, however."* Jeanne had touched her very much by sending her a picture and an affectionate letter. It was after she received these marks of affection that she told me this. The cream cheese appeared exquisite to her; never has she eaten anything so good. She said: *"It must have cost at least five francs."* It gave her indigestion.

From M. Guérin to Mme. La Néele, September 25, 1897.

Thérèse has spent a very bad night. This morning, she's as usual. It appears Dr. de Cornière was admiring his patient's gentleness and patience. It seems she's suffering atrociously. He can't understand how she continues to live and attributes this prolongation to a supernatural cause; this was the case with Mother Geneviève formerly.

From Mme. Guérin to Mme. La Néele,
September 30, 1897.

Her condition is the same this morning. Last night, she wasn't too good, which is to be understood, but her condition is the same. She is truly a little victim chosen by God. In the midst of her sufferings, she always has the same appearance, the same angelic air about her. Father Faucon, who saw her yesterday, told me through Mme. Lahaye, the seamstress, that he admires her. He had to hear her confession, and she asked him for his blessing, always with her smiling and angelic manner which never abandons her. She has always remained lucid.

Father Youf said things are going better, but it's the delirium which makes him talk this way. He believes that it's only weakness which prevents him from getting up.[18]

Our poor Carmelites are very much tried. The days they are passing through at this time are very painful.

* * *

From Mother Agnes of Jesus to M. and Mme. Guérin, and to Léonie Martin.
September 30, 1897.

J.M.J.T.
Dear Aunt and Uncle,
Dear Léonie,
Our Angel is in heaven. She gave up her last sigh at seven o'clock, pressing her Crucifix to her heart and saying: *"Oh! I love You!"* She had just lifted her eyes to heaven; what was she seeing!

Your little girl
who loves you more than ever
Sister Agnes of Jesus
r.c.i.

[18] He died October 7, 1897.

# CHRONOLOGY
## APRIL 3—SEPTEMBER 30, 1897

### APRIL

Outset of April  (End of Lent): Thérèse becomes gravely ill.

April 6          Beginning of the Last Conversations.

### MAY

May 18        She is freed from all duties.

May 30        She reveals to Mother Agnes the incident of her first hemoptysis, April 3, 1896. During the final days of the month, she is freed from her charge of the novices.

### JUNE

*June 3*        *Mother Marie de Gonzague asks her to continue the writing of her memories (Story of a Soul).*

June 4        Thérèse begins Manuscript C: she will write one part in her wheelchair, under the chestnut trees.

June 5        The illness makes rapid progress. Beginning of a novena to Our Lady of Victories. "Everything is a grace."

June 7        Sister Geneviève photographs her sister in three poses. Incident of the little white hen and her chicks.

June 9        Second anniversary of her Act of Oblation to Merciful Love. Thérèse describes the trial of faith on p. 214 *Story of a Soul. She is certain of her approaching death.* During the week, the milk diet begins.

June 11      In the garden, she casts flowers before the statue of St. Joseph.

June 13      Trinity Sunday was the last day of the novena; the patient was greatly improved.

June 25      Feast of the Sacred Heart; she has great pain in her side.

June 30      Last visit in the speakroom with her uncle, M. Guérin.

## JULY

| | |
|---|---|
| July 2 | Thérèse is at the end of her strength; Manuscript C remains unfinished. |
| July 6 | A serious recurrence of the hemoptyses (until August 5). The community is in a state of anxiety. |
| July 7 | Strong fever; she vomits blood continually. Suffocation; she is dying. Prescription of ice as a drink. |
| *July 8* | *Thérèse is taken down to the infirmary.* Sister Geneviève sleeps in cell next to infirmary. |
| July 14 | She receives blessing *in articulo mortis* from Rome, through intervention of Brother Simeon. |
| July 16 | Feast of Our Lady of Mount Carmel. Father Troude's First Mass; he brings Communion to Thérèse; Sister Marie of the Eucharist sings *"Mourir d'Amour"*. |
| *July 17* | Explicit announcement of her mission after death. *"I want to spend my heaven in doing good upon earth."* |
| July 20 | Her right lung is damaged; several cavities in it. |
| July 25 | She still stays up two hours a day. |
| July 28 | Beginning of "great sufferings." |
| *July 30* | Continual hemoptyses; suffocations. They think she will not last through the night. *At six o'clock in the evening, she receives Extreme Unction and Viaticum from Father Maupas.* |
| July 31 | Thérèse jokes about the funeral preparations being made for her. |

## AUGUST

| | |
|---|---|
| August 3 | Great physical and moral sufferings; last letter to Sister Geneviève: "The Good Shepherd." |
| August 4 | Nightmares and heavy perspirings; violent pains in her side. She was given an ear of corn. |
| August 5 | End of the hemoptyses. The picture of the Holy Face, taken from the choir, is installed in the infirmary. |
| August 6 | Transfiguration. Thérèse awaits death all through the night; temptations against the faith. |

| | |
|---|---|
| August 8 | Her condition becomes stable. Dr. de Cornière leaves for vacation. |
| August 10 | Thérèse sees a similarity between herself and Joan of Arc, whose picture she was shown. Last letter to Father Bellière. Speaks more openly than ever before about her temptations against faith. |
| August 15 | Assumption. Her sickness worsens. |
| August 16 | A very intense pain in her left side. Her temptations lessen when Sister Geneviève lights a blessed candle. |
| August 17 | Dr. La Néele's visit; the right lung is totally lost; the left is diseased in its lower region. |
| August 19 | Her last Holy Communion. Thérèse becomes very nervous during the chanting of the *"Miserere"* which preceded reception of Communion. She offers this one for Father Hyacinthe Loyson, who lost his faith. |
| August 22 | Beginning of her intestinal pains. A day of continual sufferings. It is feared she has gangrene. |
| August 23 | "The worst night so far." Thérèse understands that one can commit suicide when one is suffering so much. |
| August 24 | Intestinal pains bad enough to make her cry out. The patient suffers violently at each breath. |
| August 28 | Assuagement of the intestinal pains. Thérèse's bed is placed in the center of the infirmary. |
| August 30 | Peaceful night. Thérèse is rolled out on a bed and placed on the outside cloister walk to be photographed. |
| August 31 | Extreme weakness. Thérèse can no longer make the sign of the cross; she is famished. The patient's desires for food. |

### SEPTEMBER

| | |
|---|---|
| September 1 | She asks for a chocolate éclair. |
| September 5 | Fourth and final visit of Dr. La Néele. |
| September 6 | She cries when she is brought a relic of Théophane Vénard. |
| September 8 | Seventh anniversary of Thérèse's Profession. She traces her last lines for the Blessed Virgin. |

| | |
|---|---|
| September 11 | She weaves two crowns for the Blessed Virgin's statue from some cornflowers. |
| September 12 | Her feet begin to swell. |
| September 14 | Thérèse unpetals a rose over her Crucifix. |
| September 18 | In the morning, they believe she is dying. |
| September 19 | Father Denis' First Mass at the Carmel. Thérèse looks at her reflection in his chalice. |
| September 24 | Seventh anniversary of her taking of the Veil. |
| September 27 | Her suffering is extreme. |
| September 28 | Her breathing is very short. Thérèse hardly speaks a word. |
| September 29 | Saint Michael. In the morning, Thérèse seems to be in the agony of death. The community recites the prayers for the dying in the infirmary. Confession of Thérèse to Father Faucon. |
| *September 30* | *THURSDAY.* Thérèse is watched over by Sister Marie of the Sacred Heart and Sister Geneviève. During the Mass, all three of her sisters remain with her. All day long indescribable agony. She recovers in the afternoon, lifts herself up in bed; at three o'clock she holds her arms out in the form of a cross. Towards half-past four, signs of the last moments. Around five, terrible death rattle which will last two hours. The Community returns to the Infirmary. At six, the Angelus bell rings, and Thérèse looks at the statue of the Blessed Virgin. Around seven, her head falls back upon her pillow. The community, which had just been sent away, is recalled in haste. Around twenty minutes after seven, Thérèse lifts her eyes to heaven for the space of a *Credo;* Sister Marie of the Eucharist passes a lighted candle before Thérèse's eyes. Thérèse closes her eyes, sighs a few times, and dies. |

## OCTOBER

| | |
|---|---|
| October 1 | Photo is taken of Thérèse dead. |
| October 4 | Thérèse is buried in the Lisieux cemetery. |

# BIOGRAPHICAL GUIDE FOR PROPER NAMES

## ACARD, AGUSUT FERDINAND (1864-1931)

Gardener, workman, and sacristan at the Carmel of Lisieux from 1889 to 1912. See *Last Conversations,* p. 186.

## AGNES OF JESUS, MOTHER (1861-1951)

Marie Pauline Martin, sister and "little Mother" to Thérèse; born at Alençon, second child of the Martin family; made her studies at the Visitation convent at Le Mans from 1868 to 1877; upon her mother's death, she undertook the care and education of Thérèse, who was four and a half; she entered Carmel of Lisieux on October 2, 1882, received the Habit on April 6, 1883, and made Profession on May 8, 1884, the same day that Thérèse received her First Communion.

She was elected Prioress on February 20, 1893; was re-elected on April 19, 1902, and, with the exception of eighteen months, from May, 1908 to November, 1909, she was to remain in this office until her death in 1951.

## AIMÉE OF JESUS, SISTER (1851-1930)

A Carmelite nun of Lisieux. She entered Carmel on October 13, 1871, received the Habit on March 19, 1872, and was professed on May 8, 1873. She was physically strong and very gentle, and upon the request of Sister Thérèse, she held the latter in her arms when she could barely be touched. Sister Aimée was the only one not present at Sister Thérèse's death on September 30, 1897, because she did not hear the infirmary bell summoning the members of the community. She testified at the Process.

## ANNE OF JESUS, VENERABLE (1545-1621)

A spanish Carmelite nun, née Anne de Lobera. She was companion to St. Teresa of Avila in the early days of the Carmelite Reform, and was to become one of the foundresses of Carmel in France in 1604. Sister Thérèse had a dream in which she saw and spoke with Venerable Anne of Jesus. Cf. *Story of a Soul,* p. 191.

## BELLIÈRE, MAURICE, REVEREND (1874-1907)

Spiritual brother to Sister Thérèse. He was born at Caen; began his studies for the priesthood in October, 1894. The following year, October 15, 1895, he wrote the Carmel of Lisieux asking that one of the nuns pray for his vocation. Mother Agnes, Prioress, assigned her sister Thérèse as his spiritual sister. He left for Algiers to enter the novitiate of the White Fathers. He was ordained on June 29, 1901, and assigned to the mission at Nyassa. He returned to France in Janaury, 1906, because of poor health and died at Caen the following year.

CLODION LE CHEVELU

A nickname given to Dr. de Cornière by Thérèse because of the way he wore his hair; historically, Clodion was the chief of a Frankish tribe (d. 447).

DE CORNIÈRE, ALEXANDRE DAMASE (1841-1922)

This was the doctor who took care of Thérèse. He was born at Bonnebosq (Calvados); made his medical studies at Caen and Paris, and began to practice medicine at Lisieux in 1869. He was doctor at the Carmel for a period of almost thirty years, 1886-1920. He took care of Thérèse during her last illness, with the exception of the month of August when he was away on vacation. (She was then attended to by Dr. La Néele, a relative of Thérèse through marriage). Dr. de Cornière was the father of seven children; was a fervent Christian and took care of many poor people free of charge. He died at Lisieux.

DE CORNIÈRE, JOSEPH, REVEREND (1874-1939)

The oldest son of Dr. de Cornière, born at Lisieux. He made an attempt to become a Redemptorist in Holland (1892) and in South America (1893). He was invited by the Guérin family to La Musse for the summer vacations of 1893 and 1894. He was ordained a priest for the Bayeux diocese where he worked until his death.

DENIS DE MAROY, JOSEPH, REVEREND (1871-1962)

Born at Paris, ordained at Bayeux on September 18, 1897, and said his first Mass at the Carmel of Lisieux the following day, September 19.

Cf. *Last Conversations*, p. 192.

DUCELLIER, ALCIDE, REVEREND (1849-1916)

Born at Chicheboville (Calvados), ordained priest in 1874, and worked as one of the assistants at St. Peter's in Lisieux from 1877 to 1884. He heard Thérèse's first confession around 1880 and remained her confessor until her entrance at the Benedictine Abbey for her studies in October, 1881. He preached the sermon for Pauline's reception of the Habit; also preached for Céline's reception of the Habit and the Veil. Spiritual director to Mother Agnes of Jesus. Testified at the Process.

## FAUCON, PIERRE, REVEREND (1842-1918)

Born at Ondefontaine (Calvados), he was ordained a priest on June 29, 1868. Father Faucon was extraordinary confessor at the Carmel from 1886-1891; he heard Thérèse last confession on September 29, 1897. He testified at the Process.

## FOURNET, ELISA-ERNESTINE (1816-1901)

Born at Lisieux, daughter of Pierre-Antoine Petit and Marie-Rosalie Monsaint, she married Pierre-Celestin Fournet on November 11, 1839 and had four children, one of whom, Céline, was the future Mme. Guérin, aunt to Thérèse. On May 12, 1866, the Fournets sold their pharmacy to M. Isidore Guérin. Céline Martin and her sister Thérèse gave the name of "grandmamma" to Mme. Fournet.

## GENEVIÈVE OF ST. TERESA, SISTER (1869-1959)

Sister to Thérèse and one of her novices.

Céline, born at Alençon, the seventh child of the nine of the Martin family, she made her first Communion on May 13, 1880 at the Benedictine Abbey where she made her studies from 1877-1885. She stayed with her father, Louis Martin, during his long illness at Caen, Lisieux, La Musse (1889-1894). She entered Carmel on September 14, 1894, taking the name of Sister Marie of the Holy Face; she received the Habit on February 5, 1895, her name being changed to Sister Geneviève of St. Teresa in memory of the foundress; she was professed on February 24, 1896, and received the Veil on March 17, 1896. Céline made her novitiate under Thérèse's guidance. She was assigned as infirmarian-aide and later on became infirmarian to her sister during the last months of her life. In 1916, she took the name of Sister Geneviève of the Holy Face. Sister Geneviève played an important role in the spread of St. Thérèse's message, both through her writing and her portraits of St. Thérèse. She was the one who took the many photos of Thérèse that we still have today. She testified at the Process.

GENEVIEVE OF ST. TERESA, MOTHER (1805-1891)
Claire Bertrand, born at Poitiers, entered the Carmel of that city on March 26, 1830. She became Mistress of novices in 1837, and was sent as foundress to Lisieux on March 16, 1838. She was elected Prioress for five terms. De. de Cornière attended to her during her last illness and admired her for her courage. Thérèse witnessed her death in the infirmary (cf. *Story of a Soul*, p. 169), in the very same bed she was to occupy later on in her last illness in 1897.

GUÉRIN, CÉLINE (1847-1900)
Aunt of Thérèse.
Born at Lisieux to Pierre-Celestin Fournet and Elisa-Ernestine Petit. She married Isidore Guérin on September 11, 1866, and had three children, two girls, Jeanne and Marie, and a boy who was stillborn; upon the death of Mme. Martin, sister to Isidore Guérin, the Martin family moved to Lisieux from Alençon, and Mme. Guérin played a mother's role to her five nieces: Pauline, Marie, Léonie, Céline, and Thérèse. These visited the Guérin home each week with their father, Louis Martin. At the time of her illness, Thérèse was supplied by Mme. Guérin with choice dishes to tempt her to eat more. She died in Lisieux.

GUÉRIN, ISIDORE (1841-1909)
Uncle of Thérèse.
Born at Saint-Denis-sur-Sarthon (Orne) to Isidore Guérin and Louise-Jeanne Mace, who had three children, one of whom, Zélie, was to become the mother of St. Thérèse. Isidore made his studies as a pharmacist in Paris (1862) and received his license to practice in 1866. He set up his business at Lisieux, place St. Pierre, buying the Fournet pharmacy, whose daughter, Céline, he married on September 11, 1866.

He was named deputy guardian of his nieces on September 16, 1877, upon the death of their mother, and he established them in Les Buissonnets at Lisieux. Isidore inherited the château at La Musse in

August of 1888 and sold his pharmacy to Victor Lahaye (see Lahaye below). He took on the role of father to his nieces when their own father, Louis Martin, had a paralytic stroke, taking him into his own home in order to tend to his needs in his old age. A militant Christian, he established the work of the nocturnal adoration in Lisieux in June, 1895. He was to play an important role in the publication of *Histoire d'une Ame* in 1898. His old age was saddened by the death of his wife, February 13, 1900, and his younger daughter, Marie, in 1905. She had entered the Carmel of Lisieux and was one of Thérèse's novices, taking the name of Sister Marie of the Eucharist.

## HERMANCE OF THE HEART OF JESUS, MOTHER (1833-1898)

Madeleine Pichery, born at Honfleur; she entered the Lisieux Carmel on May 14, 1858, received the Habit on November 24, 1858, and was professed on December 2, 1859. In 1866, she became foundress of the Carmel at Coutances, returning to the Lisieux Carmel in 1882 because of sickness. She was quite a trial to the infirmarians because of her difficult character. Sister Thérèse predicted her death.

## HUGONIN, FLAVIEN-ABEL-ANTOINE, BISHOP (1823-1898)

Bishop of Bayeux and Lisieux during the lifetime of Thérèse.

Born at Thodure (Isère), he was made bishop of Bayeux on July 13, 1866. He was the one who confirmed Thérèse, June 6, 1884, and was later to receive M. Martin and his daughter, Thérèse, October 31, 1887, when she was seeking permission to enter Carmel at the age of fifteen. Two years later, he gave her the Habit, Janaury 10, 1889; he presided at Célin's taking of the Veil and Marie Guérin's reception of the Habit on March 17, 1896. He was later on to grant the imprimatur for the publishing of *Histoire d'une Ame (Story of a Soul),* March 7, 1898.

## LAHAYE, VICTOR, PHARMACIST (1855-1936)

Born at Aignerville (Calvados). Succeeded M. Guérin, after buying his pharmacy, December 8, 1888. He was closely associated with the Guérin family and assisted at Thérèse reception of the Veil on September 24, 1890. He recounted his own memories of her in a small publication entitled: *Portrait descriptif de la Bienheureuse Thérèse de l'Enfant Jésus.* This was published on March 19, 1923, when Victor

Lahaye was president of the Historical Society of Lisieux. He was pharmacist for the Carmel during Thérèse's illness. He had six children. His wife died of tuberculosis on October 22, 1898.

LA NÉELE, FRANSICQUE-LUCIEN-SULPICE, DOCTOR (1858-1916)
Doctor of Thérèse during the absence of Dr. de Cornière, and her cousin through his marriage to Jeanne Guérin.

Born at Paris, he made his studies with the Jesuits; pharmacist and medical doctor. Married Jeanne Guérin on October 1, 1890. Sold his pharmacy, November 26, 1891, and opened a doctor's office at Caen, 24 rue de l'Oratoire. He was called in to take care of Thérèse during her own doctor's absence, and he visited her three times during the months of August and September of 1897.

LA NÉELE, JEANNE-MARIE-ELISA (1868-1938)
First cousin to Thérèse.

Daughter of Isidore and Céline Guérin, born at Lisieux. Married Dr. Francis La Néele on October 1, 1890. Thérèse helped her in accepting the sacrifice of not having children of her own. She testified at the Process. After her husband's death, she adopted one of her grand-nieces. She died at Nogent-le-Rotrou.

MARIE DE GONZAGUE, MOTHER (1834-1904)
Prioress of the Carmel of Lisieux.

Marie-Adèle-Rosalie Davy de Virville, born at Caen. She entered the Carmel on November 29, 1860, received the Habit, May 30, 1861, and made Profession on June 27, 1862.

Elected Subprioress in 1866 and 1869, she then served six terms as Prioress, leaving upon the community the mark of her strong personality. She was elected again after Mother Agnes of Jesus had served out her first term from 1893-96, and she was in office until April 19, 1902. Mother Marie de Gonzague died of cancer on December 17, 1904, with sentiments of great devotion to Thérèse.

MARIE OF JESUS, SISTER (1862-1938)
Eugénie Corceau was born in Rouen. She entered the Carmel of Lisieux on April 26, 1883, received the Habit on October 15, 1883,

and was professed on December 5, 1884. She tried the patience of Thérèse during the hours of prayer through a strange habit she had of clicking her teeth together (cf. *Story of a Soul,* p. 249). In 1897, she occasionally helped the infirmarians, and thus she witnessed some of the sessions of painful cauterization which Thérèse was subjected to.

## MARIE OF THE TRINITY AND THE HOLY FACE (1874-1944)
A novice of Thérèse.

Marie Castel, born at St. Pierre-sur-Dives (Calvados), the thirteenth in a family of nineteen children. She entered the Carmel of Paris, l'avenue de Messine, April 30, 1891; she received the Habit on March 12, 1892, however, poor health forced her to leave on July 8, 1893. The Carmel of Lisieux received her as a postulant on June 16, 1894. Thérèse did all in her power to help her realize her vocation. Her Profession took place on April 30, 1896. As infirmarian-aide, Sister Marie of the Trinity was aware of Thérèse's hemoptysis in April, 1896, but she did not take care of Thérèse in 1897 in the infirmary because of her youth and the fear she would contract the disease. She wrote down her memories of the novice mistress; her testimony at the Process was important.

## MARIE OF THE EUCHARIST, SISTER (1870-1905)
First cousin of Thérèse and one of her novices.

Marie Guérin, born at Lisieux, was the second daughter of Isidore and Céline Guérin. She made her studies at the Benedictine abbey of Lisieux with Thérèse. She entered Carmel on August 15, 1895, received the Habit on March 17, 1896, and was professed on March 25, 1897. Thérèse helped her novice overcome her scruples. Marie's correspondence with her family remains a precious source of information on the last months of Thérèse, giving minute details of the progress of her illness. She died of tuberculosis at the age of thirty-five in spite of the cares of her brother-in-law, Dr. La Néele, and the use of new treatments introduced at this time.

## MARIE OF THE INCARNATION, LAY SISTER (1828-1911)
Born Zephirine Lecouturier at Firfol, near Lisieux. She entered Carmel on August 10, 1852, received the Habit August 3, 1853, and was professed November 14, 1854. This Sister was the one mentioned

by Thérèse (cf. *Story of a Soul*, p. 227) who stopped to chatter with her about all sorts of things: hay, ducks, hens, in order to distract her when she was sick in June, 1897.

MARIE OF ST. JOSEPH, SISTER (1858-1936)
Born Marie Campain at Valognes (Manche). She entered the Carmel on April 28, 1881, received the Habit on October 15, 1881, and was professed on October 15, 1882. She had a very difficult temperament and was a trial to the community. In 1896, Thérèse volunteered her services to help this Sister in the linen room where no other Sister was able to remain. Marie of St. Joseph left the Carmel in June 1909.

MARIE OF THE ANGELS AND THE SACRED HEART, SISTER (1845-1924)
Mistress of Novices at the time of Thérèse's entrance.
Born Jeanne de Chaumontel at Montpinçon (Calvados), she entered Carmel on October 29, 1866, received the Habit on March 19, 1867, and was professed on March 25, 1868. Marie of the Angels was Subprioress from 1883 to 1886, and was placed in charge of the novices from October, 1886, to February, 1893. From 1893 to 1899 she was again Subprioress; besides, she took charge of the novitiate after the death of Thérèse and remained in this charge until 1909. She testified at the Process.

MARIE OF THE SACRED HEART, SISTER (1860-1940)
Sister and godmother of Thérèse.
Marie, born at Alençon, was the oldest of the Martin children. She acted as godmother to Thérèse on January 4, 1873. Father Pichon, S.J., aided her in finding her vocation. She entered the Carmel of Lisieux on October 15, 1886, received the Habit on March 19, 1887, and was professed on May 22, 1888. For a short time she was a novice with Thérèse, who had entered on April 9, 1888. She was the one who had suggested that Thérèse write her "childhood memories" and requested that Thérèse write her retreat inspirations out for her. Thus we owe to her Mss. A and B of the *Story of a Soul*.
She suffered for many years and right up to her death from rheumatism in the joints.

## MARIE-ELIZABETH OF ST. TERESA, SISTER (1860-1935)

Marie Hamard, born at Couterne (Orne), entered the Carmel of Lisieux on July 7, 1890, but not as one of the cloistered nuns; she was an extern. She made her profession on October 15, 1891. Sister Marie-Elizabeth knew Thérèse through the latter's duties at the turn and in the sacristy; on several occasions, she entered the infirmary to take care of Thérèse while the nuns were attending Sunday Mass. She represented the community at the burial of Thérèse, who was buried in the city cemetery, October 4, 1897. Sister testified at the Process.

## MARIE-MADELEINE OF THE BLESSED SACRAMENT, LAY SISTER (1869-1916)

One of Thérèse novices.

Born Mélanie Le Bon at Plouguenast (Côtes-du-Nord), she entered Carmel on July 22, 1892, received the Habit on September 7, 1893, and was professed in November, 1894. On this occasion, Thérèse wrote her poem entitled: *"Histoire d'une bergère devenue Reine."* ("Story of a shepherdess become Queen.") She testified at the Process.

## MARIE-PHILOMÈNE OF JESUS, SISTER (1839-1924)

Noémie Jacquemin, born at Langrune (Calvados), entered Carmel on October 13, 1876, but she had to leave it in order to take care of her dying mother; she entered again on November 7, 1884, and made her Profession at forty-six, March 25, 1886.

## MARTHA OF JESUS, LAY SISTER (1865-1916)

Novice of Thérèse.

Désirée Cauvin, born at Giverville (Eure), entered Carmel on December 23, 1887, received the Habit on May 2, 1889, and was professed on September 23, 1890. She wanted to remain in the novitiate with Thérèse. The latter aided her in freeing herself from the too strong influence of Mother Marie de Gonzague (cf. *Story of a Soul*, p. 236). She testified at the Process.

## MARTIN, MARIE-LÉONIE, SISTER OF THÉRÈSE (1863-1941)

The third of the Martin children, born at Alençon, of a delicate and difficult temperament, she was the cause of much anxiety to her mother. She made several attempts at the religious life: the Poor Clares at Alençon (October, 1886), the Visitation at Caen (from July, 1887 to January 6, 1888). At the age of thirty, she was postulant once more in this order (June 24, 1893), but had to leave in 1895. She lived then with her Uncle Guérin. After the death of Thérèse, she entered definitively the visitation at Caen (January 28, 1899) and took the name of Sister Françoise-Thérèse. She carried on a great correspondence with her sisters at Lisieux Carmel until her death. She testified at the Process.

## MAUPAS, ALEXANDRE-CHARLES, REVEREND (1850-1920)

Ecclesiastical Superior of the Lisieux Carmel.

Born at Mesnil-Auzouf (Calvados). Attended the seminaries of Vire, Sommervieu, and Bayeux. Ordained priest on June 29, 1874; eventually became assistant at St. Jacques parish at Lisieux in 1895, where he succeeded his cousin, Reverend Delatoëtte. He replaced the latter also as Superior of the Carmel. He administered the last sacraments to Thérèse on September 30, 1897. He testified at the Process.

## MAZEL, FREDERIC, REVEREND (1871-1897)

A missionary and fellow-student of Father Roulland. He was assassinated in China on April 1, 1897.

## PICHON, ALMIRE, REVEREND (1843-1919)

Born at Carrouges (Orne), he entered the novitiate of the Company of Jesus on October 30, 1863, was ordained priest on September 8, 1873. In 1882, he became spiritual director of Marie Martin. In August, 1883, he met Thérèse. Father Pichon preached a retreat at the Carmel of Lisieux in October, 1887, and again in May, 1888, Thérèse being then a postulant. He reassured her after she had made a general confession (cf. *Story of a Soul,* p. 149). He was sent to Canada as a missionary (1884-1886; 1888-1907) and Thérèse corresponded with him. He did not keep any of her letters. Father Pichon testified at the Process.

## POTTIER, CÉLINE (1873-1949)

A childhood friend of Thérèse.

Céline Maudelonde, daughter of Marie-Rosalie Fournet (sister of

Mme. Guérin) and Césard-Alexandre Maudelonde, was exactly the same age as Thérèse; they played together as children (cf. *Story of a Soul,* p. 54). She married Gaston Pottier on June 19, 1894, and had two children

## PROU, ALEXIS, REVEREND (1844-1914)

Born at St. Pazanne (Loire-Etlantique), he entered the Franciscans when already a subdeacon (September 4, 1869) and was ordained priest on June 29, 1871. Guardian or Superior of the Franciscan house of St. Nazaire, he preached a retreat at the Carmel of Lisieux (October 8-15, 1891), which was the occasion of important graces for Thérèse (cf. *Story of a Soul,* p. 173).

## ROULLAND, ADOLPHE, REVEREND (1870-1934)

Spiritual brother to Thérèse.

Born at Cahagnolles (Calvados), he entered the Foreign Missions seminary at Paris. On May 30, 1896, he asked Mother Marie de Gonzague that one of her religious be associated with him in his missionary apostolate. Thérèse was assigned to this by the Prioress. He was ordained a priest (June 28, 1896), and he said his first Mass and met Thérèse at the Carmel on July 3, 1896. He sailed for China on August 2, 1896. Father Roulland carried on an important correspondence with his spriitual sister. He was recalled to France in 1909, and he testified at the Process.

## ST. JOHN OF THE CROSS, SISTER (1851-1906)

Alice Bougeret, born at Torigny-sur-Vire (Manche), entered the Carmel on April 21, 1876, received the Habit on December 8, 1876, and was professed on Janaury 17, 1878. She used to visit Thérèse in the infirmary, and her visits were not too consoling to Thérèse because she seemed somewhat unsympathetic towards the patient. Cf. *Last conversations,* p. 167.

## SAINT RAPHAEL OF THE HEART OF MARY, SISTER (1840-1918)

Born Laure Gayat at Le Havre, she entered Carmel on February 24, 1868, received the Habit on June 26 of the same year. She made her Profession on July 6, 1869. Thérèse was her helper at the turn and had to practice much patience with her because of her difficult character.

SAINT STANISLAUS OF THE SACRED HEARTS, SISTER (1824-1914)

Thérèse's infirmarian; oldest member of the community.

Marie-Rosalie Guéret, born at Lisieux, was one of the first Carmelites of the foundation (founded in 1838); she entered on April 6, 1845, received the Habit on January 15, 1846, and was professed on February 8, 1847. She carried out many functions during her long life, being sacristan, infirmarian, etc. Thérèse was her helper in the sacristy. Sister St. Stanislaus was her infirmarian during the beginning stages of her illness.

ST. VINCENT DE PAUL, LAY SISTER (1841-1905)

Born Zoé-Adèle Alaterre at Cherbourg, she entered the Carmel on February 2, 1864, received the Habit on December 8, 1864, and was professed on December 14, 1865. She made Thérèse suffer much as a novice by reproaching her for her slowness in carrying out her duties. After the death of the Saint, she was the first to benefit from one of her miracles: she was cured of cerebral anemia after kissing the feet of the dead Thérèse.

THÉRÈSE OF ST. AUGUSTINE, SISTER (1856-1929)

Julia Leroyer, born at Cressonnière (Calvados) entered the Carmel on May 1, 1875, received the Habit on October 15 of the same year, and was professed on May 1, 1877. Thérèse experienced a natural antipathy for the good religious (cf. *Story of a Soul,* p. 222), but her exterior charity persuaded Sister Therese of St. Augustine of just the opposite. After the death of St. Thérèse, this Sister wrote her memories of a holy friendship which brought out some of her last conversations with Thérèse. She testified at the Process.

TROUDE, PAUL-FRANÇOIS, REVEREND (1873-1900)

Born at Langrune (Calvados), fellow-student of Reverend Bellière (first spiritual brother of St. Thérèse), he was ordained a priest on June 29, 1897. He was a nephew to Sister Marie-Philomène, and he celebrated Mass on the feast of Our Lady of Mount Carmel, July 16, 1897, in the chapel of the Lisieux Carmel. A contemporary of St. Thérèse, he died only a few years after her.

## VÉNARD, THÉOPHANE, MARTYR (1829-1861)

Born at St. Loup-sur-Thouet (Deux-Sèvres), he was a young priest from the Foreign Missions at Paris, who was beheaded in Hanoi. He was beatified by Pius X on May 2, 1909. Thérèse had read his biography and letters. She composed a poem in his honor on February 2, 1897, and she kept his portrait before her eyes during her illness, having it pinned to the curtains of her bed. Very frequently in her last conversations she made direct references to him.

## YOUF, LOUIS-AUGUSTE, REVEREND (1842-1897)

Chaplain of the Lisieux Carmel.

Born at Caen, he attended the seminaries of Villiers, Bayeux, and was ordained a priest in 1869. He became assistant at St. Jacques' parish in Lisieux and chaplain of the Carmel from July, 1873 till his death, a week after that of Thérèse, October 7, 1897. He was Thérèse's ordinary confessor all through her religious life.

# APPENDIX

The "last conversations" of St. Thérèse of the Child Jesus in this popular edition are identical with those in the critical edition which has already been mentioned. The following information, however, will prove helpful to the reader:

## 1. LAST CONVERSATIONS WITH HER THREE SISTERS

a) *Mother Agnes of Jesus.*—From the many conversations she held with her dying sister, from April to September 30, 1897, Mother Agnes of Jesus made several copies over the years. There are four of these extant in the archives of the Lisieux Carmel, and they are referred to as: les *Cahiers verts* (1909); le *Procès de l'Ordinaire* (1910); le *Carnet jaune* (1922-1923); *Novissima Verba* (1927).

I will give a short explanation of the origin of each of these copies, referring the reader to the critical edition for a more complete history of them.[1] The *Cahiers verts* ("Green copybooks") was a very definite selection of St. Thérèse's "last conversations" made specifically for one person, namely, Monsignor de Teil. He was appointed vice-postulator for Sister Thérèse's "cause" on January 26, 1909, and was seeking information on her at the Carmel as early as February 4, 1909. He was already acquainted with the famous *Histoire d'une Ame (Story of a Soul),* but he wanted definite information about her last illness and death. Mother Agnes supplied him with a copy of Thérèse's "last conversations." She did not give these in their entirety, but selected a certain number (306 to be exact) which would manifest Thérèse's attitudes, bring out the practice of certain virtues, etc. Within a short period of ten days, she filled 132 pages of five green-covered copybooks (hence the title), sending them to him for his private use. Monsignor de Teil was very much impressed by what he read, writing the following note to Mother Agnes, March 1, 1909:

"... the copybooks you sent me have broken down the greater part of my objections. God was assuredly guiding you during the sickness of Thérèse in order to prepare the glorification of His little servant. Thank you for this precious communication. . . ."[2]

---

[1]  See *Derniers Entretiens,* 1:58ff.
[2]  See *Derniers Entretiens,* 1:72.

On March 5, 1910, the Sacred Congregation of Rites invited the bishop of Bayeux (diocese where Thérèse lived and died) to examine into the writings of the Servant of God. It was Monsignor de Teil's task to prepare the nuns for this very important step. Mother Agnes set to work once more on Thérèse's "last conversations." This time she was providing a number of these "conversations" (275 to be exact) to be examined by the judges on the "diocesan tribunal," which was set up in the summer months of 1910. This second copy of the "conversations," therefore, is now referred to as: *le Procès de l'Ordinaire* (the bishop's process).

When Mother Agnes was about to begin this work for the "diocesan process," she wrote the vice-postulator the following note, May 14, 1910:

> ". . . I forgot to ask you to kindly send me the green copybooks on Monday. I shall be able to return them to you within a few days, once I have marked off, in my little copybook of memories, the incidents and words I had selected for making the copy you had requested, Monsignor, and which, I saw with very much joy and consolation, served you as a guide. . . ."³

What is noteworthy here is Mother Agnes' reference to her "little copybook of memories." It has been conjectured that she finally transcribed all the "conversations" she had taken down on slips of paper, during Thérèse's illness, into this "little copybook of memories," possibly around the years 1904-1905. This "copybook" served her well as a source for making copies in the future.

We come now to the "Yellow Notebook." Some years after the ecclesiastical investigation into the "life" and "writings" of Sister Thérèse of the Child Jesus, possibly around 1922-1923, Mother Agnes decided to gather together in a definitive form the "memories" of her saintly sister. She chose for this purpose three large notebooks. The first was to contain the "last conversations"; the other two, the autobiographical manuscripts. We are interested here only with the first. It was later on referred to as the *"Carnet jaune"* (the "Yellow Notebook"), undoubtedly because of its yellow leather binding. This is, we might say, the most acceptable of all the four copies made simply because it contains all the "last conversations" (there are 714 in all) which were taken down by Mother Agnes. These are presented in

See *Derniers Entretiens*, 1:73.

their chronological order. Mother Agnes was writing this for herself and not with a view to supplying others with information on some specific virtue as was done in the two other copies. She used her "little copybook of memories" as her source.

With regard to the last copy, *Novissima Verba,* I have already referred to this in the Introduction. It was published in 1927, two years after Thérèse's solemn canonization, May 17, 1925, in response to the many requests for more information on the saint. At this time Mother Agnes was very much opposed to publishing her sister's "last conversations," for she felt they were far too intimate for public consumption. As a consequence, this copy is rather restrained, containing only 362 of Thérèse's "conversations."

b) *Sister Geneviève.*—Novice and infirmarian of Thérèse, Sister Geneviève (her sister Céline) left Mother Agnes the task of noting down the patient's words, limiting herself to writing on little slips of paper those words that were most personal. In 1898 she wrote these partly in a little notebook, then in a more complete way, in 1925, in a large notebook entitled: "Last Conversations of Thérèse to Céline." It is this version which appears in the present book.

c) *Sister Marie of the Sacred Heart.*—There is a very small notebook entitled: "Last Conversations of Sister Thérèse of the Child Jesus, collected by Sister Marie of the Sacred Heart." This notebook goes back to the year 1925 and contains only twenty-five conversations noted down by Sister Marie of the Sacred Heart (Thérèse's sister Marie). This collection is to be found in this present edition.

## 2. ADDITIONAL CONVERSATIONS

There are also some additional conversations of all three of these main witnesses, namely, Mother Agnes, Sister Geneviève, and Sister Marie of the Sacred Heart. The reader will also find a few conversations carried on between Thérèse and other witnesses: Sister Marie of the Eucharist (her cousin Marie); Sister Marie of the Trinity; Sister Thérèse of Saint Augustine; Sister Marie of the Angels; and Sister Aimée of Jesus.

3. LETTERS

The critical edition of *Derniers Entretiens,* 1:665ff, contains a collection of seventy-five letters, from April 3 to September 30, 1897, historical documents on the last six months of Thérèse. This popular edition has only twenty-six extracts of these letters. However, the editors were careful to reproduce all Thérèse's conversations, some of which are proper to these letters, and to cite those passages which shed most light on her sickness, or on her conduct during her illness.

# INDEX

prayer *(continued)*
  things Thérèse asked in,
    14, 36-37, 45-46, 47, 55, 60, 62-
    63, 72, 90, 93, 98-99, 105, 107,
    113, 123, 133, 137, 140, 169,
    176, 181, 193, 198, 204, 210,
    216, 229-30, 240, 243, 258, 263-
    64, 264, 267;
  see Jesus, Mary (prayer to)
present moment,
  46, 64, 107, 155, 165, 241;
  and sanctity,
    253
priests, desire to help,
  95
prioress,
  252;
  advice to future,
    56, 240;
  aptitude for being,
    16, 17;
  see Marie de Gonzague
prophetic statements,
  56, 70, 91, 109-10, 126, 129, 187,
  190, 198, 214, 217, 262, 263, 301
Prou, Father Alexis,
  19, 73, 110, 307
purgatory,
  45, 56, 81, 117, 118, 137, 188,
  273, 283
Raphael, Sister,
  90, 95, 307
rationalization,
  252
reading,
  5, 11, 14, 43-44, 261
reading thoughts,
  193
recreation,
  40, 41, 103, 239;
  extraordinary,
    42, 42n;
  incident at,
    36-37
religious life a martyrdom,
  240

reputation in community, Thérèse's,
  15-19, 49
resignation,  ⸱
  45, 47, 89, 107;
  about death,
    46, 58, 59, 61, 97, 111, 204;
  see also God (will of), indiffer-
    ence, peace
rosary,
  160
roses,
  62, 190, 256, 296
Roulland, Father Adolphe,
  spiritural brother),
    41, 82, 118, 127, 183, 307
Rule of Carmel,
  36n, 142n
sacraments,
  23, 57
  Baptism,
    121, 233, 238;
  Confession and absolution,
    16, 160, 170, 185, 292, 296, 299;
  Eucharist,
    16, 26, 31, 41, 56, 57, 58, 63, 64,
    71, 91, 92, 98-99, 101n, 121,
    123, 137, 147, 152, 157, 249,
    250, 255, 260, 262, 279n, 283,
    287, 294, 295;
  see Mass; Extreme Unction
    65, 70, 79, 81, 83, 120, 237, 274,
    283, 294, 306
sacrifice,
  10, 14, 76, 82, 95, 103, 139, 266;
  acts of,
    86, 95-96, 100, 103, 108, 119,
    120, 153, 167, 172, 251, 262,
    265-66, 281;
  and little way,
    257;
  mortification,
    115, 127, 130, 178, 180, 189,
    246, 258
sadness,
  71, 87, 106, 107, 197, 261, 265,
  286

# BIBLICAL INDEX

The Institute of Carmelite Studies promotes research and publication in the field of Carmelite spirituality. Its members are Discalced Carmelites, part of a Roman Catholic community—friars, nuns and laity—who are heirs to the teaching and way of life of Teresa of Jesus and John of the Cross, men and women dedicated to contemplation and to ministry in the Church and the world. Information concerning their way of life is available through local diocesan Vocation Offices, or from the Vocation Director's Office, 1525 Carmel Road, Hubertus, WI 53033.